The Book of Mormon:
First Nephi, The Doctrinal Foundation

RELIGIOUS STUDIES CENTER PUBLICATIONS

BOOK OF MORMON SYMPOSIUM SERIES

The Book of Mormon: The
  Keystone Scripture

The Book of Mormon: First
  Nephi, the Doctrinal
  Foundation

MONOGRAPH SERIES

Nibley on the Timely and the
  Timeless
Deity and Death
The Glory of God Is Intelligence
Reflections on Mormonism
Literature of Belief
The Words of Joseph Smith
Book of Mormon Authorship

Mormons and Muslims
The Temple in Antiquity
Isaiah and the Prophets
Scriptures for the Modern World
The Joseph Smith Translation:
  The Restoration of Plain and
  Precious Things
Apocryphal Writings and the
  Latter-Day Saints

SPECIALIZED MONOGRAPH SERIES

Supporting Saints: Life Stories
  of Nineteenth-Century
  Mormons
The Call of Zion: The Story of
  the First Welsh Mormon
  Emigration

The Religion and Family
  Connection: Social Science
  Perspectives

The Book of Mormon:
First Nephi, The Doctrinal Foundation

Papers from the Second Annual Book of Mormon Symposium

Edited with a Preface by
Monte S. Nyman and Charles D. Tate, Jr.

Religious Studies Center
Brigham Young University
Provo, Utah

Copyright © 1988 by
Religious Studies Center
Brigham Young University

Library of Congress Catalog Card Number 87-62540
ISBN 0-88494-647-9

First Printing — 1988

Produced and Distributed by
BOOKCRAFT, INC.
Salt Lake City, UT

Printed in the United States of America

CONTENTS

PREFACE

President Jeffrey R. Holland proposed that the Religious Studies Center at Brigham Young University hold an annual Book of Mormon symposium on the campus. The First Annual Book of Mormon Symposium was held in the fall of 1985 under the coordination of Dr. Paul R. Cheesman, who was then the director of Book of Mormon research at the center.

Upon the retirement of Dr. Cheesman, Dr. Monte S. Nyman assumed leadership of the Book of Mormon research area in the center and also the responsibility of coordinating the second annual symposium in 1986. He and Dr. Charles D. Tate, Jr., edited the papers presented at the second symposium for publication in this volume.

Since we plan several symposia in this series on the Book of Mormon, we will follow a basically chronological path. The first symposium was an overview, with papers concerned about the Book of Mormon in general. The second symposium focused on the book of 1 Nephi, which in fulfillment of a prophecy of Isaiah forms the doctrinal foundation of the Book of Mormon. Isaiah prophesied that the Book of Mormon would bring a spiritually blind generation to understanding and from it they would learn doctrine (2 Nephi 27:35; Isaiah 29:24). The book of 1 Nephi firmly establishes the major doctrine of the Book of Mormon—that Jesus Christ is the Savior of the world—and amply demonstrates his foreknowledge of world events by which he can bring about his eternal purposes. Other doctrines such as faith in Christ, the value of his word, the power of the Holy Ghost, and the relevance of his prophets are among many substantiated in that first book.

We hope that our readers will gain further knowledge, deeper testimonies, and greater motivation to live by the basic doctrines found in the book of 1 Nephi from reading the papers in this volume.

We emphasize that the views expressed in the various papers are not necessarily those endorsed by The Church of Jesus Christ of Latter-day Saints, Brigham Young University, or the Religious

Studies Center collectively or individually. Each author takes sole responsibility for the views presented in his or her paper.

MONTE S. NYMAN
CHARLES D. TATE, JR.

1

THE BOOK OF MORMON: A GREAT ANSWER TO "THE GREAT QUESTION"

Elder Neal A. Maxwell

I commend BYU and the Religious Studies Center for sponsoring this symposium focusing on such a vital book. My remarks will focus upon my impressions during my rereading of the Book of Mormon during this past summer.

To begin with, the Book of Mormon provides resounding and great answers to what Amulek designated as "the great question"; namely, is there really a redeeming Christ? (Alma 34:5–6.) The Book of Mormon with clarity and with evidence says, "Yes! Yes! Yes!" Moreover, in its recurring theme, the book even declares that "all things which have been given of God from the beginning of the world, unto man, are the typifying of [Christ]" (2 Nephi 11:4). How striking its answers are, considering all that God might have chosen to tell us! He, before whom all things—past, present, and future—are continually (D&C 130:7), has chosen to tell us about the "gospel" (3 Nephi 27:13–14, 21; D&C 33:12; D&C 39:6; 76:40–41)—the transcending "good news," the resplendent answers to "the great question."

Elder Neal A. Maxwell is a member of the Council of the Twelve Apostles of The Church of Jesus Christ of Latter-day Saints.

Astoundingly, too, God, who has created "worlds without number" (Moses 1:33, 37–38; see Isaiah 45:18), has chosen to reassure us on this tiny "speck of sand" that he "doeth not anything save it be for the benefit of [this] world; for he loveth [this] world" (2 Nephi 26:24); and "For behold, this is my work and my glory—to bring to pass the immortality and eternal life of man" (Moses 1:39).

It should not surprise us that this glorious gospel message is more perfect than any of its messengers, save Jesus only. Nor should it surprise us that the gospel message is more comprehensive than the comprehension of any of its bearers or hearers, save Jesus only.

Apparently translated by Joseph Smith at an average rate of eight or more of its printed pages a day, the Book of Mormon's full significance could not have been immediately and fully savored by the Prophet Joseph. Given this average, according to Professor Jack Welch, only one and a half days, for instance, would have been spent translating all of the first five chapters of Mosiah, a remarkable sermon about which books will be written.

Coming forth as it did in Bible Belt and revival conditions early in this dispensation, we of the Church have been slow to appreciate the special relevance of the Book of Mormon to the erosive conditions in ours, the latter part of this dispensation. Questioning and doubting has grown rapidly on the part of some scholars and even some clerics about the historicity of Jesus. Such, however, was not the America of 1830. Demographically speaking, therefore, the majority of the ministry of the Book of Mormon is occurring in a time of deep uncertainty and unrest concerning "the great question"—the very question which the Book of Mormon was created to answer!

And all this in a time that has been called the post-Christian era—an era, in the irony of ironies, which will come to an abrupt end when Christ, the King of kings, comes to reign over his kingdom.

Another strong reimpression is how the Book of Mormon foretells the latter-day emergence of "other books" of scripture (1 Nephi 13:39), of which it is one: "Proving to the world that the holy scriptures are true, and that God does inspire men and call them to his holy work in this age and generation, as well as in generations of old" (D&C 20:11).

With regard to omissions from the precious Holy Bible, in only one chapter of 1 Nephi, chapter 13, four phrases appear:

taken away, four times; *taken out*, once; *kept back*, twice; and *taken away out of*, once. Eight indications of omissions because of transmission deficiencies appear in one chapter! Moreover, as Nephi indicated, it was the "precious things" which had been lost. You will recall that Joseph Smith's translation of Luke 11:52 shows Jesus criticizing those, then, who had "taken away the key of knowledge, the fulness of the scriptures" (JST, Luke 11:53).

While we do not know precisely what was "kept back" or "taken away" (see 1 Nephi 13:40), logically there would be a heavy representation of such plain and precious truths in the Restoration. Therefore, the "other books" provide precisely that which God is most anxious to have "had again" among the children of men, so that we might know the truth of things, in Jacob's felicitous phrase, of "things as they really are" (Jacob 4:13).

The convergence of these "other books" of scripture with the precious Bible is part of the rhythm of the Restoration. The rhythm would have been impossible except for devoted and heroic individuals including the Jewish prophets and the Jewish people of antiquity who, in the words of the Book of Mormon, had "travails," "labors," and "pains" to preserve the Bible for us. Lamentably, as foreseen, for that contribution the Jews have been unthanked as a people, and instead have been "cursed," "hated," and made "game" of. (See 2 Nephi 29:4–5; 3 Nephi 29:4, 8.) A much later expression of the rhythm of the Restoration is symbolically reflected, too, in the graves of some Church members of the 1830s buried in Ohio and Indiana. Recently discovered, there is a trail of testifying tombstones which display, in stone, replicas of both the Bible *and* the Book of Mormon. These members felt doubly blessed and wanted the world to know it.

The existing scriptures advise of more than twenty other books to come forth[1] (see 1 Nephi 19:10–16). One day, in fact, "all things shall be revealed unto the children of men which ever have been . . . and which ever will be" (2 Nephi 27:11). Hence the ninth Article of Faith is such an impressive statement! My personal opinion, however, is that we will not get additional scriptures until we learn to appreciate fully those we already have.

The "other books," particularly the Book of Mormon, fulfill—if constitutional lawyers will forgive me—Nephi's "establishment clause": "These last records . . . shall *establish* the truth of the first, which are of the twelve apostles of the Lamb"

(1 Nephi 13:40; italics added). What the latter-day seer, Joseph Smith, brought forth will actually aid some people in accepting God's word which had already gone forth, namely the Bible (2 Nephi 3:11), by convincing them "that the records of the prophets and of the twelve apostles of the Lamb are true" (1 Nephi 13:39). There is high drama ahead!

Meanwhile, even as the criticism of the Book of Mormon continues to intensify, the book continues to testify and to diversify its displays of interior consistency, conceptual richness, and its connections with antiquity.

The plentitude of the Restoration followed as foreseen by Amos: "a famine in the land, not a famine of bread, nor a thirst for water, but of hearing the words of the Lord" (Amos 8:11). The end of that famine was marked by the coming of the Book of Mormon and the "other books."

Such books have been and are the Lord's means of preserving the spiritual memory of centuries past. Without moral memory, spiritual tragedy soon follows: "Now . . . there were many of the rising generation that . . . did not believe what had been said concerning the resurrection of the dead, neither did they believe concerning the coming of Christ" (Mosiah 26:1–2). And on another occasion, "And at the time that Mosiah discovered them . . . they had brought no records with them; and they denied the being of their Creator" (Omni 1:17).

Belief in Deity and the Resurrection are usually the first to go. Ironically, though we gratefully accept the Bible as the word of God, the very process of its emergence has, alas, caused an unnecessary slackening of the Christian faith on the part of some. Because available Bible sources are not original, but represent dated derivations and translations, this makes the "other books" of scripture, which have come to us directly from ancient records and modern revelations, even more prized.

Paul, for instance, wrote his first epistle to the Corinthians about A.D. 56. We do not, of course, have that original parchment. Instead, the earliest document involving the first epistle to the Corinthians was discovered in the 1930s and is dated about A.D. 200. By comparison, King Benjamin's sermon was given in about 124 B.C. by a prophet. In the late fourth century A.D. it was selected by another prophet—Mormon—to be a part of the Book of Mormon. Benjamin's sermon was translated into English in A.D. 1829 by Joseph Smith, another prophet. There was, therefore, an unbroken chain of a prophet-originator, a prophet-

4

editor, and a prophet-translator collaborating in a remarkable process.

Even so, some discount the Book of Mormon because they cannot see the plates from which it was translated. Furthermore, they say that we do not know enough about the process of translation. But Moroni's promise to serious readers, to be discussed shortly, involves reading and praying over the book's substance —not over the process of its production. We are "looking beyond the mark" (Jacob 4:14), therefore, when, figuratively speaking, we are more interested in the physical dimensions of the cross than what was achieved thereon by Jesus. Or, when we neglect Alma's words on faith because we are too fascinated by the light-shielding hat reportedly used by Joseph Smith during some of the translating of the Book of Mormon.[2]

Most of all, I have been especially struck in rereading and pondering the Book of Mormon with how, for the serious reader, it provides a very, very significant response to what might be called modern man's architectonic needs—that is, our deep needs to discern some design, purpose, pattern, or plan regarding human existence.

No less than fifteen times, the Book of Mormon uses the word *plan* in connection with the plan of salvation or its components. The very use of the word *plan* is itself striking. In bringing back this particular "plain and precious" truth—namely, God not only lives but does have a plan for mankind—the Book of Mormon is unusually relevant for our age and time. Phrases about God's planning from the "foundation of the world" appear not at all in the Old Testament, but ten times in the New Testament, and three times as often in the other books.[3] *Foundation*, of course, thus denotes a creation overseen by a loving and planning God.

The Book of Mormon lays further and heavy emphasis on how the gospel, in fact, has been with mankind from Adam on down. Only six pages into the book, we read of the testifying words of all the prophets "since the world began" (1 Nephi 3:20); five pages later, a recitation notes the words of the "holy prophets, from the beginning" (1 Nephi 5:13). This one verse represents many:

> For behold, did not Moses prophesy unto them concerning the coming of the Messiah, and that God should redeem his people? Yea, and even all the prophets who have prophesied ever

since the world began—have they not spoken more or less concerning these things? (Mosiah 13:33; see 2 Nephi 25:19.)

It seems probable that there will be some additional discoveries of ancient records pertaining to the Old and New Testaments, further shrinking the time between the origination of those scriptures and the earliest available documentation. However, this *shrinking* will not automatically lead to an *enlarging* of the faith—at least of some. Future discoveries of ancient documents which may "throw greater views on [His] gospel" (D&C 10:45) may also focus on portions of Jesus' gospel which existed *before* Jesus' mortal ministry. Unfortunately, a few may unjustifiably use such discoveries to diminish the divinity of the Redeemer, inferring that Jesus is, therefore, not the originator, as previously thought. However, the restored gospel, including the Book of Mormon, gives us such a clear reading of the spiritual history of mankind, showing God's "tender mercies" (see 1 Nephi 1:20; Ether 6:12) from Adam on down. There is thus no need for us to be anxious about finding a reliable portion of Christ's gospel before Christ's mortal ministry. The gospel was preached and known from the beginning (see Moses 5:58–59).

The detailed, interior correlation of the Book of Mormon—indeed of all true scripture—is marvelous to behold. Centuries before Christ's birth, King Benjamin prophesied: "And he shall be called Jesus Christ, the Son of God, the Father of heaven and earth, the Creator of all things from the beginning" (Mosiah 3:8).

The resurrected Jesus introduced himself to the Nephites with strikingly similar words centuries later: "Behold, I am Jesus Christ the Son of God. I created the heavens and the earth, and all things that in them are. I was with the Father from the beginning." (3 Nephi 9:15.)

But back to God's enfolding plan. Alma, after a discussion of the Fall, declared it was "expedient that man should know concerning the things whereof [God] had appointed unto them; therefore [God] sent angels to converse with them . . . and [make] known unto them the plan of redemption, which had been prepared from the foundation of the world" (Alma 12:28–30). This is the very process which was followed, of course, in North America in the first half of the nineteenth century through angelic visitations to Joseph Smith.

At the center of this architectonic responsiveness, with its related dispensational emphasis, is the Book of Mormon's steady, Christian core. Jacob wrote: "We knew of Christ . . . many hundred years before his coming . . . also all the holy prophets which were before us. Behold, they believed in Christ and worshipped the Father in his name . . . [keeping] the law of Moses, it pointing our souls to him." (Jacob 4:4–5.) Jacob was emphatic: "None of the prophets have written . . . save they have spoken concerning this Christ" (Jacob 7:11).

God witnesses to us in so many ways: "Yea, and all things denote there is a God; yea, even the earth, and all things that are upon the face of it, yea, and its motion, yea, and also all the planets which move in their regular form do witness that there is a Supreme Creator" (Alma 30:44; see also Moses 6:63).

A believing British scientist has observed the following of our especially situated planet:

> [Just a bit nearer to the sun, and Planet Earth's seas would soon be boiling; just a little farther out, and the whole world would become a frozen wilderness.]
> . . . If our orbit happened to be the wrong shape . . . then we should alternately freeze like Mars and fry like Venus once a year. Fortunately for us, our planet's orbit is very nearly a circle.
> The 21 percent of oxygen is another critical figure. Animals would have difficulty breathing if the oxygen content fell very far below that value. But an oxygen level much higher than this would also be disastrous, since the extra oxygen would act as a fire-raising material. Forests and grasslands would flare up every time lightning struck during a dry spell, and life on earth would become extremely hazardous.[4]

When, therefore, we know the affirmative answers to "the great question," we can, in Amulek's phrase, "live in thanksgiving daily" (Alma 34:38), including gratitude for the many special conditions which make daily life on this earth possible.

God's encompassing purposes are set forth to the very end of the Book of Mormon. Moroni urged a precise method of study and verification which, if followed, will show among other things how merciful the Lord has been unto mankind "from the creation of Adam" (Moroni 10:3). Foretelling can be convincing, too, along with remembering, in showing the sweep of God's love. We read in the Book of Mormon, "Telling them of things which must shortly come, that they might know and remember at the time of their coming that they had been made known unto them beforehand, to the intent that they might believe" (Helaman 16:5; see also Mormon 8:34–35).

Every age needs this architectonic message, but none more desperately than our age, which is preoccupied with skepticism and hedonism: "For how knoweth a man the master whom he has not served, and who is a stranger unto him, and is far from the thoughts and intents of his heart?" (Mosiah 5:13).

If, however, one gets too caught up in the warfare in the Book of Mormon, or if he is too preoccupied with the process of the book's emergence, such transcendant truths as the foregoing can easily be overlooked.

Even the title page[5] declares, among other things, that the Book of Mormon was to advise posterity "what great things the Lord hath done for their fathers." The very lack of such a spiritual memory once led to a decline of ancient Israel: "There arose another generation after them, which knew not the Lord, nor yet the works which he had done for Israel" (Judges 2:10).

Why was it so difficult for a whole people—or for Laman and Lemuel—to maintain faith? Because they were uninformed and unbelieving as to "the dealings of that God who had created them." (1 Nephi 2:12; 2 Nephi 1:10.) Many efforts were made: "I, Nephi, did teach my brethren these things; . . . I did read many things to them, which were engraven upon the plates of brass, that they might know concerning the doings of the Lord in other lands, among people of old" (1 Nephi 19:22).

The current prophetic emphasis by President Benson on the Book of Mormon, therefore, is so timely!

Even the criticisms of the book will end up having their usefulness in God's further plans. Granted, the great answers in the book will not now be accepted by disbelievers. Such people would not believe the Lord's words—whether coming through Paul or Joseph Smith—even if they had an original Pauline parchment or direct access to the gold plates. The Lord once comforted Joseph Smith by saying such individuals "would not believe my words . . . if [shown] all these things" (D&C 5:7).

Thus, at the same time some decry the Book of Mormon, for those who have ears to hear, it represents an informing but haunting "cry from the dust" (2 Nephi 3:20). It is the voice of a fallen people sent to lift us. Described as a "whisper out of the dust" (2 Nephi 26:16) from "those who have slumbered" (2 Nephi 27:9), this sound from the dust is the choral cry of many anguished voices with but a single, simple message. Their spiritual struggles span a few centuries but concern the message of the ages—the gospel of Jesus Christ! The peoples of the Book of Mormon were not on the center stage of secular history. Instead, theirs was a comparatively little theater. Yet it featured history's largest message.

Not pleasing to those who crave other kinds of history, the Book of Mormon is pleasing to those who genuinely seek answers to "the great question" (Alma 34:5). Contrary to the sad conclusion now reached by many, the Book of Mormon declares to us again and again that the universe is not comprised of what has been called "godless geometric space."[6]

Granted, too, usually the "learned shall not read [these things], for they have rejected them" (2 Nephi 27:20). This is not solely a reference to Professor Anthon, since the plural pronoun *they* is used. The reference suggests a mind-set of most of the learned of the world, who, by and large, do not take the Book of Mormon seriously. Even when they read it, they do not *really* read it, except with a mind-set which excludes miracles, including the miracle of the book's coming forth by the "gift and power of God." Their flawed approach diverts them from scrutinizing the substance. Sometimes, as has been said, certain mortals are so afraid of being "taken in," they cannot be "taken out" of their mind-sets.[7]

How dependent mankind is, therefore, upon emancipating revelation: "Behold, great and marvelous are the works of the Lord. How unsearchable are the depths of the mysteries of him; and it is impossible that man should find out all his ways. And no man knoweth of his ways save it be revealed unto him; wherefore, brethren, despise not the revelations of God." (Jacob 4:8.)

Now to Moroni's promise, which is a promise that rests on a premise; a promise with several parts. The reader is (1) to read and ponder, (2) while remembering God's mercies to mankind from Adam until now, and (3) to pray in the name of Christ and ask God with real intent if the book is true—(4) while having faith in Christ—then (5) God will manifest the truth of the book. The reverse approach, scanning while doubting, is the flip side of Moroni's methodology and produces flippant conclusions. Moroni's process of verification is surely not followed by many readers or reviewers of this book. This leads to misapprehension on their part—something like mistakenly labeling rumor with her thousand tongues as the gift of tongues!

Therefore, we should not be deluded into thinking that these "other books" will be welcomed, especially by those whose sense of sufficiency is expressed thus: "There cannot be any more" such books and "we need no more" such books (2 Nephi 29:3, 6).

Another strong impression from my rereading is how the Book of Mormon peoples, though Christians, were tied, until Jesus came, much more strictly to the pre-exilic law of Moses than we in the Church have fully appreciated. "And, notwithstanding we believe in Christ, we keep the law of Moses, and look forward with steadfastness unto Christ, until the law shall be fulfilled" (2 Nephi 25:24).

People back then were thus to "look forward unto the Messiah, and believe in him to come as though he already was" (Jarom 1:11). Moses indeed prophesied of the Messiah, but not all of his words are in the treasured Old Testament. Recall the walk of the resurrected Jesus with two disciples on the road to Emmaus? Their walk probably covered about twelve kilometers and provided ample time for Jesus' recitation of not merely three or four, but many prophecies by Moses and others concerning Christ's mortal ministry (Luke 24:27).

Scriptures attesting to Jesus' divinity are vital in any age. Otherwise, as the Book of Mormon prophesies, he will be considered a mere man (Mosiah 3:9) or a person of "naught" (1 Nephi 19:9). Over the decades, what has been called the "dilution of Christianity from within"[8] has resulted in a number of theologians not only diminishing their regard for Christ, but likewise regarding the Resurrection as merely "a symbolic expression for the renewal of life for the disciple."[9] Once again we see the supernal importance of the "other books" of scripture: they reinforce the reality of the Resurrection, especially the Book of Mormon's additional gospel with its report of the visitation of and instruction by the resurrected Jesus. The resurrection of many others occurred and, by Jesus' pointed instruction, was made record of. (See 3 Nephi 23:6–13.)

Thus the Book of Mormon resoundingly, richly, and grandly answers the "great question." Granted, in our day, the post-Christian era, many who are preoccupied are not even asking that great question anymore, regarding Christianity "not as untrue or even as unthinkable, but simply irrelevant,"[10] just like some in Benjamin and Mosiah's times (see Mosiah 28:1–2; Omni 1:17).

If the answer to "the great question" were "No," there

would quickly come a wrenching surge of what Professor Hugh Nibley has called the "terrible questions."

Even the historical, political, and geographical setting of the emergence of the Book of Mormon was special. President Brigham Young boldly declared:

> Could that book have been brought forth and published to the world under any other government but the Government of the United States? No. [God] has governed and controlled the settling of this continent. He led our fathers from Europe to this land . . . and inspired the guaranteed freedom in our Government, though that guarantee is too often disregarded. (JD 8:67.)

In the midst of this continually unfolding drama, a few members of the Church, alas, desert the cause; they are like one who abandons an oasis to search for water in the desert. Some of these few will doubtless become critics, and they will be welcomed into the "great and spacious building." Henceforth, however, so far as their theological accommodations are concerned, they are in a spacious but third-rate hotel. All dressed up, as the Book of Mormon says, "exceedingly fine" (1 Nephi 8:27), they have no place to go except—one day, hopefully, home.

The great answers to the "great question" repeatedly focus us, therefore, on the reality of the "great and last sacrifice." "This is the whole meaning of the law, every whit pointing to that great and last sacrifice; and that great and last sacrifice will be the Son of God, yea, infinite and eternal" (Alma 34:14). These great answers reaffirm that mortal melancholy need not be, however frequently and poignantly expressed.

Furthermore, what we receive in the Book of Mormon is not a mere assemblage of aphorisms, nor is it merely a few individuals offering their philosophical opinions. Instead, we receive the cumulative witness of prophetic individuals, especially those who were eyewitnesses of Jesus, including Lehi, Nephi, Jacob, Alma, the brother of Jared, Mormon, and Moroni. The biblical account of the five hundred brothers and sisters witnessing the resurrected Jesus (1 Corinthians 15:6) is joined by the witnessing throng of twenty-five hundred in the land of Bountiful (3 Nephi 17:25). All of these are thus added to the burgeoning cloud of witnesses about whom the apostle Paul wrote (Hebrews 12:1).

The Book of Mormon might have been another kind of book, of course. It could have been chiefly concerned with the ebb and flow of governmental history; that is, "Princes come and princes go, an hour of pomp, an hour of show." Such would not have offset, however, the many despairing books and the literature of lamentation so much of which we have already, each reminiscent in one way or another of the hopelessness of these lines from Shelley:

> . . . Two vast and trunkless legs of stone
> Stand in the desert. Near them, on the sand,
> Half sunk, a shattered visage lies, . . .
> And on the pedestal, these words appear:
> "My name is Ozymandias, king of kings:
> Look on my works, ye Mighty, and despair!"
> Nothing beside remains. Round the decay
> Of that colossal wreck, boundless and bare
> The lone and level sands stretch far away.[11]

Because the editing of the Book of Mormon, with its gospel of hope, occurred under divine direction, it has a focus which is essentially spiritual. Yet some still criticize the Book of Mormon for not being what it was never intended to be, as if one could justifiably criticize the phone directory for lack of a plot!

Some verses in the Book of Mormon are of tremendous salvational significance, others less so. The book of Ether has a verse about lineage history: "And Jared had four sons" (and names them) (Ether 6:14). However, Ether also contains another verse of tremendous salvational significance:

> And if men come unto me I will show unto them their weakness. I give unto men weakness that they may be humble; and my grace is sufficient for all men that humble themselves before me; for if they humble themselves before me, and have faith in me, then will I make weak things become strong unto them. (Ether 12:27.)

We read of a battle "when . . . they slept upon their swords . . . were drunken with anger, even as a man who is drunken with wine. . . . And when the night came there were thirty and two of the people of Shiz, and twenty and seven of the people of Coriantumr." (Ether 15:20–26.) Such, however, is of a much lower spiritual significance for the development of our discipleship than are these next lines. In all of scripture, these constitute the most complete delineation of Jesus' requirement that we become as little children (see Matthew 18:3): ". . . and becometh as a child, submissive, meek, humble, patient, full of love, willing to submit to all things which the Lord seeth fit to inflict upon him, even as a child doth submit to his father" (Mosiah 3:19).

One reason to "search the scriptures" is to discover these sudden luxuriant meadows of meaning, these green pastures to nourish us in our individual times of need. The Book of Mormon surely has its share and more of these. Immediately after words about economic conditions in the now vanished city of Helam, we encounter an enduring and bracing truth: "Nevertheless the Lord seeth fit to chasten his people; yea, he trieth their patience and their faith" (Mosiah 23:20–21; see also D&C 98:12; Abraham 3:25).

Similarly, the Book of Mormon provides us with insights we may not yet be ready to manage fully. Astonishingly, Alma includes our pains, sicknesses, and infirmities, along with our sins, as being among that which Jesus would also "take upon him" (Alma 7:11, 12). It was part of the perfecting of Christ's mercy by his experiencing "according to the flesh." Nephi in exclaiming "O how great the plan of our God" (2 Nephi 9:13) also declared how Jesus would suffer "the pains of all . . . men, women, and children, who belong to the family of Adam" (2 Nephi 9:21). The soul trembles at those implications. One comes away weeping from such verses, deepened in his adoration of our Redeemer.

Given such richness, it is unsurprising that the prophets urge us to read the Book of Mormon. In closing his writings to those who do not respect (1) the words of the Jews (the Bible), (2) his words (as found in the Book of Mormon), and (3) also the words from Jesus (from the future New Testament), Nephi said simply, "I bid you an everlasting farewell" (2 Nephi 33:14).

Mormon is equally emphatic regarding this interactiveness between the Bible and the Book of Mormon (see Mormon 7:8–9). The interactiveness and cross-supportiveness of holy scripture was attested to by Jesus. "For had ye believed Moses, ye would have believed me: for he wrote of me. But if ye believe not his writings, how shall ye believe my words?" (John 5:46–47.)

Meanwhile, from those who say "We have enough, from them shall be taken away even that which they have" (2 Nephi

28:30). Obviously, this refers not to the physical loss of the Bible, which may still be on the bookshelf or may be used as a bookend, but to a sad loss of conviction concerning it on the part of some.

When we "search the scriptures," the luminosity of various verses in the various books is focused, laserlike. This illumination arcs and then converges, even though we are dealing with different authors, people, places, and times: "Wherefore, I speak the same words unto one nation like unto another. And when the two nations shall run together the testimony of the two nations shall run together also." (2 Nephi 29:8.)

Believing, however, is not a matter of accessing antiquity with all its evidence, though we welcome such evidence. Nor is it dependent upon accumulating welcomed historical evidence either. Rather, it is a matter of believing in Jesus' words. Real faith, like real humility, is developed "because of the word"— and not because of surrounding circumstances! (Alma 32:13–14.)

How fitting it is that it should be so! The test is focused on the message, not on the messengers; on principles, not on process; on doctrines, not on plot. The emphasis is on belief "because of the word." As Jesus told Thomas on the Eastern Hemisphere, "Blessed are they that have not seen, and yet have believed" (John 20:29). He proclaimed to the Nephites: "More blessed are they who shall believe in your words because that ye shall testify that ye have seen me" (3 Nephi 12:2).

True faith, therefore, is brought about by overwhelming and intimidating divine intervention. The Lord, the Book of Mormon tells us, is a shepherd with a mild and pleasant voice (see Helaman 5:30–31; 3 Nephi 11:3)—not a shouting and scolding sheepherder. Others may, if they choose, demand a "voiceprint" of the "voice of the Lord," but even if so supplied, they would not like his doctrines anyway (see John 6:66). The things of the Spirit are to be "sought by faith" and they are not to be seen through slit-eyed skepticism.

Without real faith, individuals sooner or later find one thing or another to stumble over (Romans 9:32). After all, it is a very difficult thing to show the proud things which they "never had supposed," especially things they do not really want to know. When Jesus was speaking about himself as the bread of life, a powerful doctrine laden with life-changing implications, there was murmuring. Jesus asked them, "Doth this offend you?" (John 6:61.) "Blessed is he, whosoever shall not be offended in me" (Luke 7:23).

As if all this were not enough, the splendid Book of Mormon advises that a third scriptural witness is yet to come from the lost tribes (see 2 Nephi 29:12–14). Its coming is likely to be even more dramatic than the coming forth of the second testament. Those who doubt or disdain the second testament of Christ will not accept the third either. But believers will then possess a triumphant triad of truth (see 2 Nephi 29:12–14). Were it not for the Book of Mormon, we would not even know about the third set of records!

We do not know when and how this will occur, but we are safe in assuming that the third book will have the same fundamental focus as the Book of Mormon—"that . . . their seed [too] . . . may be brought to a knowledge of me, their Redeemer" (3 Nephi 16:4). If there is a title page in that third set of sacred records, it is not likely to differ in purpose from the title page in the Book of Mormon, except for its focus on still other peoples who likewise received a personal visit from the resurrected Jesus (see 3 Nephi 15:20–24; 16:1–4).

Thus, in the dispensation of the fulness of times there is not only a "welding together" (D&C 128:18) of the keys of all the dispensations, but there will also be a "welding together" of all the sacred books of scripture given by the Lord over the sweep of human history. Then, as prophesied, "my word also shall be gathered in one" (2 Nephi 29:14). Then there will be one fold, one shepherd, and one stunning scriptural witness for the Christ!

Given all the foregoing, it is touching that a jailed Joseph Smith, during his last mortal night, 26 June 1844, bore "a powerful testimony to the guards of the divine authenticity of the Book of Mormon, the restoration of the Gospel, the administration of angels"[12] (see Alma 12:28–30). The guards apparently did not hearken then any more than most of the world hearkens now. Heeded or unheeded, however, the Book of Mormon has a further rendezvous to keep: "Wherefore, these things shall go from generation to generation as long as the earth shall stand; and they shall go according to the will and pleasure of God; and the nations who shall possess them shall be judged of them according to the words which are written" (2 Nephi 25:22).

For my part, I am glad the book will be with us "as long as the earth shall stand." I need and want additional time. For me, towers, courtyards, and wings await inspection. My tour of it has never been completed. Some rooms I have yet to enter, and there are more flaming fireplaces waiting to warm me. Even the rooms

I have glimpsed contain further furnishings and rich detail yet to be savored. There are panels inlaid with incredible insights and design and decor dating from Eden. There are also sumptuous banquet tables painstakingly prepared by predecessors which await all of us. Yet, we as Church members sometimes behave like hurried tourists, scarcely venturing beyond the entry hall to the mansion.

May we come to feel as a whole people beckoned beyond the entry hall. May we go inside far enough to hear clearly the whispered truths from those who have "slumbered," which whisperings will awaken in us individually the life of discipleship as never before.

That it may be so for the people of the Church, spurred by this symposium and, more important, by the Spirit is my witness to you, in the name of Jesus Christ. Amen.

NOTES AND REFERENCES

1. Wars of the Lord, Jasher, more from Samuel, the Acts of Solomon, the book of Nathan, Shemaiah, Ahijah, Iddo, Jehu, the Sayings of the Seers, at least two epistles of Paul, books of Enoch, Ezias, Adam's Book of Remembrance, and Gad the Seer. Thus we are dealing with over twenty missing books. We also have certain prophecies from Jacob, or Israel, and extensive prophecies by Joseph in Egypt, only a portion of which we have (2 Nephi 3:1–25 and 4:1–3; JST, Genesis 50:24–37; Alma 46:24–26).

2. Furthermore, too few people are inclined to follow the counsel of Moroni regarding the book's substance: "Condemn me not because of mine imperfection, neither my father, because of his imperfection, neither them who have written before him; but rather give thanks unto God that he hath made manifest unto you our imperfections, that ye may learn to be more wise than we have been" (Mormon 9:31).

3. Twenty-two times in the Book of Mormon, ten times in the Doctrine and Covenants, and three times in the Pearl of Great Price.

4. Alan Hayward, *God Is* (Nashville: Thomas Nelson, Inc., 1980), pp. 62, 63, 68.

5. *Teachings of the Prophet Joseph Smith*, comp. Joseph Fielding Smith (Salt Lake City: Deseret Book Co., 1976), p. 7.

6. Michael Harrington, *The Politics at God's Funeral: The Spiritual Crisis of Western Civilization* (New York: Holt, Rinehart, and Winston, 1983), p. 114.

7. C. S. Lewis, *The Last Battle* (New York: Collier, 1970), p. 148.

8. Harrington, *The Politics at God's Funeral*, p. 153.

9. Ibid., p. 164.

10. Penelope Fitzgerald, *The Knox Brothers* (Coward, McCann & Geoghegen, Inc.: New York, 1977), p. 106–7.

11. Percy Bysshe Shelley, "Ozymandias," *Norton Anthology of English Literature* 2 vols. (New York: W. W. Norton & Company, 1986), 2:691.

12. *Teachings of the Prophet Joseph Smith*, p. 383.

2

THE TITLE PAGE

Daniel H. Ludlow

I am grateful to have been asked to discuss the title page of the Book of Mormon.[1] I was both surprised and dismayed when I reviewed my book *A Companion to Your Study of the Book of Mormon*—in which I consider each book in the Book of Mormon, chapter by chapter and verse by verse—to find that I did not discuss there or even mention the title page. As I reviewed other commentaries on the Book of Mormon, I found that, almost without exception, they begin with the first verse of the first chapter of 1 Nephi and end with the last verse of the tenth chapter of Moroni. I soon became convinced that the title page of the Book of Mormon is one of the least studied and least understood parts of this holy scripture. Articles and comments on the title page are, indeed, few and far between.

Perhaps more disturbing, some of us may have been applying a misleading "personal interpretation" to the origin and the meaning of some of the statements in the title page because of the lack of thoughtful consideration given to these statements. For

Daniel H. Ludlow is Director of Correlation Review for The Church of Jesus Christ of Latter-day Saints.

example, one statement in the title page is quoted very frequently (and I believe correctly) as referring to the entire Book of Mormon: "Which is to show unto the remnant of the House of Israel what great things the Lord hath done for their fathers; and that they may know the covenants of the Lord, that they are not cast off forever—And also to the convincing of the Jew and Gentile that JESUS is the CHRIST, the ETERNAL GOD, manifesting himself unto all nations." Yet most English professors would say that in the present paragraphing of the title page that passage should refer only to Moroni's abridgment of the book of Ether.

Now let me share with you the steps I followed in my study of the title page. First, I read and reread the following statement by Joseph Smith about the title page, which appears in the standard histories of the Church:

> I wish to mention here that the title-page of the Book of Mormon is a literal translation, taken from the very last leaf, on the left hand side of the collection or book of plates, which contained the record which has been translated, the language of the whole running the same as all Hebrew writing in general; and that said title page is not by any means a modern composition, either of mine or of any other man who has lived or does live in this generation.[2]

Next, I obtained copies of the title pages from all major editions of the Book of Mormon: 1830, 1837, 1840, 1852, 1879, 1920, and 1981. I noted that in the current edition (1981) the text of the title page is divided into twelve major statements. I then compared the wording, spelling, capitalization, and punctuation of each of the twelve statements in all of the major editions. Later in our discussion I will share with you the results of these comparisons.

I also studied the earliest sources of the title page text. The earliest available source is the "printer's manuscript," which is largely in the handwriting of Oliver Cowdery. It is now in the possession of the Reorganized Church of Jesus Christ of Latter Day Saints in Independence, Missouri. With assistance from the staff of the Church Historical Library in Salt Lake City, I obtained a copy of the title page from that manuscript. I have prepared a typewritten copy of that manuscript page, listing its text word for word and letter by letter. I will include that copy at a later point.

Furthermore, I obtained copies of the two other early documents which contain the title page. The first is a handwritten copy on the copyright application form of 11 June 1829, and the second is a printed copy from the 26 June 1829 *Wayne Sentinel*.

With all these copies gathered, let us now examine some of the items I have noted in analyzing the text of the Book of Mormon title page.

But first, let me propose an experiment. Below is a typewritten copy of the title page of the Book of Mormon as it appears in the printer's manuscript. The spelling, capitalization, and punctuation are as shown.

Assume that (1) you are a typesetter working in a publishing house in 1830, and (2) you have the assignment to set this material in type after correcting obvious errors. Now go ahead, edit the material, and punctuate it into sentences and paragraphs.

The Book of Mormon An account written by the hand of Mormon upon plates taken from the plates of Nephi Wherefore it is an abridgment of the record of the People of Nephi & also of the Lamanites written to the Lamanites which are a remnant of the house of Israel & also to Jew & Gentile written by way of commandment & also by the spirit of Prophesy & of revelation written & sealed up & hid up unto the Lord that they might not be destroid to come forth by the gift & power of God unto the interpretation thereof sealed by the hand of Moroni & hid up unto the Lord to come forth in due time by the way of Gentile the enterpretation thereof by the gift of God an abridgment taken from the Book of Ether also which is a record of the People of Jared which were scattered at the time the Lord confounded the language of the People when they were building a tower to get to heaven which is to shew unto the remnant of the house of Israel how great things the Lord hath done for their fathers & that they may know the covenants of the Lord that they are not cast off forever & also to the convincing of the Jew & Gentile that Jesus is the Christ the Eternal God manifesting himself unto all Nations & now if there be fault it be the mistake of men wherefore condemn not the things of God that ye may be found spotless at the judgment seat of Christ

—By Joseph Smith Juniour, Author & proprietor

How did you do? Did you edit it in the same way it was edited for the first edition (1830)? The possibility that you did it differently is quite high. You saw that the copy of the title page in the printer's manuscript contains virtually no punctuation marks, but you also saw that it is capitalized quite carefully. The experiment you just completed is what the typesetter for E. B. Grandin had to do. According to the following statement by B. H. Roberts in the *Comprehensive History of the Church*, the foreman in the Grandin printing establishment, John H. Gilbert, claimed that he was largely responsible for the punctuation and capitalization (possibly not all) of the first edition, which would include determining the sentences and the paragraphs: "It is said by Mr. Gilbert, Grandin's foreman printer and chief compositor on the *Book of Mormon*, that the manuscript as sent to him was neither capitalized nor punctuated, and that the capitalization and punctuation in the first edition was done by him."[3]

Previously I mentioned two early documents of the title page text. The earliest of these two versions is the copy of the copyright application of 11 June 1829 (see figure 1). You will note that in the space on the application form for the title of the book, the Prophet Joseph Smith included all of the text of what we now call the title page. You will note also that the text is written with some capitalization and a considerable degree of punctuation, but is not divided into paragraphs.

The later of these two documents is the *Wayne Sentinel* dated 26 June 1829 (see figure 2). You will note that the text is separated into the following clauses, sentences, and paragraphs:

1. An introduction: "The Book of Mormon, an account, written by the hand of Mormon upon plates, taken from the plates of Nephi."

2. A first paragraph beginning: "Wherefore it is an abridgment of the record of the people of Nephi," and ending, "an abridgment taken from the book of Ether."

3. A second paragraph beginning: "Also, which is a record of the people of Jared," and ending, "that ye may be found spotless at the judgment seat of Christ."

The *Wayne Sentinel* was published by the E. B. Grandin publishing concern. Undoubtedly this 26 June 1829 version reflects the punctuation and paragraphing that had already been determined for the first printing of the Book of Mormon.

You will notice (see figure 3) in the reproduction of the title page in the first edition (1830) that the wording, the essential

Northern District
of New-York. } To wit:

Be it remembered, That on the *eleventh* day of *June* in the *fifty third* year of the Independence of the United States of America, A. D. *1829* *Joseph Smith Junior* of the said District, ha*th* deposited in this Office the title of a *Book* the right whereof *he* claim*s* as *Author* in the words following, to wit: *The Book of Mormon, an account written by the hand of Mormon upon plates taken from the plates of Nephi; Wherefore it is an abridgment of the record of the people of Nephi: and also of the Lamanites, which are a remnant of the House of Israel, and also to Jew & Gentile written by way of commandment and also by the spirit of prophesy & of revelation, written & sealed & hid up unto the Lord, that they might not be destroyed, to come forth by the gift & power of God unto the interpretation thereof — sealed up by the hand of Moroni & hid up unto the Lord, to come forth in due time by the way of Gentile, the interpretation thereof by the gift of God; an abridgment taken from the book of Ether: Also, which is a record of the people of Jared, which were scattered at the time the Lord confounded the language of the people, when they were building a tower to get to Heaven; which is to shew unto the remnant of the house of Israel how great things the Lord hath done for their fathers; & that they may know the covenants of the Lord, that they are not cast off forever: and also to the convincing of the Jew & Gentile that Jesus is the Christ, the eternal God, manifesting himself unto all nations. And now if there be fault, it be the mistake of men; wherefore condemn not the things of God, that ye maybe found spotless at the judgment seat of Christ. By Joseph Smith Junior, author & proprietor.*

In conformity to the act of the Congress of the United States, entitled "An act for the encouragement of learning, by securing the copies of Maps, Charts, and Books, to the authors and proprietors of such copies, during the times therein mentioned." and also, to the act entitled "An act supplementary to an act entitled 'An act for the encouragement of learning, by securing the copies of Maps, Charts, and Books, to the authors and proprietors of such copies during the times therein mentioned;' and extending the benefits thereof to the arts of Designing, Engraving, and Etching historical and other prints."

R.R. Lansing, Clerk of the Dist.
Court of the United States for the Northern District of New York

It is pretended that it will be published as soon as the translation is completed. Meanwhile we have been furnished with the following, which is represented to us as intended for the title page of the work—we give it as a curiosity :—

" The *Book of Mormon*, an account, written by the hand of Mormon upon plates, taken from the plates of Nephi :—

" Wherefore it is an abridgment of the record of the people of Nephi, and also of the Lamanites, written to the Lamanites, which are a remnant of the house of Israel ; and also to Jew and Gentile ; written by way of commandment, and also by the spirit of prophecy, and of revelation ; written and sealed and hid up unto the Lord, that they might not be destroyed,—to come forth by the gift and power of God unto the interpretation thereof—sealed up by the hand of Mormni, and hid up unto the Lord, to come forth in due time by the way of Gentile—the interpretation thereof by the gift of God : an abridgment taken from the book of Ether.

" Also, which is a record of the people of Jared, which were scattered at the time the Lord confounded the language of the people, when they were building a tower to get to Heaven ; which is to shew unto the remnant of the house of Israel how great things the Lord hath done for their fathers : and that they may know the covenants of the Lord, that they are not cast off forever : and also to the convincing of the Jew and Gentile that Jesus is the Christ, the Eternal God, manifesting himself unto all nations. And now, if there be fault, it be the mistake of men : wherefore condemn not the things of God, that ye may be found spotless at the judgment seat of Christ.—By JOSEPH SMITH, Junior, Author and Proprietor "

Figure 2

THE

BOOK OF MORMON:

AN ACCOUNT WRITTEN BY THE HAND OF MORMON, UPON PLATES TAKEN FROM THE PLATES OF NEPHI.

Wherefore it is an abridgment of the Record of the People of Nephi; and also of the Lamanites; written to the Lamanites, which are a remnant of the House of Israel; and also to Jew and Gentile; written by way of commandment, and also by the spirit of Prophesy and of Revelation. Written, and sealed up, and hid up unto the LORD, that they might not be destroyed; to come forth by the gift and power of GOD, unto the interpretation thereof; sealed by the hand of Moroni, and hid up unto the LORD, to come forth in due time by the way of Gentile; the interpretation thereof by the gift of GOD; an abridgment taken from the Book of Ether.

Also, which is a Record of the People of Jared, which were scattered at the time the LORD confounded the language of the people when they were building a tower to get to Heaven: which is to shew unto the remnant of the House of Israel how great things the LORD hath done for their fathers; and that they may know the covenants of the LORD, that they are not cast off forever; and also to the convincing of the Jew and Gentile that JESUS is the CHRIST, the ETERNAL GOD, manifesting Himself unto all nations. And now if there be fault, it be the mistake of men; wherefore condemn not the things of GOD, that ye may be found spotless at the judgment seat of CHRIST.

BY JOSEPH SMITH, JUNIOR,

AUTHOR AND PROPRIETOR.

PALMYRA:

PRINTED BY E. B. GRANDIN, FOR THE AUTHOR.

1830.

Figure 3

punctuation, and the paragraphing are identical to that in the article already published in the *Wayne Sentinel*. These two versions established the pattern of publishing the title page in three sections: a brief introduction and two paragraphs. This same format has been used in all subsequent editions published in English.

One change was made in the title page in the second edition (1837). The clause "An abridgment taken from the book of Ether" was moved from the last part of the first paragraph to the beginning of the second paragraph, bringing the two elements about the book of Ether together. This clause has remained in this position in all subsequent editions in English, including both those of The Church of Jesus Christ of Latter-day Saints and those of the Reorganized Church of Jesus Christ of Latter Day Saints.

The 1840 edition of the title page is virtually identical to the 1837 edition, except that the word *Moroni* appears after the second paragraph. The name *Moroni* also is printed in the same place both in the LDS edition of 1852 and in the RLDS editions of 1874 and 1908.

The only changes between the 1830 and the 1981 editions in the words used, spelling, or word order are shown in the following list:

1830 Edition	*1981 Edition*
which [are a remnant]	who [are a remnant]
[spirit of] prophesy	[spirit of] prophecy
by the way of Gentile	by way of the Gentile
which [were scattered]	who [were scattered]
[Which is to] shew	[Which is to] show
how [great things the Lord hath done]	what [great things the Lord hath done]
if there be fault, it be the mistake of men	if there are faults they are the mistakes of men
judgment seat	judgment-seat
By Joseph Smith, Junior, Author and Proprietor	Translated by Joseph Smith, Jun.

Some of the non-English editions of the title page have paragraphing different from that of the English editions. The 1980 edition in Fijian has four paragraphs, and the Rarotongan edition has three paragraphs.

Interestingly, changing the number of paragraphs might lead to additional insights as we ask such questions as: (1) *who* the author is (or who the authors are) of the various statements of the title page, and (2) *when* the various statements were written. For example, publishing the title page in two paragraphs and adding the word *Moroni* in some editions undoubtedly influenced virtually all early students of the Book of Mormon to conclude that Moroni was the only author of the title page. According to this reasoning, one would conclude that the title page must have been written after about A.D. 385 when Moroni received the plates from his father, Mormon. This view has been expressed by different scholars, including Dr. Sidney B. Sperry, who concluded that Moroni wrote the entire title page at two distinctively different times in his life:

> In the opinion of the writer this statement [Mormon 8:12–13] was Moroni's original farewell. A careful study of what precedes and what follows these words must lead one to realize the possibility of this being so. Verse 13 is a logical point for a chapter division.
>
> It is quite likely that at this point Moroni wrote the first paragraph (as we now have it) of the title page of the Book of Mormon.
>
> "Wherefore, it is an abridgment of the record of the people of Nephi, and also of the Lamanites—Written to the Lamanites, who are a remnant of the house of Israel; and also to Jew and Gentile—Written by way of commandment, and also by the spirit of prophecy and of revelation—Written and sealed up, and hid up unto the Lord, that they might not be destroyed—To come forth by the gift and power of God unto the interpretation thereof—Sealed by the hand of Moroni, and hid up unto the Lord, to come forth in due time by way of the Gentile—The interpretation thereof by the gift of God."
>
> He did not write the second paragraph of the title page at this time for the very good and sufficient reason that he had not yet abridged the Book of Ether which is mentioned therein.[4]

Dr. Sperry then reviewed the contents of Mormon 8:14–9:37 and added:

There may be those who will prefer to believe that this is the point at which Moroni wrote the first paragraph of the title page rather than at Mormon 8:13, as I have advocated. But no matter— Moroni finds that he still has space left on the plates upon which he may write something of value. He ponders the matter and finally decides on making an abridgment of the Book of Ether for the benefit of future generations. . . .

Having finished his task of abridgment, Moroni then proceeded to add another paragraph to his title page. This was a logical necessity. Thus we read:

"An abridgment taken from the Book of Ether also, which is a record of the people of Jared, who were scattered at the time the Lord confounded the language of the people, when they were building a tower to get to heaven—Which is to show unto the remnant of the House of Israel what great things the Lord hath done for their fathers; and that they may know the covenants of the Lord, that they are not cast off forever—And also, to the convincing of the Jew and Gentile that JESUS is the CHRIST, the ETERNAL GOD, manifesting himself unto all nations—And now, if there are faults they are the mistakes of men; wherefore, condemn not the things of God, that ye may be found spotless at the judgment-seat of Christ."[5]

According to Dr. Sperry, Moroni then proceeded to give us the text now found in Moroni chapters 1 through 10.

Virtually all other scholars and students of the Book of Mormon who have written commentary about the title page have reached exactly the same two conclusions: (1) the title page was written entirely by Moroni, and (2) he wrote it at two different times in his life.

Just as a matter of interest, however, let us change the paragraphing of the title page into a brief title (The Book of Mormon) and six paragraphs that we will number 1 through 6 for ease of reference in this discussion. The title page then would appear as follows:

THE
BOOK OF MORMON

1. An account written by the hand of Mormon upon plates taken from the plates of Nephi. Wherefore, it is an abridgment of the record of the people of Nephi, and also of the Lamanites. Written to the Lamanites, who are a remnant of the house of Israel; and also to Jew and Gentile. Written by way of commandment, and also by the spirit of prophecy and of revelation. Written

and sealed up, and hid up unto the Lord, that they might not be destroyed, to come forth by the gift and power of God unto the interpretation thereof.

2. Sealed by the hand of Moroni, and hid up unto the Lord, to come forth in due time by way of the Gentile, the interpretation thereof by the gift of God.

3. An abridgment taken from the Book of Ether also, which is a record of the people of Jared, who were scattered at the time the Lord confounded the language of the people, when they were building a tower to get to heaven.

4. Which is to show unto the remnant of the house of Israel what great things the Lord hath done for their fathers, and that they may know the covenants of the Lord that they are not cast off forever.

5. And also to the convincing of the Jew and Gentile that JESUS is the CHRIST, the ETERNAL GOD, manifesting himself unto all nations.

6. And now, if there are faults they are the mistakes of men; wherefore, condemn not the things of God, that ye may be found spotless at the judgment seat of Christ.

Let us now reread the entire title page word for word but with this new paragraphing, and consider additional possibilities as to the *person* who might have written certain paragraphs and as to the *time* when those paragraphs might have been written.

The brief four-word title (The Book of Mormon) is the same title that has appeared on the cover and title page of all editions and appears first on the title page of the current edition.

In reading the first paragraph, let us change our mind-set and assume that Mormon wrote it rather than Moroni. After all, Mormon was the major abridger or compiler of the writings we have in our present Book of Mormon. Surely, he would have been justified in writing a preface of some type for his work.

An account, written by the hand of Mormon upon plates, taken from the plates of Nephi. Wherefore, it is an abridgment of the record of the people of Nephi, and also of the Lamanites. Written to the Lamanites, who are a remnant of the house of Israel, and also to Jew and Gentile. Written by way of commandment, and also by the spirit of prophecy and of revelation. Written and sealed up, and hid up unto the Lord, that they might not be destroyed, to come forth by the gift and power of God unto the interpretation thereof.

Don't you agree that everything in that paragraph could reasonably and logically have been written by Mormon? Some might say that Mormon would have been too modest to include his own name. But at the time he would have written this paragraph, he was the *only* writer who had written on the plates that he refers to throughout the record as the "plates of Mormon." Also, the word *Mormon* appears only twice on the entire title page: once in the four-word title, and once in the first paragraph of ninety-eight words. In Mosiah 18:30, however, Mormon used the word *Mormon* six times in the first forty-two words of the verse!

Let us now read the next paragraph, assuming as we do so that Moroni is its author. He has received the plates from his father and has engraved on the plates the text of Mormon chapters 8 and 9. Then he adds these words to the title page that his father had written:

> Sealed by the hand of Moroni, and hid up unto the Lord, to come forth in due time by way of the Gentile, the interpretation thereof by the gift of God.

These words obviously were written by Moroni. Therefore, the remainder of the title page also must have been written by Moroni, because he was the only one to engrave on the plates after his father, Mormon.

The assumption that Mormon wrote the first paragraph and Moroni wrote the second paragraph helps explain other difficulties that scholars have pointed out. Note, for example, the close parallels in wording and thought patterns between the last sentence of the first paragraph and the sentence now comprising the second paragraph of our illustration:

> Written and sealed up, and hid up unto the Lord, that they might not be destroyed, to come forth by the gift and power of God unto the interpretation thereof.
> Sealed by the hand of Moroni, and hid up unto the Lord, to come forth in due time by way of the Gentile, the interpretation thereof by the gift of God.

If Moroni had written both of these sentences, why would he have repeated himself so closely? But if Mormon wrote the first of these sentences and intended it to be the final sentence of his title page, could not Moroni logically have used almost the same wording in writing his sentence, which at that time he intended to be the final sentence of the title page?

As indicated earlier, Moroni definitely wrote the remainder of the title *after* he had completed his abridgment of the plates of Ether. Notice the wording of the next sentence, which in our example forms one paragraph:

> An abridgment taken from the Book of Ether also, which is a record of the people of Jared, who were scattered at the time the Lord confounded the language of the people, when they were building a tower to get to heaven.

Now let us read the final three paragraphs, knowing that Moroni wrote them at the very end of his writing and assuming that they pertain to the entire record on the plates of Mormon, both to the writings of Mormon and to the writings of Moroni:

> Which is to show unto the remnant of the house of Israel what great things the Lord hath done for their fathers, and that they may know the covenants of the Lord that they are not cast off forever.
>
> And also to the convincing of the Jew and Gentile that JESUS is the CHRIST, the ETERNAL GOD, manifesting himself unto all nations.
>
> And now, if there are faults they are the mistakes of men; wherefore, condemn not the things of God, that ye may be found spotless at the judgment seat of Christ.

In the traditional printings, these paragraphs appear to pertain *only* to the "abridgment taken from the Book of Ether," although most of us have quoted them as though they pertain to the entire Book of Mormon. The paragraphing suggested here would indicate that they do indeed pertain to the entire book, which is the most logical interpretation.

Let me emphasize that I am not suggesting that the present paragraphing of the title page is necessarily wrong. However, the decision to publish the title page text in two paragraphs was not determined by the Prophet Joseph Smith but by John H. Gilbert, the typesetter at E. B. Grandin's publishing house, *before* he had the opportunity to read and study the entire Book of Mormon. Thus he would not have understood the separate and different contributions of Mormon and Moroni in the Book of Mormon: Mormon's contribution to "the record of the people of Nephi" and Moroni's contribution to the "abridgment taken from the Book of Ether." This lack of understanding by Mr. Gilbert is evident in his decision to divide the introductory statement pertaining to the book of Ether in the title page into two sentences in two different paragraphs. Thus in the first edition of the Book of Mormon the wording "an abridgment taken from the Book of Ether" appears as the last part of paragraph 1, whereas the wording, "also, which is a record of the people of Jared," appears as the first part of paragraph 2. As noted earlier, these two elements were combined in the 1837 edition to comprise the beginning of paragraph two, where they have remained ever since.

Concerning the setting of the type for the title page, Mr. Gilbert has written:

> In the forepart of June 1829, Mr. E. B. Grandin, the printer of the "Wayne Sentinel," came to me and said he wanted I should assist him in . . . printing 5000 copies of a book. . . . Hyrum Smith brought the first installment of manuscript, of 24 pages, closely written on common foolscap paper. . . . The title page was first set up, and after proof was read and corrected, several copies were printed.[6]

That first setting of the type for the title page text into two paragraphs by Mr. Gilbert in "the forepart of June 1829" obviously established the two-paragraph pattern followed (1) in the 26 June 1829 article in the *Wayne Sentinel*, (2) in the first edition of the Book of Mormon, and (3) in all subsequent editions of the Book of Mormon in English.

Thus I believe we may at least consider dividing the text of the title page into more than two paragraphs, knowing that the Book of Mormon is true and that the paragraphing of the title page in no way detracts from its divine nature.

In closing, I bear my testimony that I know the Book of Mormon is the true word of God, revealed to and written by earlier prophets and translated by the Prophet Joseph Smith through the gift and power of God. Of these things I bear witness in the name of Jesus Christ. Amen.

NOTES AND REFERENCES

1. Brother Ludlow gave two different presentations on this subject at the symposium. This written account contains material from both presentations.

2. Joseph Smith, Jr., *History of The Church of Jesus Christ of Latter-day Saints*, ed. B. H. Roberts, 7 vols. (Salt Lake City: Deseret News, 1932–1951), 1:71.

3. B. H. Roberts, *A Comprehensive History of The Church of Jesus Christ of Latter-day Saints*, 6 vols. (Salt Lake City: The Church of Jesus Christ of Latter-day Saints, 1930), 1:159.

4. Sidney B. Sperry in *A Book of Mormon Treasury* (Salt Lake City: Bookcraft, 1959), pp. 123–24.

5. Ibid., pp. 124–25.

6. Wilford C. Wood, *Joseph Smith Begins His Work*, Introductory section (Salt Lake City: Wilford C. Wood, 1958).

3

THE CALLING OF
A PROPHET

John W. Welch

Chapter 1 of 1 Nephi reports in very brief but significant terms the essential facts about the call and public ministry of the prophet Lehi. These rich verses reward close examination. While many approaches can be taken to enhance our understanding and appreciation of the inspiration and courageous dedication of this father-prophet,[1] the approach taken in this paper seeks to examine several details in the text of 1 Nephi 1, attempting, among other things, to see Lehi's prophetic call in light of his world by inquiring how his words and experiences may have been understood by his contemporaries. It is concluded that in many remarkable respects Lehi had much in common with other prophets of God called in that classic era of ancient Israelite prophecy.

Despite the fact that the text reporting the call of Lehi is very brief,[2] it employs several key words and images that were full of tradition and conveyed much meaning in the world in which Lehi lived. By understanding the significance of these ancient words

John W. Welch is Professor of Law at Brigham Young University.

and phrases, modern readers can appreciate many interesting aspects of Lehi's prophetic call. Especially important is Lehi's vision in which he sees God "sitting upon his throne, surrounded with numberless concourses of angels" (1 Nephi 1:8). It appears that by this experience, which compares closely with the so-called "council visions" of Old Testament prophets,[3] Lehi became a prophet.

The commencement of the first year of the reign of Zedekiah. The engaging story of Lehi's call is familiar to virtually every person who has ever begun to read the Book of Mormon. It came in the commencement of the first year of the reign of Zedekiah,[4] king of Judah, in 597/96 B.C. This was undoubtedly an unforgettably troubling year, for in the first part of December, 598 B.C., Jehoiakim, king of Judah, had died. His son Jehoiachin, who was probably only an adolescent, was made king.[5] Three months and ten days later, on 16 March (2 Adar) 597 B.C., Jerusalem fell, having been besieged by the Babylonians (2 Kings 24:10–16).[6] They deposed king Jehoiachin and deported him to Babylon, along with many of the leading citizens, soldiers, and craftsmen of Jerusalem (Jeremiah 24:1),[7] leaving Jehoiachin's uncle, the mere twenty-one-year-old Zedekiah, on the throne as a puppet king.[8] Therefore, at the time when Lehi became concerned about the welfare of his people, the still insurgent Jews at Jerusalem already knew well the indomitable military power of the Babylonians and were in a weakened political position with an inexperienced, twenty-one-year-old king at their helm. The situation in Jerusalem was grave and volatile, if not already desperate.

Such circumstances as trouble in the land and the coronation of a new king often precipitated prophetic action in the ancient world. One scholar, for example, has argued from circumstantial evidence in the Old Testament that prophecy played an especially important role at or around the coronation of each new king. He suggests that the distinctive council visions and messenger prophecies of Micaiah (1 Kings 22:1–38), Isaiah (Isaiah 6, 40), Ezekiel (Ezekiel 1–10), and Amos (Amos 7:1–3, 4–6, 7–9; 8:1–3; 9:1), as well as Jeremiah's temple sermon (Jeremiah 26:1)—which have much in common with 1 Nephi 1—all occurred around the New Year, at the "epiphany and enthronement of Yahweh," the day when the king was typically crowned and the fates or destinies pronounced.[9] If there is any merit to such suggestions, we may understand more clearly the sharply negative reaction which Lehi's public message evoked,[10] since it was apparently near the day when the Israelites were celebrating Zedekiah's enthronement, or at least "in the commencement" of the first year of his troubled reign, that many prophets including Lehi came forth and spoke out pessimistically against Zedekiah's newly installed regime.

Many prophets. Nephi reports that "there came many prophets, prophesying unto the people that they must repent, or the great city Jerusalem must be destroyed" (1 Nephi 1:4). Who were these other prophets and how do their words compare with Lehi's? Prophetic messages of judgment and destruction were in fact common among the so-called classical prophets of Israel who are known to have been active at this time. For example during Lehi's lifetime, Nahum (ca. 612 B.C.) proclaimed the vengeance of the Lord on his enemies and marked the fall of Nineveh. Zephaniah (who also lived during this time) prophesied that God would sweep the earth completely clean and would stretch his hand over Judah to punish its royal house and to wipe out of Jerusalem all remnants of Baal (Zephaniah 1:2−9). "The whole land shall be devoured by the fire of his jealousy," he prophesied (Zephaniah 1:18). "Gather yourselves together, . . . O nation, . . . before the fierce anger of the Lord come upon you," he exhorted (Zephaniah 2:1−2; cf. 3:8).[11] Zephaniah spoke doom against Jerusalem, calling it a tyrant city, filthy and foul (Zephaniah 3:1−8), while he also promised that a poor and afflicted remnant would be preserved by finding refuge in the Lord (Zephaniah 3:11−13; cf. Isaiah 6:13, which also holds out some optimism for the return or repentance of a remnant through the power of the "holy seed") and that the survivors would be rescued and gathered when the proper time would come (Zephaniah 3:19−20). Habakkuk (ca. 609−598 B.C.) prophesied during the reign of Jehoiakim[12] of the destruction of the treacherous and of the overconfident, pronouncing five woes upon extortioners, exploiters, debauchery, and idolatry (Habakkuk 2:5−20), while also offering a prayer to God that He be merciful (Habakkuk 3:2). Jeremiah was also similarly active during and after Lehi's day. And indeed, there were undoubtedly many other prophets who arose during this time for whom we have no names (2 Chronicles 36:15−16).[13]

It is significant in seeing Lehi among his contemporaries that he was not a lone voice delivering the messages of woe, destruction, mercy, and redemption. He likewise prophesied that Jerusalem would be destroyed and that its inhabitants would perish by the sword (1 Nephi 1:13), yet he also praised the mercy of God and looked forward to the "redemption of the world" (1 Nephi 1:14, 19). Although 1 Nephi makes no explicit statement relating Lehi's message to that of his contemporaries, the point is evident: The people in Jerusalem in Lehi's day had been warned expressly and repeatedly.

Nephi also leaves the ill fate of these other prophets unstated. Only a few years earlier, for example, the prophet Urijah had been persecuted, had fled to Egypt, was extradited, convicted, and ignominiously executed for preaching the same message that the prophets were again preaching in the first year of the reign of Zedekiah (Jeremiah 26:20–23). Similarly 2 Chronicles 36:15–16 later explains what had happened to these prophets and why: "And the Lord God of their fathers sent to them by his messengers . . . because he had compassion on his people, and on his dwelling place: But they mocked the messengers of God, and despised his words, and misused his prophets, until the wrath of the Lord arose against his people, till there was no remedy." The fact that he was willing to deliver that very message entrusted to him by God, knowing full well that precisely the same thing would undoubtedly happen to him as had already happened to others delivering that identical message only a few months or years before, marks Lehi as a man of extraordinary courage, commitment, and devotion to the Lord and to his people, one of the hallmarks of a true prophet of the Lord.

It was also typical at this time for these prophets to work largely by themselves. They fulfilled "their missions alone as individuals,"[14] although this does not imply that they were "detached from the mainstream of Israel's religious tradition."[15] Lehi appears to have worked this way, acting on his own inspiration and initiative,[16] for Nephi's account is silent on any involvement Lehi might have had with his fellow prophets. He may have gone forth and prayed unto the Lord (1 Nephi 1:5) because he was among the prophets who were already actively crying repentance in Jerusalem, but it appears more likely that he was profoundly moved to pray, motivated by the problems in Jerusalem and by the messages of the prophets whom he had just heard.

Prayed . . . on behalf of his people. Lehi's first recorded impulse was to pray on behalf of his people (1 Nephi 1:5). In so doing, he was in harmony with the spirit of classic Hebrew prophecy which flourished during his day. A prophet who knows with moral certainty what will happen to his people has been characterized as having an "irresistible" need not only to deliver his message, but "to intercede on behalf of his people."[17] Such attempts by the prophets to try through prayer to offset the impending doom of all their people as a whole community have been identified as one of the notable functions of the classic Israelite prophets during the time of Lehi.[18] Thus, Lehi's action would probably have been viewed by his contemporaries as being in tune with the spirit of prophecy in his day.

A pillar of fire. As Lehi prayed, he beheld a pillar of fire dwelling upon a rock in front of him. From this pillar Lehi saw and heard many powerful things,[19] but Nephi does not elaborate on who or what Lehi saw in this pillar of fire. Joseph Smith described how God, angels, and spirits appear in fiery manifestations; he taught, for instance, that "spirits can only be revealed in flaming fire and glory."[20] From ancient sources, too, one learns that the appearance of fire, especially a pillar of fire, was a frequent mode of heavenly manifestation, sometimes of God and other times of his messengers or of the holy beings who surrounded him. God appeared to Moses in a burning bush (Exodus 3:2) and on a flaming Mount Sinai (Exodus 19:18); he also appeared over the tabernacle at night in a fire (Numbers 9:15) and over the door of the tabernacle by day in a similar "pillar of cloud" (Deuteronomy 31:15). On some occasions in the Old Testament, fire was associated with God's messengers, especially those emanating from God's council (discussed further below; see, for example, Psalm 104:4), whose fiery description can be compared with the appearance of Moroni in Joseph Smith—History 1:30–32; and in other ancient accounts fire was used to combat God's enemies.[21] Thus, we cannot be certain who or what[22] Lehi saw in the pillar of fire that appeared to him. Lehi could have seen God in this pillar, but since his vision of God himself is reported as the next stage of the vision, it seems more likely to me that what he beheld at this time was a messenger of God whose threatening words and presence, perhaps summoning Lehi, caused Lehi to "quake and tremble exceedingly" (1 Nephi 1:6).

He thought he saw God sitting upon his throne, surrounded with numberless concourses of angels. Lehi returned directly to his bed, where the next part of his vision opened. There, most significantly, he beheld "God sitting upon his throne, surrounded with numberless concourses of angels." Such visions of God seated in the midst of his host assembled in heaven appear to have been particularly meaningful for people in Lehi's day.[23] If the prevailing understanding is correct, it was by such a vision that the prophet received his commission, his authorization, his perspective, his knowledge of God, and his information about God's judgments and decrees. Similarly, from the texts of the Book of Mormon one can assume that in connection with his encounter with God and the heavenly council Lehi likewise received his call to serve as a prophet of God, as the following details further show.

In many other texts from the ancient Near East, God is visualized presiding over and working with his council. Important relationships between this council and God's prophets have been scrutinized in recent years by several scholars.[24] While the members of this council served several functions, such as accompanying their God in battle[25] and giving "praise to his glorious position,"[26] the council's most distinctive purpose was to govern the world by delivering the decrees of God.[27] These decrees were typically issued to messengers or prophets who would deliver them to those affected. In earlier years, the prophets of Israel had delivered their messages primarily to the kings of Israel, but in Lehi's day, they typically directed these edicts, like imperial heralds, to the entire population.[28]

Three main elements common to most accounts of such council visions in the Bible have been identified. They are, first, that God was described as surrounded by his numerous host; second, that the discussion of the council was brought to a conclusion by a council leader; and third, that the word of God was then stated to determine the fate of a person or group.[29] The heralds of the council who delivered God's decrees were sometimes deities or angels; other times they were human prophets, messengers, or apostles who were admitted in a vision into the council, made privy to the judgment of the council, and then dispatched to make their assigned proclamation. From the fact that many ancient Near Eastern accounts show the messenger delivering the identical words he received from the council, it has been concluded that it was apparently important to these people that "the message [be] delivered in precisely the same words that had been given to the divine couriers,"[30] and that this gave divine authority and legitimacy to the decrees the prophet or messenger delivered.[31] That council, its decrees, its intimate confidences, and the heavenly principles upon which this council was based, were known in Hebrew as the *sod* (Greek *mysterion*),[32] and knowing the *sod* conferred great power and wisdom.

This understanding of God, his heavenly council, and the prophet's role as a messenger of that council has been derived from several passages in the Old Testament and in ancient Near Eastern literature. It was apparently fairly well understood in Lehi's day. For example, 1 Kings 22:19–23, as noted earlier, records the experience of the prophet Micaiah, who saw God and his council, heard its deliberation and resolution, and was sent forth with the decree of God:

> And he said, Hear thou therefore the word of the Lord: I saw the Lord sitting on his throne, and all the host of heaven standing by him on his right hand and on his left. And the Lord said, Who shall persuade Ahab, that he may go up and fall at Ramoth-gilead? And one said on this manner, and another said on that manner. And there came forth a spirit, and stood before the Lord, and said, I will persuade him. And the Lord said unto him . . . Thou shalt persuade him, and prevail also: go forth, and do so.

Likewise, Jeremiah 23:18 (contemporaneous with Lehi) asks rhetorically about those who are true prophets: "For who hath stood in Yahweh's council [*sod*], and seen and heard his word? Who has carefully marked [obeyed] his word?"[33] This passage not only stresses the importance in Lehi's day for a prophet to stand in the council of God, but also to both "see and hear" what goes on there, and then to carry out his assignment meticulously by delivering the precise words of the council's decree, just as Lehi does. To so report and do, it has been concluded, was certification in that day that the prophet was a true messenger of God.[34]

Our understanding of Lehi's mission as a prophet can be increased in this light. As Jeremiah demands of a true prophet, Lehi indeed beheld God and his assembly, "saw and heard" (1 Nephi 1:18, 19; also 1:6) what transpired there, and then "went forth . . . to declare unto [the people of Jerusalem] concerning the things which he had both seen and heard" (verse 18).

Angels. In Lehi's vision, God was surrounded by his numerous host. As described above, it appears that the host was typically viewed in antiquity as serving three functions, namely, praising God, delivering the decrees of the council, and accompanying God in battle. The first two of these functions are quite clearly present in Lehi's vision, and the third may be inferred. First, in 1 Nephi 1:8, the host was "singing and praising their God." [35] Second, Lehi describes the members of the host as angels (literally "messengers"). In both Hebrew and Greek the words translated as "angel" or "apostle" can literally mean "messenger," indicating the likely presence here of the messenger function of these individuals in God's council. As in the paradigm above, a conspicuous council leader also came forth in Lehi's vision to deliver a book to him and to send him forth as a messenger. Third, while that was done, twelve others from the council then "went forth upon the face of the earth." Perhaps they were viewed as fulfilling the warrior function often served by these heavenly beings. The vision of Ezekiel appears to have been grounded in a similar manifestation. He saw "six men" come forth, each with "a slaughter weapon in his hand; and one man among them was clothed with linen, with a writer's inkhorn by his side" (Ezekiel 9:2–3).[36] It is possible that the twelve whom Lehi saw were likewise coming forth to take their battle stations or warning posts, imminently prepared to execute judgment upon Jerusalem, but there is no express indication in 1 Nephi who these twelve were or what they did. They probably should not be thought of as archangels, as understood in later Judaism.[37] Perhaps more relevant is the possibility that the number twelve may have had significance in the minds of Lehi and his contemporaries because multiples of twelve often had judicial and administrative significance in the courts and official bodies of Israel. Later, Lehi would learn more about the coming of the Messiah and his Twelve Apostles, but in the context of Lehi's vision up to this particular point, these twelve would probably have been thought of as functioning in the role of executing God's judgment, rather than in the other roles they would later fulfill during Jesus' earthly ministry.[38]

One descending. The leader of this council was exceptionally glorious ("his luster was above that of the sun at noon-day," 1 Nephi 1:9; cf. Acts 22:6; Joseph Smith—History 1:30), but beyond that he is not specifically identified in the text. It may be that this principal messenger was one of the angels, if the pronoun *one* in verse 9 refers to "one" of the angels, which would be the closest plural antecedent out of which "one" might have been identified. On the other hand, it seems more likely that the "one descending" was "the Holy One of Israel," the Lord himself, who then had left his throne to deliver in person his decree to his messenger the prophet,[39] for as in Amos 3:7 the Lord God himself reveals his secrets (*sod*) unto his servants, the prophets. Under this understanding, the one who came down[40] to speak to Lehi was the God himself who had been initially seated on his throne, and thus Lehi's exclamation "unto the Lord" at the conclusion of his vision, extolling the highness of his throne (verse 14), should be understood as having been made in a direct personal statement to that God, Christ himself, as he stood right before Lehi (verse 11).[41]

Book. The edict delivered to Lehi contained the judgments of God and his council upon the city of Jerusalem.[42] It began with a curse upon the city: "Wo, wo, unto Jerusalem, for I have seen thine abominations!" (1 Nephi 1:13; cf. Ezekiel 2:10).[43] From this decree, Lehi learned many other things about the destruction of Jerusalem by the sword (verse 13, cf. David's vision in 1 Chronicles 21:16); he also read there about the coming of a Messiah and, as others too had prophesied about the eventual recovery of the scattered remnant (cf. Zephaniah 3:19–20 above), about the redemption of the world (1 Nephi 1:19).

It is interesting that Lehi read this information in a "book" (verse 11).[44] The book may have been a scroll, or it could have been comprised of tablets. A close analogue to 1 Nephi 1:11 is found in the contemporary writings of Habakkuk, where the Lord spoke to Habakkuk about the preparation of a book that a herald from the Lord's council was to carry forth with speed: "And the Lord answered me, and said, Write the vision, and make it plain upon tables, that he may run that readeth it" (Habakkuk 2:2). Equally, it appears that the unstated instruction to Lehi was that he should deliver his message post haste.[45] The fact that Lehi was handed a written decree may also reflect the contemporary legal and political practices of his day. Some have theorized that preclassical, nonwritten prophecy flourished in the ninth and tenth centuries B.C. in part because at that time an oral message was still regarded as an authoritative decree.[46] During Lehi's day, however, written edicts under the Assyrian practice had become the standard legal mode of issuing proclamations, and prophets were more concerned with writing, and thus the authoritativeness of Lehi's words in the minds of his listeners was probably enhanced by the fact that he could report that he had read these words in a written decree.

He did exclaim many things. Lehi's reaction to this edict was profoundly spiritual. He was "filled with the Spirit of the Lord" and his "soul did rejoice, and his whole heart was filled" (1 Nephi 1:12, 15). He spontaneously and eloquently joined the heavenly host in praising God. By so doing, he functionally, if not constitutionally, joined the council as one of its members. Since his words seem to reflect poetic composition similar to exaltations of God's controlling power and wisdom found in ancient Near Eastern literature,[47] it may have been that Lehi, too, sang his words of praise, like the other hymns or psalms of praise in his day were sung:

> Great and marvelous are thy works,
> O Lord God Almighty!
> Thy throne is high in the heavens.
>
> Thy power, and goodness, and mercy
> Are over all the inhabitants of the earth
>
> Because thou art merciful
> thou wilt not suffer those who come unto thee
> that they shall perish! (verse 14.)

He truly testified. Lehi next "went forth among the people, and began to prophesy and to declare unto them" what he had "seen and heard" (verse 18). He had little choice but to speak out, in the sense that he, like the other prophets of God, was impelled and constrained by the Spirit. Prophets speak because they must, and because they cannot hold back what they know. Lehi probably also knew, like Ezekiel, that if he did not deliver the warning that God had commanded him to speak, the blood of all the wicked would be required at his hand; but if he warned the wicked then he would save his own soul (Ezekiel 3:17–19).

His message was one of testimony. "He truly testified of their wickedness and their abominations" (1 Nephi 1:19). Since Lehi had seen the facts in the council and in the book, he could stand as a witness and testify against the people, much as a plaintiff would lodge a complaint or accusation against a defendant or lawbreaker. If he spoke like the other prophets of his day, Lehi's testimony was punctuated with blunt declarative statements, offering no excuses, rationales, theological justifications, or explanations. He simply declared the message he had been told to give. Thus, like several other prophets at this time who brought so-called "prophetic lawsuits" against the people of Israel or in the Book of Mormon,[48] Lehi issued a declarative testimony or affidavit against the wickedness of the people in Jerusalem. In addition, he could also deliver the verdict, as in the formulaic "prophetic judgment-speeches" of other contemporaneous prophets,[49] for the verdict in heaven had already been handed down.

While Lehi's reference to the redemption of the world offered hope to the people of Jerusalem that they would someday be bought back from this foreclosure, and that the world would eventually be saved (1 Nephi 1:19) even though it be utterly wasted (cf. Zephaniah 1:2), the reaction to his message was still predictable. The people became angry and tried to kill him. Since they were law-abiding citizens, they probably raised some technical charge of treason or false prophecy against Lehi, as they did against Jeremiah (Jeremiah 26:11), but their underlying motive would more likely be found in the fact that Lehi, like so many prophets, spoke concerning the coming of a Messiah to overthrow the wicked establishment. In the face of this threat, and just as the Lord also promised to protect Jeremiah, he delivered Lehi, for, as Nephi explains, "the tender mercies of the Lord are over all those whom he hath chosen, because of their faith, to make them mighty even unto the power of deliverance" (1 Nephi 1:20). In a dream, Lehi was blessed by the Lord for having faithfully fulfilled the assignment he had been given. He was permitted and commanded to leave his post and depart into the wilderness (1 Nephi 2:1–2), so that he could become an instrument "unto the fulfilling of the word of the Lord, that [Israel] should be scattered upon all the face of the earth" (1 Nephi 10:13).

The mysteries. Not everyone, however, rejected Lehi's message. At least Nephi desired to know of the truthfulness of the words of his father. In faith, with great desires and lowliness of heart,[50] and being willing to be obedient and not rebellious, Nephi sought and received a confirmation from God so that he "did believe all the words which had been spoken" by Lehi (1

Nephi 2:16). In a comparable way, the Lord will make known to all his children the truthfulness of the words of his messengers, the prophets.

It is significant to me that Nephi specifically says here that he desired to know "of the mysteries of God" (verse 16). While all are invited to seek and all are promised knowledge (1 Nephi 15:8; Matthew 7:7; Moroni 10:4−5), this is not an open invitation for all men and women to seek "mysteries" beyond the declarative words of the prophets. When Nephi said that he desired to know of the "mysteries," he was most likely referring quite precisely to the information that Lehi had just learned through his visions in 1 Nephi 1.[51] As stated above, the Hebrew word *sod* basically means "council," but by association it also came to mean the "decree of the council" itself.[52] Because the council and its actions were not open to the general public, they were thought of as being very confidential, esoteric, or secret, also "conveying the notion of intimate friendship."[53] Hence, the word *sod* can also be translated as "mystery": "*Sod* also came to be used for the secret decision rendered at such councils . . . and in the Hebrew represented by Prov, Sir, and Qumran, *sod* is used simply for secrets or mysteries."[54] Just as Raymond E. Brown has concluded that "the background of such a concept is that of the prophets being introduced into the heavenly assembly and gaining a knowledge of its secret decrees,"[55] so it would appear that Lehi, in just such a way, had attained access on this occasion to the "mysteries" of God. From this, one can see that while the decrees of the divine council (*sod*) were confidential and privileged information (and that in this sense they can be called *mysteria*), they were not puzzles or cryptic information. Hence when Nephi has great desires to "know of the mysteries of God," so shortly after Lehi had experienced the *sod*, it would appear that Nephi is similarly seeking to know the *sod* and the decrees and glories of that council, just as Lehi had known them and as Jeremiah speaks of them. He is blessed with a visit of the Lord and a belief in "all the words" which Lehi had spoken, that is, the words which Lehi had delivered as he had received them from the Lord (1 Nephi 2:16).

Conclusion. First Nephi 1 can clearly be approached in many ways to better understand and appreciate the call of Lehi as a prophet of God. This presentation has tried to use a variety of information about the gospel and about Lehi's own day to elucidate the possible meanings of his visions in 1 Nephi 1.

From this, one can see how Lehi's dedication and inspiration can be confirmed in terms of several universally applicable aspects of prophecy. Under generally applicable definitions of what it means to be a prophet, Lehi certainly qualifies. Hugh B. Brown has defined eleven characteristics that "should distinguish a man who claims to be a prophet."[56] Lehi manifests them all: (1) He boldly claims that God has spoken to him; (2) he is a dignified man bearing a dignified message; (3) he declares his message without fear; (4) he bears witness without argument or concession; (5) he speaks in the name of the Lord; (6) he predicts future events that come to pass; (7) his message pertains to future as well as present generations; (8) he endures persecution; (9) he denounces wickedness fearlessly; (10) he does things that no man could do without God's help; and (11) his teachings are in strict agreement with scripture. Other criteria can be added to this list; for example, (12) that he prophesies of Christ.[57] Each of these characteristics are found in 1 Nephi 1:4–20 and in the life and courageous deeds of the prophet Lehi.[58]

Additionally and equally so, Lehi's prophetic attributes can be understood and confirmed in light of classical Israelite prophecy specific to his own contemporaneous world. Like other prophets in the seventh century, Lehi was steeped in the precise terminology and conception of the divine heavenly council (verse 8) and in its many particular functions and its distinctive images and protocol, which gave meaning and power to his message. Like his many prophetic contemporaries, Lehi also abhorred and testified against the abominations he saw in Jerusalem (verse 19); he and they rejected the arrogant nationalism of many Jews in Jerusalem and spoke instead of a worldwide redemption (verse 19); he spoke out publicly, triggered by events at the commencement of a new king's reign (verse 4); he pleaded with God in behalf of his people (verse 5); he called for simple righteousness, addressing the general population as opposed to the king (verse 18); he worked essentially alone, and was greatly concerned that his prophecies be written down. These were typical characteristics of prophets of this time; they and several others like them are reflected in remarkable detail in the abbreviated account of 1 Nephi 1.

It is clear that prophets have been called upon by God to say and do many different things over the centuries. Some have been called like Moses as lawgivers, or like Joshua as military leaders. Abraham served as a paragon of faith, peace, and covenant making, while others like Elijah were outspoken dissidents decrying the wickedness of kings and idolatry.[59] Similarly, Lehi's role among the prophets of God was specifically suited to the needs of the Lord in that day. He was called as a messenger of the Lord, faithfully delivering God's decree against Jerusalem, and obediently following the direction of the Lord during that pivotal period in the history of Jerusalem and of the world as well. By all eternal and historical criteria, Lehi qualifies functionally, archetypally, literarily, spiritually, and scripturally as one of the great prophets of God. His call as a prophet in 1 Nephi 1 gives a foundation of divine authority, revelation, and guidance for everything that follows father Lehi's posterity throughout the Book of Mormon.

NOTES AND REFERENCES

1. For various approaches, see George Reynolds and J. Sjodahl, *Commentary on the Book of Mormon* (Salt Lake City: Deseret Book Co., 1955) 1:7–12; Hugh Nibley, *Lehi in the Desert* (Salt Lake City: Bookcraft, 1952), pp. 4–13; Hugh Nibley, *An Approach to the Book of Mormon* (Salt Lake City: Deseret Book Co., 1957), pp. 25–54; Sidney Sperry, *Book of Mormon Compendium* (Salt Lake City: Bookcraft, 1968), p. 97; S. Kent Brown, "Lehi's Personal Record: Quest for a Missing Source," *BYU Studies* 24 (1984), pp. 19–42; Blake Thomas Ostler, "The Throne-Theophany and Prophetic Commission in 1 Nephi: A Form-Critical Analysis," F.A.R.M.S. Preliminary Report, OST–82 (1982), in *BYU Studies*, 26:4 (Fall 1986), 67–95.

2. 1 Nephi 1 contains only an abridgment of the record of Lehi (verse 17). Sometimes Nephi appears to paraphrase his father's words, as in verse 15, "after this manner was the language of my father"; other times he is quoting verbatim, as in verse 8 (compare Alma 36:22, also quoting these twenty-one words of Lehi) and 1:13.

3. Throughout this article, I speak of Lehi's vision as a "council vision." I do this for several reasons, primarily because it is similar to the council visions of Old Testament prophets. Also, the word *concourse* in Joseph Smith's day meant "a moving, flowing or running together; a concourse of men," and it is used in this sense in 1 Nephi 8:21; but the word also meant "a meeting; an assembly of men; an assembly of things," thus indicating that the idea of a council might be more expressly present in Lehi's account than a modern reader is likely to notice. Noah Webster, *American Dictionary of the English Language*

(1828). See also Hugh Nibley, *Since Cumorah* (Salt Lake City: Deseret Book Co., 1967), pp. 212–13, describing Lehi's vision as one that takes us "back to a council in heaven as a fitting prologue to a religious history." The term *council*, of course, should not be understood to describe a small group. Like the premortal Council in Heaven, the council which Lehi beheld was not a small cabinet meeting, but was multitudinous, as is reflected in the fact that the word *concourses* is plural. However, comparisons between Lehi's vision and the "council visions" of his contemporaries or others should not be overstated. Like all comparisons, there will be differences as well as similarities.

4. Events in the ancient world were normally dated by reference to regnal years. A similar reference introduces Isaiah's council vision in Isaiah 6:1, "In the year that king Uzziah died."

5. According to 2 Chronicles 36:9, Jehoiachin was eight years old when he was placed on the throne. According to 2 Kings 24:8, he was eighteen, but since his father Jehoiakim only lived to be thirty-six, the younger age for Jehoiachin seems more likely.

6. A contemporaneous cuneiform tablet records the specific events surrounding this conquest. See D. Winton Thomas, ed., *Documents from Old Testament Times* (Edinburgh: Nelson, 1958), p. 80. A different account is given in 2 Chronicles 36:5–7, which reports that Jehoiakim was still king when the Babylonians attacked, that Jehoiachin was placed on the throne for three months and ten days and then was brought to Babylon and replaced by Zedekiah.

7. Jeremiah 52:28 numbers them at 3,023. 2 Kings 24:14 reports that ten thousand were taken captive, perhaps in a second stage of deportation. See Robert Smith, "Book of Mormon Event Structure: Ancient Near East," F.A.R.M.S Preliminary Report, SMI–84, pp. 14–15; John W. Welch, "They Came from Jerusalem," *Ensign* (Sept. 1976), pp. 27–30.

8. Zedekiah was apparently placed on the throne on 22 April (10 Nisan) 597 B.C. but his coronation would have taken place either on 1 Tishri, or 1 Nisan of the following year, and thus it is unclear whether the Book of Mormon phrase "in the commencement of the first year of the reign of Zedekiah," 1 Nephi 1:4, cf. Jeremiah 49:34, refers to the day he began to rule or the day of his coronation. See Smith, "Book of Mormon Event Structure," p. 15.

9. Edwin Kingsbury, "The Prophets and the Council of Yahweh," *Journal of Biblical Literature* 83 (1964), p. 284, pointing especially to parallels in the determination of destiny in the council of the gods following the re-enthronement of Marduk in the Babylonian year-rite. Cf. G. Widengren, *The Ascension of the Apostle and the Heavenly Book (King and Saviour III)* (Uppsala: Lundequistska/Leipzig: Harrasowitz, 1950), p. 10. These sources help us understand reasons why the New Year was an effective time for a prophetic call.

10. The reaction of the people in Jerusalem was political in the sense that his message indicted and condemned the city whose inhabitants then collectively sought Lehi's life. This would have involved, in my opinion, several forms of legal and political action, much like the lawsuit brought against Jeremiah and the extradition procedure initiated in the case of Urijah discussed in Jeremiah 26.

11. J. Watts's translation, in *The Books of Joel, Obadiah, Jonah, Nahum, Habakkuk and Zephaniah* (Cambridge: University Press, 1975).

12. John Bright, *Jeremiah* (Garden City: Doubleday, 1965), p. 333. There may have been others. Although they cannot be dated precisely, prophecies such as Joel's predictions of the disastrous "day of the Lord" and his pleas for repentance also can "most naturally . . . be understood [in] reference to the cataclysmic events of 587 B.C.," L. Allen, *The Books of Joel, Obadiah, Jonah and Micah* (Grand Rapids: Eerdmans, 1976), p. 24, and Obadiah's prophecies, particularly in verses 11–14, speaking of an overthrow of Jerusalem and of God's justice, may also relate to events in Lehi's day. Ibid., p. 130. J. Watts, p. 13, sees the "Day of the Lord" as the liturgical high day of the great autumn festival (1 Tishri?) from the time of Amos through Joel.

13. This exemplifies the eternal principle that God will warn all nations of his judgments; see Marion G. Romney, Conference Report, April 1958, p. 128.

14. Compare Abinadi, Samuel the Lamanite, John the Baptist, and other such prophets who stand alone in crying out the word of the Lord. See also *Encyclopaedia Judaica* 13:1162 (hereafter cited as *EJ*); E. W. Heaton, *Hebrew Kingdoms* (Oxford: University Press, 1968), pp. 237–44.

15. Heaton, *Hebrew Kingdoms,* p. 243.

16. Compare Lehi with the description of the "independent prophets" in ibid., pp. 238–39.

17. *EJ* 13:1169.

18. For example, Jeremiah was told to cease praying on behalf of his people, Jeremiah 14:11; *EJ* 13:1170. This prophetic and intercessory function was also served by prophets such as Abraham (Genesis 20:7), Samuel (1 Samuel 7:5–9), and in the Book of Mormon notably by Enos (Enos 1:9–17).

19. Nephi does not indicate whether this was Lehi's first vision. It seems probable that it was, although a similar vision in Isaiah 6 is thought by some to have come in the midst of Isaiah's work as a prophet, rather than as his first revelatory experience.

20. *Teachings of the Prophet Joseph Smith*, comp. Joseph Fielding Smith (Salt Lake City: Deseret Book, 1978) p. 325; hereafter *TPJS*. See also D&C 29:12, prophesying that Christ will come "in a pillar of fire" with his Twelve Apostles "to judge the whole house of Israel." Similarly, here the function of the pillar of fire seems to be associated with God's judgment upon Jerusalem. See note 21.

21. See Exodus 14:24; Numbers 21:27–30; Deuteronomy 9:3; Genesis 3:24; 19:24; Malachi 4:1. Compare especially Psalm 104:4 with the description of the messengers of Yamm in the Ugaritic Text *CTA* 2.I.32–33: "A fire, two fires, they appear / / / Their tongues a sharpened sword." Discussed in E. Theodore Mullen, *The Divine Council in Canaanite and Early Hebrew Literature* (Chico: Scholars Press, 1980), p. 199. It has been concluded that, among the Israelites and the peoples of the ancient Near East, fire was "intimately associated with those divine beings who attend the great gods, and the fire appears to be a sort of weapon." P. Miller, "Fire in the Mythology of Canaan and Israel," *Catholic Biblical Quarterly* 27 (1965), 259.

22. It is possible that the pillar contained things having to do with the destruction of Jerusalem. Amos had prophesied that the fire of God would destroy the walls and palaces of Tyre (Amos 1:4, 10). Perhaps in Lehi's vision the rock upon which the pillar dwelt was symbolic of the hardhearted Jerusalem, or of its walls, or of Jerusalem as the mountain of the Lord. Possibly a flaming sword was involved. The sword of God's justice which hangs over people threatening their destruction (1 Nephi 15:30; Alma 54:30; 60:29; Helaman 13:5; 3 Nephi 20:20; Moroni 8:41) may be related to God's destroying fire, since the Hebrew words *lahat* and *lahab* each mean both "flame" and "sword blade," and since God's messengers are not only "accompanied by the imagery of fire" but also frequently come bearing swords. See Genesis 3:24; Numbers 22:31; Joshua 5:13; Mullen, p. 199. If a flaming sword was involved, Lehi's vision may have been similar to one given to king David, when he "saw the angel of the Lord stand between the earth and the heaven, having a drawn sword in his hand stretched out over Jerusalem" (1 Chronicles 21:14–16). See also Isaiah 29, which prophesied that God would wage a holy war against Jerusalem to visit that city "with the flame [*lahab*] of devouring fire" (Isaiah 29:6). Heavenly armies and council visions generally were connected with this fire motif. P. Miller, "The Divine Council and the Prophetic Call to War," *Vetus Testamentum* 18 (1968), 100–107.

23. See note 24. Blake Ostler, "Throne Theophany," has demonstrated that Lehi's throne theophany, in addition to being similar to other prophetic accounts from Lehi's day, also resembles several visions in the later pseudepigrapha; but one need not go beyond sources from Lehi's day in order to find historical analogues for each aspect of Lehi's vision. For example, Ostler looks to the pseudepigrapha for an instance of a prophet acting as an intercessor on behalf of his people, whereas Jeremiah 14:11, 18:20, and other texts place this prophetic function in preexilic times. He also places more emphasis on the throne and less on the council than appears appropriate. For a discussion of another form of prophetic call that was current in Lehi's day, in which the prophet meets God, is commissioned, objects, is reassured, and is given a sign, see Stephen Ricks, "The Narrative Call Pattern in the Prophetic Commission of Enoch (Moses 6)," *BYU Studies* 26 (Fall, 1986), 97–105.

24. See, for example, Mullen; Claus Westermann, *Basic Forms of Prophetic Speech* (Philadelphia: Westminster, 1967), pp. 98–128; Widengren; Frank M. Cross, "The Council of Yahweh in Second Isaiah," *JNES* 12 (1953), 274–77; E. Kingsbury, "The Prophets and the Council of Yahweh," *JBL* 83 (1964), 279–86; P. Miller, "The Divine Council and the Prophetic Call to War," *VT* 18 (1968), 100–107; John S. Holladay, "Assyrian Statecraft and the Prophets of Israel," *HTR* 63 (1970), 29–51; N. Tidwell, "*Wa'omar* (Zechariah 3:5) and the Genre of Zechariah's Fourth Vision," *JBL* 94 (1975), 343–55; Joseph F. McConkie, "Premortal Existence, Foreordinations and Heavenly Councils," in *Apocryphal Writings and the Latter-day Saints*, C. Wilfred Griggs, ed. (Provo, Utah: BYU Religious Studies Center, 1986), pp. 173–98. Similar conceptions of the assembly of the gods convened in heaven are found among the Canaanites, the Babylonians, the Greeks, and others in the ancient Near East.

25. Mullen, pp. 181–85; see, for example, Deuteronomy 33:2–3; Psalm 89:6–9.

26. Mullen, pp. 145–46, 200.

27. Ibid., p. 209. Those verdicts were issued by God pursuant to eternal principles, divine laws, and immutable regulations. In the Sumerian Hymns, one frequently encounters terms involving the word *ME*, whose precise meaning cannot be determined, but which embraces "world order," "divine command or edict," "divine norms," "secrets, mysteries," "fate or destiny" and "divine powers." Karl Oberhuber, *Der Numinose Begriff ME in Sumerischen* (Innsbruck: Leopold-Franzens-Universitaet, 1963), p. 3. R. Otto describes the *numina*, or eternal things, which existed before the gods and the world came into being, and Oberhuber points out the possible relation between the meaning of *ME* and the *numina*. Ibid., pp. 5–8. The *MEs* may be related historically to the principles, decrees, edicts, fates, and powers of the divine council in the Semitic sources. See also G. Farber-Fluegge, *Der Mythos "Inanna und Enki,"* Studia Pohl 10 (Rome: Biblical Institute, 1973); T. Jacobsen, *Toward the Image of Tammuz* (Cambridge, Mass.: Harvard University Press, 1976), pp. 359–60, n.20; Y. Rosengarten, *Sumer et le sacre* (Paris: Boccard, 1977). I am grateful to Paul Hoskisson for bringing these Mesopotamian materials to my attention. Cf. Kingsbury, pp. 284–85, briefly comparing Israelite prophecies with the Babylonian year-rite determination of destinies; Widengren, p. 91. Compare also Alma 42, similarly affirming that God is subject to eternal law.

28. Holladay, pp. 42–46.

29. Mullen, p. 218, n.180, summarizing Tidwell, "Wa'omar." See 1 Kings 22:19–22; Isaiah 6:1–10; 40:1–8; Job 1:6–12; 2:1–6; Zechariah 1:8–13; 3:1–7; 6:1–8. Mullen notes that Psalm 29, 82, 89:6–9 and Deuteronomy 32:8–9 do not entirely fit the pattern.

30. Mullen, pp. 209–10. Cf. Mosiah 3:23, where the angel of God certifies that he has "spoken *the words* which the Lord God hath commanded me" (italics added). See also Mosiah 11:20; 12:1.

31. "It would seem that the question of the messenger's authority could be answered simply: it is that of the one who sends him." J. Ross, "The Prophet as Yahweh's Messenger," in *Israel's Prophetic Heritage* (New York: Harper, 1962), p. 101. Joseph Smith explained how this authority was conferred: "All the prophets had the Melchizedek Priesthood and were ordained by God himself," *TPJS*, p. 181.

32. Also in Hebrew as the *èdat*, or *dor*. See Mullen, pp. 118–19.

33. J. Bright's translation.

34. Mullen, p. 221.

35. This compares with Isaiah's vision of God seated in the presence of the seraphim (literally "fiery things"), who praised his holiness and glory (Isaiah 6:1–3). See also Ezekiel 1:4–28; 1 Enoch 14:22. Michael Carter has suggested to me that such singing and circumambulation "surrounding" God may have cosmogonic and cultic significance.

36. The overall character of Ezekiel's vision is "the proclamation of an act of judgement"; Walther Zimmerli, *Ezekiel* (Philadelphia: Fortress, 1979), p. 247; thus these six come forth to execute judgment.

37. Since he wrote at a time when the council members typically remained anonymous in deference to the Supreme Deity (see Mullen, p. 178), it is unlikely that Lehi would have thought in terms of the intricate angelology which developed under Babylonian influence during the sixth and fifth centuries, and thus Reynold's reference, *Commentary*, pp. 8−9, 11−12, to the angelic names and personalities found in Daniel, 1 Enoch, and other Old Testament pseudepigrapha, is probably out of place.

38. Nephi later calls the twelve "the apostles of the Lamb" (1 Nephi 11:29, 34). Both the Hebrew word *shaliach*, meaning "sent one" or "agent," and the Greek word *apostolos*, "one sent forth," also mean "messenger," and thus Nephi's word is not inapposite to messengers of the heavenly council; see Widengren, pp. 31−36, 47.

39. Thus it is appropriate that the word *one* was capitalized in the 1981 LDS edition of the Book of Mormon.

40. On God's position in the heavens or on his mountain, see Exodus 19−20; 1 Nephi 11:1; Moses 1; Richard J. Clifford, *The Cosmic Mountain in Canaan and the Old Testament* (Cambridge, Mass.: Harvard University Press, 1972). On God coming down, compare Ugaritic Text *CTA* 14.II.57−58, which Mullen reconstructs to describe how the council of the gods there, led by El and Ba`al, "descended" to the earthly meeting place.

41. Elder Marion G. Romney affirms that this being was Christ the Lord. Conference Report, October 1970, p. 28.

42. "This contained the decision of the court. It was the judgment of that great court." Reynolds, p. 9.

43. On the connection between the curse and the announcement of judgment, see Westermann, pp. 190−98.

44. Another appearance of the heavenly book is discussed in D&C 77:14; see also G. Widengren, who connects this book with the book of law that (like the Urim and Thummim) was worn on the king's breast at his coronation (2 Kings 11:12), p. 25, and was related to the Book of Life associated with New Year's (cf. Mosiah 5:11, 6:1−2), pp. 10, 38, cf. 1 Nephi 1:4, discussed above. The heavenly book appears often in Mesopotamian, Jewish, Samaritan, Gnostic, and other sources.

45. The scroll which Ezekiel sees, reads, and eats (Ezekiel 2:9−3:2; cf. Revelation 10:9) is a subsequent development of this motif. Going beyond the prophets like Lehi and Habakkuk a generation before him, Ezekiel not only reads, but eats, the words he is commanded to deliver. Like Lehi's book, however, Ezekiel's roll spelled out "lamentations, and mourning, and woe" (Ezekiel 2:10).

46. For example, Mullen, p. 216.

47. Compare, for example, the tricolon in Ugaritic Text *CTA* 3.V.38−39, "Your decree, O 'El, is wise / / Your wisdom is eternal / / A life of fortune your decree," discussed in Mullen, p. 145. Cf. Psalm 29:1−2. David N. Freedman, *Pottery, Poetry and Prophecy: Studies in Early Hebrew Poetry* (Winona Lake, Indiana: Eisenbrauns, 1980), argues convincingly that poetry was a concomitant of ancient Israelite prophecy.

48. See Kirsten Nielsen, *Yahweh as Prosecutor and Judge*, JSOT Supp. Series 9 (Sheffield: JSOT, 1978); Antoon Schoors, *I Am God Your Saviour: A Form-critical Study of the Main Genres in Israel XL-LV* (Leiden: Brill, 1973), pp. 189–244. For an analysis of several such cases in the Book of Mormon, see Richard McGuire, "Prophetic Lawsuits in the Hebrew Bible and Book of Mormon," F.A.R.M.S Preliminary Report, MCG–83.

49. See Westermann, pp. 169–204. We have too little of Lehi's public statement, however, to know whether his words were couched in terms of a "prophetic lawsuit," a "prophetic judgment speech," or in some other form of prophetic rhetoric.

50. Compare "At times God does reveal His secrets especially to the humble. Sir 42, 18–9. . . . It is to the humble that He reveals His secrets (*mysteria-sodaw*)," Raymond E. Brown, "The Pre-Christian Semitic Concept of 'Mystery,' " *CBQ* 20 (1958), 417–43; the quote is from p. 424 and n.32.

51. This is not to limit the meaning of the phrase *the mysteries of God* in other contexts. But at the time Nephi inquired of the Lord in 1 Nephi 2:16, it seems that what he was seeking to know was the truth of the things that Lehi had learned in his vision in 1 Nephi 1:6–14.

52. Ross, p. 103. Discussed further in John Tvedtnes, "Hebraisms in the Book of Mormon," *BYU Studies* 11 (1970), pp. 50–60, showing Book of Mormon usages consistent with the semantic range of meaning of the Hebrew *sod*.

53. Brown, pp. 417–21.

54. Ibid., p. 421.

55. Ibid.

56. Hugh B. Brown, *Eternal Quest* (Salt Lake City: Bookcraft, 1956), pp. 130–31.

57. Both the Book of Mormon (Jacob 4:4; 7:11) and Jewish rabbinic tradition, TB *Berakoth* 34b, affirm that all the prophets know of Christ. The Talmud states: "R. Hayya b. Abba said in the name of R. Johanan: All the prophets prophesied only for the days of the Messiah, but as for the world to come, 'Eye hath not seen, oh God, beside Thee.' "

58. Compare also the similarly defining attributes of a prophet given in *EJ* 13:1151–52, and Truman G. Madsen, *Joseph Smith Among the Prophets* (Salt Lake City: Deseret Book Co., 1965), pp. 1–35. *EJ* 13:1160–61 also offers a helpful summary of the attributes of classical Israelite prophets as distinguished from prophets in other periods of Israelite history.

59. See generally H. Wheeler Robinson, *Inspiration and Revelation in the Old Testament* (Oxford: Clarendon, 1946).

4

FATHER LEHI

H. Donl Peterson

Lehi is the prominent and dominant figure in the opening of the Book of Mormon record. But because the chief role soon shifts to Nephi, the reader may be prone to overlook the importance and personality of this great prophet and patriarch who was the original founder of the Nephite nation. Let us examine, in the manner suggested by Brigham Young, the part played by this courageous ancient prophet:

> Do you read the Scriptures, my brethren and sisters, as though you were writing them a thousand, two thousand, or five thousand years ago? Do you read them as though you stood in the place of the men who wrote them? If you do not feel thus, it is your privilege to do so, that you may be as familiar with the spirit and meaning of the written word of God as you are with your daily walk and conversation, or as you are with your workmen or with your households.[1]

H. Donl Peterson is Director of the Pearl of Great Price Studies in the Religious Studies Center and Professor of Ancient Scripture at Brigham Young University.

Lehi the Man

Lehi was of the house of Joseph through his son Manasseh (Alma 10:3). The land apportioned by the prophet Joshua to the sons of Joseph (Manasseh and Ephraim) was north of Jerusalem and south of the Sea of Galilee in the area generally known as Samaria at the time of Christ. We are not told when Lehi's ancestors first lived in Judah. Many people fled from their lands in Israel to Judah in 721 B.C. when the Assyrians captured the Northern Kingdom and carried off many slaves. Earlier, others of Ephraim and Manasseh had gathered to Jerusalem under King Asa (2 Chronicles 15:1–15). The scripture does tell us that Lehi "dwelt at Jerusalem in all his days" (1 Nephi 1:4).

Lehi was probably born between 650–640 B.C. This estimate is based on the fact that Lehi and Sariah had four sons of marriageable age—Laman, Lemuel, Sam, and Nephi—when the family departed from Jerusalem. They also had daughters who had apparently already married, but there is no mention of daughters leaving Jerusalem with the original company (1 Nephi 2:5).[2] Thus we estimate that Lehi would have been about forty or fifty years old.

Lehi was an educated man who was familiar with the Egyptian language as well as his own Hebrew tongue (1 Nephi 1:2). He was also a wealthy man. He may have had property in Jerusalem (see 1 Nephi 1:4), but he definitely owned some outside of Jerusalem in the land of his inheritance (1 Nephi 3:16), and that is where he apparently kept his wealth. When his four sons collected their father's gold, silver, and precious things in an attempt to purchase the plates of brass from Laban, they got it outside of Jerusalem (1 Nephi 3:16, 25).

We don't know what Lehi's occupation was, but since he was conversant in the Egyptian language and he seemed somewhat familiar with the ways of the desert, it is logical to assume that he had some occupation or some previous experiences that utilized both skills.

Lehi the Prophet

Lehi was a record keeper. He wrote "many things which he saw in visions and in dreams; and he also hath written many things which he prophesied and spake unto his children" (1

Nephi 1:16–17). If we had the record of Lehi, we would know more about him as a prophet in Jerusalem. A fuller account of Lehi's visions and dreams was recorded in the 116 pages of manuscript that were lost by Martin Harris after they were translated. Since they were not retranslated (see D&C 10), our analysis of Lehi's prophetic nature will be limited to what we can determine from the record we now have.

Lehi was a visionary man. Sariah, and Laman and Lemuel, on two different occasions used that phrase in referring to him (1 Nephi 2:11; 5:2). Both accounts carry the same uncomplimentary implications that father Jacob's older sons had when they saw Joseph approaching their camp saying "Behold, this dreamer cometh" (Genesis 37:19).

Lehi did not deny the charge of being visionary. He confirmed his sons' accusation by confounding them through the power of the Spirit (1 Nephi 2:14). To his wife, he replied: "I know that I am a visionary man; for if I had not seen the things of God in a vision I should not have known the goodness of God, but had tarried at Jerusalem, and had perished with my brethren" (1 Nephi 5:4). This response reminds one of the Prophet Joseph Smith's statement concerning his experiences:

> Though I was hated and persecuted for saying that I had seen a vision, yet it was true; and while they were persecuting me, reviling me, and speaking all manner of evil against me falsely for so saying, I was led to say in my heart: Why persecute me for telling the truth? I have actually seen a vision; and who am I that I can withstand God, or why does the world think to make me deny what I have actually seen? For I had seen a vision; I knew it, and I knew that God knew it, and I could not deny it, neither dared I do it; at least I knew that by so doing I would offend God, and come under condemnation. (Joseph Smith—History 1:25.)

First Nephi records several visions or dreams, as Lehi used these two terms. While Lehi was in prayer in behalf of his people, a pillar of fire appeared to him and dwelt upon a rock. Nephi does not say what his father saw and heard, only that he did see and hear much and it caused him to "quake and tremble exceedingly" (1 Nephi 1:6).[3] Lehi returned to his home at Jerusalem and cast himself upon his bed, being overcome by the Spirit and the things which he had witnessed. Being thus overcome with the Spirit "he was [again] carried away in a vision." In this vision Lehi "saw the heavens open, and he thought he saw God sitting upon his throne, surrounded with numberless concourses of angels in the attitude of singing and praising their God.'' He next saw "One," who undoubtedly was Jesus, "descending out of the midst of heaven.'' Jesus' luster was described as "above that of the sun at noon-day.'' Twelve others followed Jesus and their brightness exceeded the "stars in the firmament.'' Jesus presented Lehi with a book and bade him read it.⁴ As he read the account, he was filled with the Spirit of the Lord. It was confirmed to him that Jerusalem should be destroyed and many of its inhabitants should perish by the sword while others should be carried away into Babylon.

Lehi concluded from that marvelous vision that: (1) the works of God are great and marvelous; (2) God's throne is high in the heavens and his power, goodness, and mercy are over all the inhabitants of the earth; and (3) because of God's mercy those that come unto him shall not perish (see 1 Nephi 1:14). Lehi was now, if he had not been before, a special witness of Jesus Christ, a prophet in the fullest sense.

Anxious to share this great theophany with his people, Lehi went among the inhabitants of Jerusalem prophesying of those things that he had seen in the vision. But the Jews mocked him and sought his life as they had the lives of the prophets of old. A man is not warmly accepted if he does not espouse the popular cause. To speak of their defeat and capture would surely solicit such responses as "traitor," "coward," and "liar."

In a third dream, or vision, the Lord commanded Lehi to take his family and depart into the wilderness. Obedient to that command, Lehi left most of his possessions and took only his family, provisions, and tents and departed into the wilderness.

The Lord continued to instruct Lehi by dreams. In one dream, he was commanded to send his four sons back to Jerusalem to obtain the records known as the plates of brass (1 Nephi 3:1–4). After their successful return, he sent them to Jerusalem again, this time to get Ishmael and his family. The Book of Mormon does not say that this commandment came by dream but only that "the Lord spake unto him [Lehi] again" (1 Nephi 7:1). He had other dreams of his family (1 Nephi 8). He also probably saw the same visions of Jerusalem, the promised land, and the nations and kingdoms of the Gentiles which Nephi later saw (1 Nephi 11–14). Indeed Lehi was a visionary man, for that was why and how he escaped the fall of Jerusalem (2 Nephi 1:4).

Lehi, Man of Faith

Lehi was a man of great faith. He shows this in the early chapters of 1 Nephi. He prayed "with all his heart, in behalf of his people" (1 Nephi 1:5). The visions he was given in answer to this prayer is certainly evidence of his faith (compare James 1:5–6). The Lord commended him for being faithful in preaching to the Jews in spite of mockery and persecution (1 Nephi 2:1). His faith was further exemplified by his willingness to leave all of his earthly possessions and depart into the wilderness not knowing the extent of his journey or the trials he would face. All this he was willing to do to be "obedient unto the word of the Lord" (1 Nephi 2:2–4). His faith is once more verified by the Spirit accompanying his speaking with his sons in the valley of Lemuel in convincing them to do as he commanded.

One of the most famous statements in the Book of Mormon is Nephi's faithful reply to his father about returning to Jerusalem to obtain the plates because he knew that "the Lord giveth no commandments unto the children of men, save he shall prepare a way for them that they may accomplish the thing which he commandeth them" (1 Nephi 3:7). A careful reading of the text strongly suggests that it was Lehi's teachings that were reflected in Nephi's answer. Referring to the older brothers' hesitancy in fulfilling the assignment of the Lord, Lehi reminded his son that it was not his own requirement but the Lord's, "Therefore go, my son, and thou shalt be favored of the Lord" (1 Nephi 3:5–6). Nephi fit the adage "like father, like son." He was certainly reflecting his father's teachings in his own faith.

Although Lehi's faith wavered one time in the face of extreme hunger and hardship (1 Nephi 16:20), and few there are who would not have wavered under similar conditions, he had been a pillar of strength before that and would be thereafter. But even though he was a prophet, he was still a human being. Again this reminds us of a statement by the Prophet Joseph Smith.

> I was this morning introduced to a man from the east. After hearing my name, he remarked that I was nothing but a man, indicating by this expression, that he had supposed that a person to whom the Lord should see fit to reveal His will, must be something more than a man. He seemed to have forgotten the saying that fell from the lips of St. James [James 5:17–18], that Elias was a man subject to like passions as we are, yet he had such power with God,

that He, in answer to his prayers, shut the heavens that they gave no rain for the space of three years and six months; and again, in answer to his prayer, the heavens gave forth rain, and the earth gave forth fruit.[5]

Although Lehi's wavering brought chastisement from the Lord and the deepest of sorrow to Lehi himself, it did not cost him his prophetic calling. The Lord still allowed him to use the Liahona and receive instructions for the people he had been called to preside over. (1 Nephi 16:25–27.)

A Father of Nations

There are many millions of people who can trace their genealogy to the patriarch Lehi. Did he understand that this would happen when he began his prophetic career? Probably not. Although later he was shown his posterity in vision (1 Nephi 5:17), he was apparently oblivious to his destiny at the beginning of his mission. Let's examine how it all came about.

When his four sons went back to Jerusalem a second time, to invite Ishmael and his family to join the Lehi colony in the wilderness, Ishmael and his family consented. Why would Ishmael even entertain the thought of joining Lehi in the wilderness? It appears that they were not strangers. It is obvious that Ishmael accepted Lehi as a prophet of God, but there were other ties also. According to Erastus Snow, "The Prophet Joseph informed us that . . . Ishmael was of the lineage of Ephraim, and that his sons [had] married into Lehi's family, and Lehi's sons married Ishmael's daughters."[6] It is concluded from this statement that Lehi had some older daughters who had already married Ishmael's sons. It is further thought that Lehi and Ishmael had previously contracted with each other to have their children marry. Both were of the tribe of Joseph, and their families were nearly compatible in the number of matchups for marriage. When Zoram is included, there is a perfect numerical matchup of marriageable-aged people.

The marriages between these two families fulfilled prophecy. Elder Erastus Snow said that Joseph Smith explained that this marriage fulfilled the words of Jacob as he blessed Ephraim and Manasseh in Genesis 48: "And let my name be named on them, and the name of my fathers Abraham and Isaac; and let them grow into a multitude in the midst of the earth" (Genesis 48:16).

> Thus these descendants of Manasseh and Ephraim grew together upon this American continent, with a sprinkling from the house of Judah, from Mulek descended, who left Jerusalem eleven years after Lehi, and founded the colony afterwards known as Zarahemla and found by Mosiah—thus making a combination, an intermixture of Ephraim and Manasseh with the remnants of Judah, and for aught we know, the remnants of some other tribes that might have accompanied Mulek.[7]

The children of Lehi and Ishmael were married while the colony was camped in the valley of Ishmael.

Lehi the Seer

After the two families of Joseph's descendants were safely out of Jerusalem, once again the voice of the Lord spoke to Lehi by night and commanded him that "on the morrow he should take his journey into the wilderness" (1 Nephi 16:9). When Lehi went to his tent door the next morning he found on the ground "a round ball of curious workmanship" made of "fine brass." Within the ball were two spindles; one pointed the way they should go into the wilderness (1 Nephi 16:10). The miraculous brass ball directed Lehi's colony into the more fertile parts of the wilderness (1 Nephi 16:16).

Nephi explained that the pointers in the ball worked according to the faith, diligence, and heed given to them. He further said that writing appeared on the ball that was plain to read and which gave them "understanding concerning the ways of the Lord" (1 Nephi 16:29). This also changed from time to time according to the group's faith and diligence. And because those who looked into the interpreters were called seers (Mosiah 8:13), it is possible that those who were commanded to look into the ball would qualify as seers. "A seer can know of things which are past, and also of things which are to come, and by them shall all things be revealed, or, rather, shall secret things be made manifest, and hidden things shall come to light, and things which are not known shall be made known by them, and also things shall be made known by them which otherwise could not be known"

(Mosiah 8:17). Regardless of the Liahona experience, Lehi was in this sense certainly a seer.

Lehi the Explorer

Another dimension of this great leader was his courage to tackle the frontier, to extend into the unknown. Lehi did just this, relying solely upon the Lord and the miraculous instrument that he had provided for them.

The group traveled south-southeast for many days and then established another camp. At that encampment Ishmael died and was buried (1 Nephi 16:34). This incident once again triggered a rebellion in the camp. The mourning daughters of Ishmael remonstrated against Lehi because of their father's death and of the great sufferings they had endured in the wilderness. And after all their sufferings they stated that they feared they would yet perish in the wilderness from hunger. They wanted to return to Jerusalem. (1 Nephi 16:35–36.)

The situation was so tense that the Lord himself had to intercede. Nephi records that "the Lord was with us, yea, even the voice of the Lord came and did speak many words unto them, and did chasten them exceedingly" (1 Nephi 16:39). As a result of the Lord's chastening, once again the rebellious temporarily repented, and the Lord blessed the caravan with food.

The weary travelers packed their provisions and journeyed on—on into the wilderness. However, the group changed directions and traveled nearly eastward from that time on, enduring hunger, thirst, and fatigue. There were ever-present murmurings, and the women were bearing children in the wilderness. Lehi and Sariah had two sons, Jacob and Joseph, born to them while in the wilderness. We have no record of any other children born to them, but the record does note that their married children were starting their families (1 Nephi 18:6, 19).

Those were difficult times. Lest anyone think that it was a joyous occasion—even ever-optimistic, positive Nephi described those days as follows: "And so great were the blessings of the Lord upon us, that while we did live upon raw meat in the wilderness, our women did give plenty of suck for their children, and were strong, yea, even like unto the men; and *they began to bear their journeyings without murmuring*" (1 Nephi 17:2; italics added).

When the weary travelers reached the Arabian Sea, they pitched their tents by the seashore. Nephi reported that notwithstanding they had suffered many afflictions and much difficulty, "even so much that we cannot write them all, we were exceedingly rejoiced when we came to the seashore; and we called the place Bountiful, because of its much fruit" (1 Nephi 17:6).

The colony spent a total of eight years in the wilderness (1 Nephi 17:4). The distance from Jerusalem to Southern Arabia then east to Bountiful is a distance of between 2,000 to 2,400 miles. The four sons made two additional round trips from the valley of Lemuel to Jerusalem, adding another 800 to 1,000 miles to their travels. By comparison, the Mormon pioneers walked about 1,100 miles—half the distance that Lehi and his colony did.

Lehi the Family Man

One role of Lehi which is often overlooked is that of being a father with a responsibility to save his family. He was shown in a vision at the very beginning that Laman and Lemuel would probably fail in their quest for eternal life (1 Nephi 8:4, 17–18). Undaunted, he sought to persuade them otherwise throughout the length and breadth of his journey. At times he was even opposed by his usually faithful wife Sariah (1 Nephi 5:1–7). Torn by his sure knowledge that they were on the Lord's errand and the opposition from those he loved most, he undoubtedly had a constant worry on his mind. Probably only those who have struggled with similar family problems will fully appreciate Lehi's dilemma, but the realities of life covered this experienced father as he struggled to help some in his family feel and see what he felt and saw. Even at death's door he still prayed and yearned for some change to take place in his wayward sons (2 Nephi 1:12–23).

Yet, how he rejoiced in the accomplishments of faithful Nephi and stalwart Sam! His love is further exemplified in his love for one of the extended family—Zoram, the servant of Laban (2 Nephi 1:30–32). He gloried in the leadership exemplified in Nephi and fervently recommended that the rest of the family follow him as he followed the Spirit of the Lord (2 Nephi 1:24, 27). As Nephi had consistently honored his father, Lehi honored and respected his son and fully recognized him as his successor on this errand of the Lord. That Lehi was respected as a father by even the rebellious sons is obvious from the fact that he kept them in one unit until his death.

One of the last acts Lehi completed in his role as father was to call each of his own sons, Zoram, and the sons of Ishmael together for one final blessing. One by one he pronounced his prophetic views upon them, extending that blessing unto their posterity for hundreds of years. The blessing to his son Joseph best exemplifies his views of the future.

Lehi Blesses Joseph

Lehi reminded his youngest son that he had been born in the wilderness "in the days of my greatest sorrow." He then spoke of Joseph, the great patriarch who was sold into Egypt, who was young Joseph's direct ancestor and namesake. Lehi, quoting from the plates of brass, stated that "Joseph truly saw our day." That is, Joseph, who lived over a thousand years before Lehi, saw his posterity, the Nephite nation, in vision. He also prophesied of two Saints of the latter days who would also be named Joseph, who would be blessed of the Most High. Those two were Joseph Smith, Sr., and Joseph Smith, Jr.

The Prophet Joseph Smith, according to the Book of Mormon, would bring the posterity of young Joseph to a knowledge of the covenants which God made with their fathers. He would be great like unto Moses. Not only would Joseph Smith bring to the world the Book of Mormon, but he would help convince the world of the truthfulness of the Bible. Lehi further quoted Joseph's ancient prophecy relative to Joseph Smith that out of weakness he would be made strong. Those that sought to kill Joseph Smith would be confounded. The Lord promised Joseph of old that Joseph Smith "shall write the writing of the fruit of thy loins, unto the fruit of thy loins" (2 Nephi 3:18). That is, Joseph Smith would be instrumental in restoring the writings on the Josephic plates of brass and the Josephic Book of Mormon to the offspring of Joseph in the last days, even the house of Ephraim and Manasseh who constitute the vast majority of the Latter-day Saints. (See also 2 Nephi 4:2.)

Conclusion

When Lehi settled in the New World, he rehearsed the great mercies of the Lord in bringing them out of the land of Jerusalem to their land of promise in spite of their rebellions. He also told them concerning the land of promise which they had obtained, that it was their land of promise and it was a land choice above all other lands, and that the Lord had covenanted with him [Lehi] that it should be a land for his children forever (2 Nephi 1:5). The Western Hemisphere had been protected of the Lord and had not been discovered as yet by other nations, so it would not be overrun and there would be no place for an inheritance (2 Nephi 1:8). Lehi's final leg of his mission was now complete. He had weathered the storm of adversity from without and within. The Lord recognized the faithfulness of this good man by giving him an assurance of his eternal life. He proclaimed to his sons: "But behold, the Lord hath redeemed my soul from hell; I have beheld his glory, and I am encircled about eternally in the arms of his love" (2 Nephi 1:15).

We honor father Lehi as one of the noble and great ones; as the head of a major dispensation of the gospel of Jesus Christ; the father of a multitude of nations; as a prophet, seer, and revelator; a loving, caring parent and husband; a man of courage and convictions; one given a land inheritance forever for himself and his posterity; a pioneer and explorer; a patriarch and inspired scribe; an exemplar and a true disciple of the Lord Jesus Christ. As his vision extended forward, may his posterity of today extend their vision backward to the greatness of this exemplary patriarch.

NOTES AND REFERENCES

1. John A. Widtsoe, comp., *Discourses of Brigham Young* (Salt Lake City: Deseret Book Co., 1961), p. 128.

2. *JD* 23:184 (will be quoted later in the text).

3. It is interesting to note that Moses described Jehovah's presence by night among the Israelites as a pillar of fire (Exodus 13:21–22). Nephi and Lehi, while in prison, were protected from bodily harm by a pillar of fire, and all who saw the miracle were so blessed (Helaman 5:24, 43). The Twelve Apostles will stand in a pillar of fire at Christ's coming (D&C 29:12). Joseph Smith, in two of his accounts of the First Vision, describes the Father and the Son descending in a "pillar of fire" (see also Paul's account in Acts 26:13).

4. It is also interesting to note that Ezekiel also saw a book in a vision wherein he was commanded to eat it (Ezekiel 2:9–3:4). John the Revelator had a similar experience (Revelation 10; see also D&C 77:14).

5. *Teachings of the Prophet Joseph Smith,* comp. Joseph Fielding Smith (Salt Lake City: Deseret Book, 1976), p. 89.

6. *JD* 23:184.

7. *JD* 23:185.

5

LEHI AND NEPHI: FAITH UNTO SALVATION

Monte S. Nyman

As Nephi began to make an abridgment of his father's record, he stated that his objective was to show "that the tender mercies of the Lord are over all those whom he has chosen, *because of their faith*, to make them mighty even unto the power of deliverance" (1 Nephi 1:20; italics added). The events described by Nephi in the abridgment certainly do illustrate his objective. However, the element of faith may not be fully understood by the reader. This is not a problem unique to the reading of the Book of Mormon. Faith has been described as the most talked about and yet the least understood principle of the gospel, probably because there are at least three different principles of faith and people often do not differentiate among them.

The different principles of faith were spoken of by the Prophet Joseph Smith in the *Lectures on Faith*.[1] In these lectures he identified the first as the principle of *action*. Said Joseph, "faith is the assurance which men have of the existence of things

Monte S. Nyman is Associate Dean of Religious Education and Professor of Ancient Scripture at Brigham Young University.

which they have not seen, and the principle of action in all intelligent beings."[2]

The second principle of faith is one of *power*. The Prophet declared, "But faith is not only the principle of action, but of power also, in all intelligent beings, whether in heaven or on earth." He said further, "It is the principle by which Jehovah works, and through which he exercises power over all temporal as well as eternal things."[3]

The third principle of faith was defined by Joseph Smith as *faith unto life and salvation*. The Prophet said that three things were necessary for any rational and intelligent being to obtain this third principle of faith:

> First, the idea that he [God] actually exists.
> Secondly, a *correct* idea of his character, perfections, and attributes.
> Thirdly, an actual knowledge that the course of life which he is pursuing is according to his will.[4]

A study of the events that Nephi records as examples of the power of the Lord's delivering his people reveals each of the above principles of faith. The attributes that developed each principle of faith are also shown in many instances. To analyze and comprehend these principles and developmental attributes should be helpful towards one's own attainment of these principles and attributes.

Faith as a Principle of Action

Lehi was concerned for his people because of the warning of destruction given by the many prophets who visited the land of Jerusalem. This concern caused him to pray for his people, a principle of action (1 Nephi 1:4–5). Lehi was rewarded for his faith with a series of visions and dreams. With this added assurance, Lehi took further action by also prophesying of the destruction of Jerusalem as had the other prophets (1 Nephi 1:18).

Having faith in his father's experience, Nephi desired to know for himself of the things of which Lehi had testified. His action of prayer was rewarded by a visit of the Lord because of his faith. (1 Nephi 2:16, 19.) This experience plus the assurance of his father's faith enabled Nephi to demonstrate his faith in contrast to his brothers' lack of it by leading the return to Jerusalem to obtain the plates of brass as the Lord had commanded (1

Nephi 3:1–6). His statement of faith is one of the best-known passages in the Book of Mormon. In answer to his father's request, Nephi said: "I will go and do the things which the Lord hath commanded, for I know that the Lord giveth no commandments unto the children of men, save he shall prepare a way for them that they may accomplish the thing which he commandeth them" (1 Nephi 3:7).

Nephi further exemplified faith as a principle of action to his brothers as he overcame each difficulty in obtaining the plates after they arrived back at Jerusalem. In response to Laman and Lemuel's threat to return without the plates, Nephi firmly decreed: "As the Lord liveth, and as we live, we will not go down unto our father in the wilderness until we have accomplished the thing which the Lord hath commanded us. Wherefore, let us be faithful in keeping the commandments of the Lord." (1 Nephi 3:15, 16.) Nephi further assured his brethren by presenting another approach to obtaining the plates from Laban and reminding them of the reasons they had come upon this important mission. He used the example of his father's knowledge as well as his own reasoning to try to convince them. (1 Nephi 3:16–20.) His reasoning with his brethren further illustrates how this kind of faith is attained, being "faithful in keeping the commandments of the Lord" (1 Nephi 3:16). When we keep the commandments, we can be assured of the Lord's help, for he has declared to this generation, "I, the Lord, am bound when ye do what I say; but when ye do not what I say, ye have no promise" (D&C 82:10).

After a second failure to obtain the records, Nephi's faith was still undaunted. In response to Laman and Lemuel's objections, Nephi cited the example of Moses and of their visitation by an angel to assure his brothers that the Lord would provide a way for them to obtain the plates (1 Nephi 4:1–3). Although Moses had lived many years earlier, Nephi knew about him from his parents' teachings or from his own reading. This illustrates another way to develop faith—the reading of the scriptures, which show us examples of the Lord's dealings with others.

Another example of faith as a principle of action is shown by Zoram, the servant of Laban. When he recognized that Nephi was not Laban as he had supposed, he decided to follow Nephi and his brethren into the wilderness after Nephi's oath assured him that the Lord had commanded them to go. (1 Nephi 4:31–35.)

The second return to Jerusalem by Lehi's sons is another example of faith as a principle of action. However, the purpose of obtaining wives for themselves may have been a more motivating force for Laman and Lemuel than faith was. We have no record of hesitancy on their part in this account. (1 Nephi 7:1–3.) A more pronounced principle of faith as action is shown by the family of Ishmael. After hearing the word of the Lord, they willingly accompanied Nephi and his brethren to the valley of Lemuel, the base camp of Lehi. Although two of the daughters and two of the sons did rebel on that journey, Ishmael, his wife, and his three other daughters were firm in their faith. Of course, as the text says, "the Lord did soften the heart of Ishmael." (1 Nephi 7:4–6.) Without the blessing of the Lord, such faith would never have been attained.

Other examples of Lehi's and Nephi's faith appear throughout Nephi's writings. These include Lehi's willingness to continue on into the wilderness (1 Nephi 16:9–11); Nephi's willingness to build a ship under the direction of the Lord (1 Nephi 17:7–10); and the entire group's willingness to set forth upon the waters to travel to the land of promise (1 Nephi 18:5–8). The rest of the Book of Mormon also contains many more examples of faith, but the above incidents certainly illustrate faith as a principle of action. They also show that faithfully keeping the commandments of God, reading the scriptures, and gaining the outpouring of the Spirit of the Lord are the ingredients for turning this kind of faith into action. The Book of Mormon also illustrates the other principles of faith.

Faith as a Principle of Power

Implementing the principle of power through faith, Lehi and Nephi were able to accomplish the purpose of the Lord—to bring a remnant of Joseph to the promised land. This faith-unto-power principle is illustrated in several instances.

After arriving in the valley of Lemuel, Lehi confounded his murmuring sons with a speech, "being filled with the Spirit." The power of this speech caused the two rebellious sons' frames to "shake before him" and made them obey his commandments. (1 Nephi 2:14.) Undoubtedly this was a blessing bestowed upon Lehi because of his faith.

Nephi was also blessed with the presence of an angel to rebuke his brothers for their anger in smiting him and his brother

Sam with a rod (1 Nephi 3:28–29). While the text makes no mention of Nephi's faith at this time, he had continually expressed his own faith and urged his brothers to be faithful. This episode illustrates that when a person has done all he can, then his faith is rewarded with power from the Lord.

One of the best examples of faith as a power principle is Nephi's encounter with Zoram, the servant of Laban. Nephi was so convincing in speaking in the voice of Laban that the servant obediently followed him. He also conversed freely with Nephi as he carried the plates of brass outside the walls of Jerusalem. The time involved and the distance covered could have been quite extensive. Therefore, this was no temporary misidentity but illustrates how completely convinced the servant was that Nephi was Laban. Furthermore, it is logical that Zoram knew Laban's voice well. It was not until Nephi spoke in his own voice to his frightened brothers who had also mistaken Nephi for Laban that the servant realized that Nephi was not Laban (1 Nephi 4:28–30). Apparently Nephi's large stature was similar to that of Laban and in the darkness of night the probable significant difference in age could not be recognized. What was the secret to Nephi's voice change? Was it not a gift of the Spirit, a form of the gift of tongues, a power poured out on him because of his faith? While such an explanation may not satisfy the learned of the world, remember that Nephi did not write the things pleasing to the world but the things pleasing to God (1 Nephi 6:5). It was God's will that Nephi obtain the plates of brass and there is no question that he was pleased with the faith of his young servant Nephi. I believe that the Lord blessed Nephi because of his faith with the power to speak as Laban.

Another great example of faith as a power principle is shown when Nephi was bound with cords by his brothers who intended to leave him "in the wilderness to be devoured by wild beasts." Through Nephi's prayer of faith, he was given strength to burst the bands from his hands and feet and obtain his freedom. (1 Nephi 7:16–18.) From this example, we can see that such power comes only through faith. Nephi prayed for strength, "according to [his] faith." The natural man would ask the Lord to break the bands or send an angel or someone to loose him. Nephi, the spiritual giant that he was, sought the power through his faith. What a great example to follow!

Another example is shown later in 1 Nephi when Nephi was so filled with the Spirit of God as he preached to his brethren with such power that they durst not "lay their hands upon [him] nor touch [him] with their fingers, even for the space of many days" (1 Nephi 17:48–52). Following these days, the Lord instructed Nephi to stretch forth his hand to his brethren and he would shock them as a witness of the power of God within him. Nephi's compliance with this instruction caused his brothers to shake before him and acknowledge the power of God (1 Nephi 17:53–55). Such power is irrefutable even to the wicked, and it is available to those who exercise faith.

After the ship was completed and the group departed for the land of promise, Laman and Lemuel again bound Nephi as they sailed upon the mighty deep. After he was bound, "the compass, which had been prepared of the Lord, did cease to work." (1 Nephi 18:11–12.) Nephi acknowledged that the judgments of God were upon them, which once more demonstrated faith unto divine power. The compass (Liahona) which operated upon faith did not work again until Nephi's brethren loosed his bands. That this power from the Lord was a result of Nephi's faith is shown by the fact that Nephi praised the Lord for his actions and did not murmur because of his afflictions. Only the power of God could refute the faithless Laman and Lemuel. (1 Nephi 18:11–21.) A positive note to this incident could well be stated— only the faith of Nephi brought his people to the promised land.

There are many other examples of the principle of power through faith in the rest of the Book of Mormon. In the *Lectures on Faith*, the Prophet Joseph cites the instance of the prison holding Alma and Amulek being tumbled to the ground (Alma 14:25–28) and the conversion of the Lamanites (Helaman 5:40–45) as examples of this power.[5] Other examples could be cited, but suffice it to say that this power comes through the Spirit of God giving strength and power to man to accomplish things beyond his natural abilities. One would do well to seek for such faith.

Faith unto Life and Salvation

The third principle of faith is almost an extension of the first principle, the moving cause of action, though the difference between the two is significant. The first is the cause of people's doing things, while the latter is a definite knowledge that what they are doing is the expressed mind and will of the Lord regardless of their own reasoning or prior understanding. To attain this principle of faith, we must follow the principle of sacrifice.

> Let us here observe, that a religion that does not require the sacrifice of all things never has power sufficient to produce the faith necessary unto life and salvation; for, from the first existence of man, the faith necessary unto the enjoyment of life and salvation never could be obtained without the sacrifice of all earthly things. It was through this sacrifice, and this only, that God has ordained that men should enjoy eternal life; and it is through the medium of the sacrifice of all earthly things that men do actually know that they are doing the things that are well pleasing in the sight of God. When a man has offered in sacrifice all that he has for the truth's sake, not even withholding his life, and believing before God that he has been called to make this sacrifice because he seeks to do his will, he does know, most assuredly, that God does and will accept his sacrifice and offering, and that he has not, nor will not seek his face in vain. Under these circumstances, then, he can obtain the faith necessary for him to lay hold on eternal life.[6]

This principle of faith also is exemplified a few times in the book of 1 Nephi. The initial example is Lehi's call to take his family and leave Jerusalem, departing into the wilderness. He was not told his destination nor the extent of his journey. He received this call because of his previous faith unto action. It was based upon the principle of sacrifice. "He left his house, and the land of his inheritance, and his gold, and his silver, and his precious things, and took nothing with him, save it were his family, and provisions, and tents." (1 Nephi 2:1–4.)

Although his temporal salvation was endangered, since the Jews sought to take away his life, his eternal salvation was also at stake. The subsequent chapters show that Lehi fully understood this. Sometime later his wife Sariah complained over the feared loss of her sons and she accused her husband of being a visionary man. Lehi testified that he was just that, for if he had not "seen the things of God in a vision [he would] not have known the goodness of God, but [would have] tarried at Jerusalem, and [would have] perished with [his] brethren." But because of his faith he had "obtained a land of promise" and he knew that the Lord would deliver his sons out of the hands of Laban. (1 Nephi 5:4–5.) Lehi knew that the course he was pursuing was the will of the Lord. This assurance through faith also came to Sariah upon the return of her sons (1 Nephi 5:8–9).

Lehi's experience verifies the teachings of Joseph Smith regarding the principle of faith unto life and salvation. Joseph said those who do sacrifice will know that the course they pursue is the will of the Lord.[7] Lehi's knowledge of his sons' safety came because of his previous sacrifices. Joseph also taught that this principle was what enabled men to endure afflictions, persecutions, the spoiling of their goods, and even suffer death.[8] Lehi had gone through these very things and thus had faith unto life and salvation. Lehi later testified that the Lord had redeemed his soul from hell, that he had beheld his glory, and that he was "encircled about eternally in the arms of his love" (2 Nephi 1:15).

Nephi is a second example of the principle of faith unto life and salvation. Because of his faith and diligence, the Lord visited him and assured him that they were all being led to a land of promise and that Nephi was to play a leadership role in this great endeavor (1 Nephi 2:19–24). Thus he knew that the course he was pursuing was the will of the Lord.

Upon returning to Jerusalem to obtain the plates of brass from Laban, Nephi again exemplified faith unto life and salvation. Being reluctantly followed by his rebellious brothers and Sam, Nephi left them outside the walls of the city of Jerusalem and "crept into the city and went forth towards the house of Laban" being "led by the Spirit, not knowing beforehand the things which [he] should do" (1 Nephi 4:4–6).

Finding Laban in a state of drunkenness, Nephi "was constrained by the Spirit that [he] should kill Laban" (1 Nephi 4:10). But Nephi could not think of taking a man's life. The Spirit commanded him a second time to slay Laban, but his heart and his mind still hesitated to follow this commandment. After giving the reasons why Laban had been delivered into Nephi's hands, the Spirit a third time commanded and gave the Lord's justification for taking Laban's life. (1 Nephi 4:11–13.) With this explanation, Nephi's mind now gave him the broader perspective of the Lord and his heart gave him knowledge of the course he was to pursue. Therefore, he followed the Spirit's command and smote off Laban's head. (1 Nephi 4:14–18.)

This incident often troubles readers of the Book of Mormon, but it wouldn't if they understood the principle of faith unto life and salvation. Nephi was being led by the Spirit and was being instructed to act according to a law of the Lord. This law had been revealed anciently, but apparently Nephi was not aware of it or had not comprehended its appropriateness. Probably no one would until the situation was presented by the Spirit. Nephi later illustrated this law to his brothers in regard to the people being driven out of the land of Canaan by the Israelites under Joshua. Nephi asked if these people who had been destroyed were righteous and then answered his own question with a resounding nay. He then asked if the people in Jerusalem who were destined to be destroyed were righteous. Again he answered no. (1 Nephi 17:33–34.) Nephi further taught that the Lord destroys only the nations of the wicked (1 Nephi 17:37). Laban was a wicked person, and thus the Lord commanded that he be destroyed.

The law that was revealed was the law of retaliation. As the Spirit pointed out to Nephi, Laban had offended the Lord three times (1 Nephi 4:11); therefore, the Lord had delivered him into Nephi's hand. The Lord, also knowing the eternal perspective of a nation about to be conceived, issued the decree to take Laban's life. This ancient law has been revealed anew in this last dispensation of the fulness of times and verifies the action commanded by the Spirit. It even verifies that this law had been revealed to Nephi. (D&C 98:23–32.) A careful study of these verses and of 1 Nephi 3:11–4:18 will show that Nephi's actions correlate with the revealed law of the Lord.

Laban had refused to heed the commandments of the Lord relayed by Lehi's sons to give them the plates. This was the first offense. After the sons had attempted to purchase the records, Laban had robbed them of their gold and silver, and precious things which they had offered for the plates, a second offense. Following this bartering session, Laban had sent his servants to slay Nephi and his brothers. After these three offenses, the Lord had delivered Laban into Nephi's hands and justified his demise because of the future destiny of Lehi and his colony.

God is a God of law. Similar incidents are recorded in the stick of Judah. Samuel's slaying of Agag (1 Samuel 15) and Elijah's slaying of the prophets of Baal (1 Kings 18) are two biblical examples.

The Prophet Joseph Smith revealed a further dimension applicable to the Laban situation.

> God said, "Thou shalt not kill;" at another time He said, "Thou shalt utterly destroy." This is the principle on which the government of heaven is conducted—by revelation adapted to the

circumstances in which the children of the kingdom are placed. Whatever God requires is right, no matter what it is, although we may not see the reason thereof till long after the events transpire.[9]

Some may reason from this statement that truth is relative, but such reasoning is faulty. God understands the eternal and long-range effects of every situation and will always reveal the absolute truth. If all the variables are the same, the same directions will be given, but man is not able to comprehend the variables as is God. Thorough study of God's word verifies his eternal nature of righteousness (Helaman 13:38) and that "the course of the Lord is one eternal round" not varying "from that which he hath said" (1 Nephi 10:19 and Alma 7:20).

After the death of Lehi, Nephi again sacrificed all and led "those who believed in the warnings and the revelations of God" into the wilderness to avoid war with Laman and his followers (2 Nephi 5:5−6). Undoubtedly Nephi's life continued to follow the will of the Lord. This is evidenced by one of the closing remarks he wrote upon the plates. He stated that he gloried in Jesus who had redeemed his soul from hell (2 Nephi 33:6). His calling and election had been made sure; his faith had led him to salvation.

As Nephi taught, the Lord "leadeth away the righteous into precious lands, and the wicked he destroyeth" (1 Nephi 17:38). Mosiah, king of Zarahemla, led a group out from the wicked (Omni 1:12). Alma baptized the repentant and led them from among the wicked (Mosiah 18 and 23). The people of Ammon (converted Lamanites) followed the will of the Lord and were reestablished in the land of Jershon (Alma 27). All of these movements are other examples of faith unto life and salvation, knowing that the course they pursued was the will of the Lord. These examples within the Book of Mormon should inspire its readers to seek to know the will of the Lord concerning the course they should follow.

Conclusion

The Prophet Joseph Smith declared that by learning and abiding by the precepts of the Book of Mormon, a man would come nearer to God than by following any other book (Introduction). One of the precepts taught by Nephi was that through faith the Lord would make those whom he had chosen mighty "even unto the power of deliverance" (1 Nephi 1:20). Those who study the scriptures and faithfully keep the commandments will be blessed with the Lord's spirit and be motivated to action. Those who are motivated to action because of their faith will have the principle of power in their lives to accomplish what they endeavor to do in righteousness beyond the natural abilities of man. Those who will sacrifice sufficiently will be led unto life and salvation by knowing that the course they pursue is the will of the Lord. Of these principles of faith, the Book of Mormon bears repeated testimony.

NOTES AND REFERENCES

1. There are those who question Joseph Smith as the author of *Lectures on Faith*. This paper will not discuss that issue but will treat them as written by the Prophet.

2. Ibid., 1:9.

3. Ibid., 1:13, 16.

4. Ibid., 3:2−5.

5. Ibid., 1:19.

6. Ibid., 6:7.

7. Ibid.

8. Ibid., 6:2−3.

9. *Teachings of the Prophet Joseph Smith*, comp. Joseph Fielding Smith (Salt Lake City: Deseret Book Co., 1976), p. 256.

6

THE PROPHET NEPHI

Rodney Turner

Some men are "morning stars" of the first magnitude, possessing a luminescence so unique, so compelling, that lesser mortals bask in their reflected glory like so many planets orbiting the sun. This eternal principle of attraction functions like a spiritual law of gravity (D&C 88:40). It originates in that God whose dominions forever flow unto him "without compulsory means" (D&C 121:46).

For the spiritually minded, the foremost of such men in this world are those towering figures comprising the prophets, seers, and revelators of the ages. Few in number, they are heaven's pillars on earth, upholding the various gospel dispensations. One of these was Nephi, a truly superlative man. Indeed, he was the prototype of those renowned Book of Mormon prophets and kings who came after him. These and many unidentified prophets reflected Nephi's faith, courage, and commitment.

Nephi not only set the prophetic tone for his people for a thousand years, but his voice rings out to the children of Lehi and

Rodney Turner is Professor of Ancient Scripture at Brigham Young University.

all mankind in our day. Indeed, his words and those of his fellow prophets in the Book of Mormon render that volume of scripture the keystone of salvation in this last gospel dispensation. Elder Bruce R. McConkie testified: "It is the book that will save the world and prepare the sons of men for joy and peace here and now and everlasting life in eternity."[1]

The House of Joseph

Lehi's lineage was foreordained. Upon acquiring the plates of brass, he learned that he was a descendant of Joseph through Manasseh (1 Nephi 3:3, 12; 5:14–16; 6:2; Alma 10:3). This knowledge inspired him to prophesy that the contents of the plates (comprising much of the Old Testament) would "go forth unto all nations, kindreds, tongues, and people who were of his seed" (1 Nephi 5:17–19). In the times of the Gentiles, the Bible was to be the scriptural Elias, or forerunner, of the Book of Mormon.

Lehi and Nephi inaugurated the American branch of a line of prophets descending from Joseph.[2] Joseph was Jacob's covenant son who, through Manasseh and Ephraim, received a double portion in Israel (Genesis 48:8–22). More important, "Joseph" was the one to whom the other tribes would look for both temporal and spiritual salvation (Genesis 37:5–10).

It was "Joseph" who was to spread abroad in the Americas (Genesis 49:22). It was "Joseph" who would write "Another Testament of Christ"—the Book of Mormon (see Ezekiel 37:16–20; 2 Nephi 3:12). It was "Joseph" whose descendant and namesake Joseph Smith was to be a choice seer and an "ensign" for the gathering of Israel in the latter days (JST, Genesis 50:30–33; 2 Nephi 3:6–8, 11, 16; D&C 113:6). It was "Joseph" who would bestow the ordinances of the house of the Lord upon redeemed Israel prior to the Savior's millennial reign (D&C 133:30–35).

Through Lehi, "Joseph" came to America. He did so for at least three reasons: (1) that his posterity might lay claim to the choicest of the lands of promise, the Americas, (2) that the Book of Mormon—the "stick of Ephraim" (D&C 27:5)—might be written as the Western Hemisphere's witness of Jesus Christ, and (3) so that the restored Church might be established in the land of Zion from whence the message of salvation would go forth to all nations (D&C 58:13).

"Joseph's" latter-day work was to be directed by his younger son, Ephraim, who received the blessing of the firstborn from his grandfather Jacob (Genesis 48:17–20). The Lord told Jeremiah: "I am a father to Israel, and Ephraim is my firstborn" (Jeremiah 31:9). As Jesus is the elder brother of the human family, so is Joseph, through Ephraim, the elder brother of Israel.

Lehi and his prophet-descendants were in a very real sense forerunners of the Restoration. As the Bible was an Elias for the Book of Mormon, so was the Book of Mormon an Elias for the restored Church. They are inseparably connected; they stand or fall together.

The Chronicle Begins

The Nephite chronicle began in Jerusalem six hundred years before the birth of Christ. Nephi's father, Lehi, a lifetime resident of the land,[3] had amassed a large fortune—probably through trade with Egypt, which had been a dominant influence in the Middle East for many centuries and controlled Palestine and Syria between 609 and 605 B.C.

But in 604 Nebuchadnezzar conquered these lands and, in the first of three major deportations, exiled a number of prominent Jewish citizens to Babylon. It was a time of great political turmoil. One faction favored submission to Babylon, another sought alliance with Egypt. It was under these conditions that many prophets, including Jeremiah (whose ministry began about 627), warned of the imminent destruction of Jerusalem.

Deeply concerned, Lehi prayed in behalf of his people. The visions that followed (1 Nephi 1:5–15, 19) establish the central theme of the Book of Mormon—the redemptive mission of Jesus Christ. Lehi testified publicly of his visions and of the Messiah's future coming. Incensed, the Jews sought his life, and, warned by the Lord, Lehi fled with his family into the wilderness. His first major encampment was in the valley of Lemuel near the Gulf of Aqabah—approximately two hundred miles south of Jerusalem. "Joseph's" American odyssey had begun.

Nephi was "exceedingly young" but "large in stature" (1 Nephi 2:16; 4:31) at the time. This suggests that he was born around 615 B.C., during the turbulent period preceding the fall of the Assyrian empire in 612 and the rise of Babylon in 605. (Jerusalem would be destroyed in about 587.)

Nephi was the fourth son of Lehi and Sariah. Two younger brothers, Jacob and Joseph, would be born during the eight or more years of wilderness sojourning. He also had two or more sisters (2 Nephi 5:6).

He must have been in his late teens when he married one of Ishmael's five daughters (1 Nephi 16:7; 18:19). The only specific incident involving his own family he mentions occurred at sea when he was bound by Laman and Lemuel. He writes: "My wife with her tears and prayers, and also my children, did not soften the hearts of my brethren that they would loose me" (1 Nephi 18:19). He later states that he and his children were actually hated by these brothers (2 Nephi 5:14).

Nephi and His Brothers

As prophesied, Nephi became the teacher of his brothers (1 Nephi 2:22). He explained to them Lehi's allegorical vision (1 Nephi 8:2–38; 15:2–36; 16:1–5), as well as his teachings concerning Israel and the prophecies of Isaiah (1 Nephi 10; 15:20; 19:22–24; 20–22).

But in spite of all they were taught, Laman, the archvillain, and his tag-along brother Lemuel emerge as fundamentally corrupt men. Their record was dismal: they were materialistic, faithless, disloyal, cowardly, complaining, cruel, lazy, untruthful, and, like Jacob's son Reuben, "unstable as water" (Genesis 49:4) —humbling themselves one day and breathing out threats the next (1 Nephi 7:20; 16:5, 32, 39; 18:4, 15, 20). The only thing that really impressed them was power (1 Nephi 18:20). Above all, they were would-be murderers of their own father and brother. In the end, they polluted their posterity with their lies and brought a curse upon them that was not to be removed for more than a half a millennium.

On the other hand, Nephi was a man of astonishing faith, profound humility, and consistent steadiness. In the latter, he was unequaled even by his parents. Fearful that her sons had perished in the wilderness, Sariah complained against Lehi in language reminiscent of that used earlier by Laman and Lemuel (1 Nephi 2:11; 5:2). And at the time of the broken bow incident even Lehi "began to murmur against the Lord his God" (1 Nephi 16:20). Chastened by the Lord, Lehi "was brought down into the depths of sorrow" (1 Nephi 16:25). These very human lapses in no way diminish the greatness of Lehi and Sariah; would that we stumbled but once on so long and arduous a journey!

Had Nephi sought the power he was accused of seeking (1 Nephi 16:38), he might then have assumed leadership over his father. Instead, he honored and sustained his patriarch by asking: "Whither shall I go to obtain food?" (1 Nephi 16:23).

But why the striking contrast between Nephi and his two brothers? Was one so good, and the others so bad? Is it a case of self-serving manipulation of the facts on Nephi's part? Hardly. If anything, Nephi has moderated his own virtues. I believe that Nephi and Laman symbolize that essential opposition between good and evil drawn so vividly in the Book of Mormon. They represent the two extremes found therein: life versus death, heaven versus hell, the kingdom of God versus the kingdom of the devil, the spiritually minded versus the carnally minded, the saved versus the lost—those sealed up to Christ and those sealed up to the devil (Alma 34:34–36; 40:23–26).

Lehi knew that Laman and Lemuel slept "the sleep of hell" (2 Nephi 1:13). He pleaded with them to repent lest they suffer "the eternal destruction of both soul and body" (2 Nephi 1:22). Nephi also grieved over them: "Behold, my soul is rent with anguish because of you, and my heart is pained; I fear lest ye shall be cast off forever" (1 Nephi 17:47).

They had seen an angel (1 Nephi 3:29; 4:3; 7:10; 17:45), had experienced the power of God (1 Nephi 7:18; 17:48, 52–55), and had heard the voice of the Lord and received of his Spirit (1 Nephi 16:39; 17:45). Yet they plotted Nephi's murder on at least four occasions (1 Nephi 7:16; 16:37; 17:48; 2 Nephi 5:2; compare 1:24), and their father's at least once (1 Nephi 16:37). Nephi accused Laman and Lemuel of being "murderers in their hearts" (1 Nephi 17:44). They were prepared to shed innocent blood.

These were not ignorant men; they stood self-condemned. When literally shocked by the Spirit, they testified: "We know of a surety that the Lord is with thee, for we know that it is the power of the Lord that has shaken us" (1 Nephi 17:55; compare 2 Nephi 4:22). Nephi adds that he had to prevent them from worshipping him at the time (1 Nephi 17:55).

The Laban Affair

Nowhere are the contrasting characters of Nephi and Laman better revealed than in the Laban affair. Unlike Laman and

Lemuel, who doubted both the source and the feasibility of the idea of getting the plates of brass, young Nephi was convinced that not only should Laban's record be obtained, but that it *would* be obtained. "I will go and do the things which the Lord hath commanded, for I know that the Lord giveth no commandments unto the children of men, save he shall prepare a way for them that they may accomplish the thing which he commandeth them" (1 Nephi 3:7; compare 17:3).

He then led his reluctant, murmuring brothers back to Jerusalem. Laman's subsequent abortive encounter with Laban convinced him that the mission was futile. But Nephi, having been blessed with the gift of faith (1 Nephi 3:8), swore an oath: "*As the Lord liveth, and as we live*, we will not go down unto our father in the wilderness until we have accomplished the thing which the Lord hath commanded us" (1 Nephi 3:15; italics added). His former testimony had not been idly spoken.

Hoping that Laban would be willing to exchange the plates of brass for their father's treasure, the four brothers went down to the land of their inheritance, obtained the treasure and brought it to Laban. And "he did lust after it" (1 Nephi 3:25). Threatened and driven out, the brothers fled for their lives. Filled with rage and humiliation, Laman and Lemuel whipped Sam and Nephi with a rod. It was then that a divine messenger appeared and revealed that the rod of authority belonged in Nephi's hand, not theirs. By their misconduct, they had forfeited the traditional right of leadership. The Lord had chosen Nephi instead; he would rule the Lehite nation. (1 Nephi 3:29.) That choice rankled the Lamanites for over five hundred years.

Assured of success by the angel and angrily yielding to Nephi's persuasive arguments, Laman and Lemuel reluctantly accompanied Sam and Nephi back to Jerusalem where they hid themselves outside its walls while Nephi crept into the darkened city alone. Faith and doubt, courage and cowardice, had parted company. "And I was led by the Spirit, not knowing beforehand the things which I should do" (1 Nephi 4:6). What, indeed, could he do? Laban had stolen his father's wealth; Nephi had nothing his adversary wanted but his life.

Approaching Laban's house, Nephi discovered him "drunken with wine" and lying in the street. As he drew Laban's magnificent sword, the Spirit that led Nephi said, "Kill him." Appalled, Nephi resisted the command: "Never at any time have I shed the blood of man" (1 Nephi 4:10). The Spirit spoke again: "The Lord hath delivered him into thy hands."

Nephi reflected on the fact that Laban was a would-be (if not actual) murderer, that he defied God's commandments, and that he had stolen Lehi's property. Confirming Nephi's thoughts, the Spirit repeated the command: "Slay him, for the Lord hath delivered him into thy hands; behold *the Lord slayeth the wicked* to bring forth his righteous purposes. It is better that one man should perish than that a nation should dwindle and perish in unbelief." (1 Nephi 4:12–13; italics added.) Commitment over-ruled conscience; Nephi obeyed the "voice of the Spirit;" he beheaded Laban.

Some critics maintain that Nephi simply rationalized a justi-fication for what was, in fact, an act of murder. They argue that a God of love would never be a party to such a crime, that it is a contradiction of his true nature as revealed by Jesus in the Sermon on the Mount. Using the same logic, they also deny that the Lord commanded Abraham to sacrifice Isaac.[4]

However, Nephi's rationalizations did not precede the Spirit's command; they *followed* it. Then, too, Nephi was over forty years old when he wrote this account. He had become well acquainted with the Holy Ghost and knew the difference between his own thoughts and divine revelation. His action had been totally unpremeditated; he had gone to Laban's house *"not knowing* beforehand the things which I should do" (1 Nephi 4:6; italics added).

As for his account, he could just as well have written that Laban was already dead when he found him, or provided some other plausible explanation. We would be none the wiser. But Nephi was a truthful man; he wrote it as it happened.

The affair was a trial of faith. The Lord could easily have procured the record some other way, but he deliberately placed Nephi in a dilemma: obtain and safeguard the plates as com-manded, or let Laban live. If Laban lived, the mission would fail. For even if the plates could be obtained by strategem, Laban would certainly know who had taken them. And without the plates of brass, Lehi's posterity would, like the later Mulekites, "perish in unbelief" (1 Nephi 4:13; Omni 1:17). Their history, if any, would have been far different. Above all, there would be no Book of Mormon as we know it. The "keystone of our religion" would be missing, and the Lord's purposes frustrated, a thing he will not tolerate (D&C 3:1).

85

Nephi was also justified from a personal standpoint. Nine hours before he was shot to death, Joseph Smith wrote his wife, Emma: "There is one principle which is eternal; it is the duty of all men to protect their lives and the lives of the household, whenever necessity requires, and no power has a right to forbid it, should the last extreme arrive."[5] If the principle of self-preservation applies to a "household," how much more does it apply to an entire nation!

But there is a larger issue: the moral nature of God. What are its bounds? Who can say what the Almighty can and cannot do? The Prophet Joseph Smith observed: "It is the constitutional disposition of mankind to set up stakes and set bounds to the works and ways of the Almighty."[6] Yet he "willeth to take even them whom he will take, and preserveth in life them whom he will preserve" (D&C 63:3). He judged Laban, found him guilty, and ordered his execution. Nephi was but the instrument of divine justice. Did Jehovah have a right to do this? Of course. The agency of man cannot delimit or circumscribe the agency of God. As Joseph Smith noted:

> That which is wrong under one circumstance, may be, and often is, right under another. God said, "Thou shalt not kill;" at another time He said, "Thou shalt utterly destroy." This is the principle on which the government of heaven is conducted—by revelation adapted to the circumstances in which the children of the kingdom are placed. Whatever God requires is right, no matter what it is, although we may not see the reason thereof till long after the events transpire.[7]

Thus we see that God cannot be bound even by his prior words or commandments. For example, he told Joseph Smith: "Abraham was commanded to offer his son Isaac; nevertheless, *it was written*: Thou shalt not kill. Abraham, however, did not refuse, and it was accounted unto him for righteousness." (D&C 132:36; italics added; compare Jacob 4:5.)

The spoken word of the Lord takes precedence over the written word of the Lord. The will of the Lord today takes precedence over the will of the Lord yesterday. That is precisely why a living prophet is indispensable, and why his inspired word supersedes written scripture. The God who proved Abraham is the God who proved Nephi, and, like Abraham, Nephi obeyed and it was accounted unto him for righteousness.

Nephi's Records

The Adamic "book of remembrance"—the pattern of which was given "by the finger of God" (Moses 6:5, 46)—was the prototype of subsequent scripture. It contained genealogical, historical, and inspirational materials. The plates of brass reflected the divine pattern and probably determined the form Nephi adopted for his own two records—known as the large and small plates of Nephi.[8] (Large and small refer to their number, not their dimensions.)

Upon arriving in America, Nephi began his record on the large plates. In addition to purely historical data, they contained certain prophecies of Lehi and Nephi as well as genealogical data (1 Nephi 9:2, 4; 19:1–2; 2 Nephi 4:14; 5:33). These plates were kept by the Nephite kings until 92 B.C. when they were transferred to a descendant of Nephi, Alma the son of Alma (Mosiah 28:11, 20). Four hundred twenty-seven years later, in A.D. 335, the large plates were retrieved from the hill Shim by Mormon who, in 385, hid them up in the hill Cumorah (Mormon 1:2–4; 2:17; 6:6). Presumably, they are still there.

The small plates (1 Nephi through Omni) were prepared in 569 B.C. when Nephi was about forty-five years old (2 Nephi 5:28–33). They were devoted to spiritual matters, especially those pertaining to the gospel. Upon discovering them, Mormon was so pleased with their Christ-centered orientation that he decided to continue that emphasis throughout the remainder of his own abridgement of the large plates (Words of Mormon 1:3–5).

The Great Vision

Like Abraham, Nephi was spiritually ambitious; he wanted to know the mysteries of God (1 Nephi 2:16; Abraham 1:2). He wanted to see what his father had seen. His desire was realized; he joined Adam, Enoch, the brother of Jared, and the Apostle John as one of the very few men God has ever granted a panoramic vision of things to come.

While still a youth, prior to his marriage, Nephi was "caught away in the Spirit of the Lord" into "an exceedingly high mountain" where he briefly conversed with the Spirit [the Holy Ghost?] face to face (1 Nephi 11:1, 11; compare 2 Nephi 4:25).

The Spirit was soon replaced by an angelic guide who explained to Nephi all that followed.

The vision spanned well over three thousand years, from the birth of Jesus to the celestialization of the earth. However, Nephi was forbidden to write that portion of the revelation reserved for John the Revelator (1 Nephi 14:24–25; 2 Nephi 4:25).[9]

He was shown the same things his father had seen: the tree of life, the rod of iron, the river, the spacious building, and so forth. These symbols reappear as the different scenes of the vision unfold, binding together its component parts like the recurring themes of a symphony.

Nephi first beheld Mary, "most beautiful and fair above all other virgins" (1 Nephi 11:15) "carried away in the Spirit for the space of a time" (1 Nephi 11:19; compare Luke 1:35). When he beheld the virgin again, she was bearing the infant Son of God in her arms. His baptism, ministry, and crucifixion followed. (1 Nephi 11:20–33.) These redeeming events were revealed in the context of the rod of iron and the tree of life or fountain of living waters which symbolize the love of God as embodied in the mission of Jesus Christ (1 Nephi 11:25).

In the vision, after Jesus' death the proud world—represented by the spacious building—was arrayed against the Apostles and the Church. In time, the building collapsed, signifying the end of all nations that fight against God. (1 Nephi 11:34–36.)

Nephi next beheld ancient America (1 Nephi 12). He saw the wars and general wickedness of Lehi's posterity end in the devastating destructions accompanying Jesus' crucifixion—an example of the "mist of darkness" (1 Nephi 12:4).

These upheavals were followed by the ministry of the resurrected Savior, the era of righteousness, the final destruction of the Nephite nation in the fifth century, and the long period of spiritual darkness thereafter (1 Nephi 12:6–23). In these latter scenes the river of filthy water, the mists of darkness, and the spacious building return again like so many somber themes.

Europe, Asia Minor, and the Middle East as they were in the early centuries of the Christian era were then seen by Nephi (1 Nephi 13). He beheld the "formation of a great church" which his angelic guide described as "most abominable above all other churches" (1 Nephi 13:4–5). Historically, this diverse "church" consisted of those vicious elements of Judaism, heathenism, apostate Christianity, and civil government which persecuted, tortured, and slew the Saints of God both before and after the passing of the ancient church. But it is yet to be destroyed. It exists today among the nations of the earth and will continue to "fight against the Lamb of God" (1 Nephi 14:13) almost until the end of the world.

Nephi then saw the discovery of America, its settlement by the Gentiles, the revolutionary war, and the white man's prophesied depredations against the Lamanites (1 Nephi 13:1–19). He saw the Gentiles bring the Bible to America—the land of Joseph. But "plain and most precious" doctrines and ordinances had been lost when certain inspired writings were "taken away" and "kept back" by that "abominable church" (1 Nephi 13:26, 32). Because of this, the Gentiles, blessed temporally, stumbled spiritually (1 Nephi 13:25–30).

However, their spiritual blindness was not to continue. Many of the "plain and most precious" things lost to them were to be recovered in the writings of the forefathers of the very peoples being "smitten" by the Gentiles.

The Church of Jesus Christ, established among the Gentiles in America, would be the instrument through which the Book of Mormon and other latter-day scriptures would restore those "most precious parts of the gospel of the Lamb" (1 Nephi 13:32) which had been deliberately omitted from the Christian canon of scripture. The combined testimonies of these new witnesses for the true Christ and the true gospel would lift the mists of spiritual darkness enveloping the world. Thus, in due time, righteous Israel—Jew and Gentile—would be saved (1 Nephi 13:31–42).

The final scenes of Nephi's vision pertained to these latter days (1 Nephi 14). Repentant Gentiles were adopted into the house of Joseph and all Israel was gathered to "no more be confounded" (1 Nephi 14:2).

Nephi saw the great and abominable church fall during the climactic judgments poured out upon the nations prior to Christ's world advent. The anti-Christ church, "the whore of all the earth," would fight against Zion no longer (2 Nephi 10:16).

The "marvelous work" of the latter days was to be "everlasting" in its consequences; the choice between salvation and damnation would be final and irrevocable (1 Nephi 14:7). For, in the final analysis there have been but two paths lying before the family of God. All walk one or the other (2 Nephi 2:27–29).

Such is the "opposition in all things" (2 Nephi 2:11), so essential to the plan of salvation. We first encountered it in our premortal estate (D&C 29:39; Abraham 3:27–28). It was there that the "two churches" came into being. They constituted the opposing powers in the war in heaven, a war which rages with ever-increasing intensity as we approach the end of telestial time. Nephi's angelic guide summed up this ongoing cosmic struggle between good and evil when he stated: "Behold there are save two churches only; the one is the church of the Lamb of God, and the other is the church of the devil; wherefore, whoso belongeth not to the church of the Lamb of God belongeth to that great church, which is the mother of abominations; and she is the whore of all the earth" (1 Nephi 14:10).

Between now and the last judgment, billions of men and women will be transferring their memberships from one church to the other! Those who repent, bow the knee, and confess that Jesus is the Christ will be numbered with the church of the Lamb of God (Mosiah 27:31; D&C 76:110−11).[10]

Those who absolutely refuse to repent will remain "filthy still"; they will retain their memberships in the church of the devil. They are sons and daughters of Perdition, suffering the damnation of the second death. (Alma 12:12−18; D&C 88:35.) Happily, the vast majority of the human family will eventually repent and obtain a measure of salvation in one of the "many mansions" comprising the Father's kingdom (John 14:2; D&C 76).

Nephi saw that enemies of the Lord's latter-day work would arise in every nation. But the "saints of the church of the Lamb" and the scattered "covenant people of the Lord" would be "armed with righteousness and with the power of God" (1 Nephi 14:14; compare D&C 45:66−69). The "wrath of God" (divine justice) would then be poured out upon the "abominable church" as wars swept through the nations belonging to it.

This condition will mark the beginning of the final phase of the Father's work in fulfilling his covenant with Abraham (1 Nephi 14:16−17; compare 3 Nephi 16:5, 17−20; 20:11−13). Nephi ended his account of the vision at that point.

The Rod of Iron and the Liahona

The marriages of Ishmael's daughters to Zoram and to Lehi's four sons marked the end of the long encampment in the valley of Lemuel. On the very day of the colony's departure, "to his great astonishment" (1 Nephi 16:10), Lehi found a ball of curious workmanship lying at his tent door. The next phase of the journey would take the colony through a more arid and dangerous country. In addition to locating food and water, they would need to avoid encountering robbers or others who might prove a threat, or even a temptation, to them. The Lord had prepared the way for them to do so—the Liahona (so called in Alma 37:38), the divine companion to the rod of iron.

The rod of iron is the "word of God" (1 Nephi 15:23–24), as found in revealed scripture. It consists of those general doctrines, ordinances, and commandments—those "correct principles"—identified with the Lord's church in every dispensation. Jesus Christ is "the Word, even the messenger of salvation" (D&C 93:8). Holding fast to the rod of iron is holding fast to him. In doing so, the Saints are united in a common bond of light and truth.

The Liahona represents the constant guidance of the Holy Spirit needed by us all as we confront the ever-changing circumstances of life (1 Nephi 16:26–27). The living prophet embodies the Liahona principle for the entire Church. He provides the Church with the word of the Lord pertaining to current matters of general concern. Because of him, revelation is an open-ended principle.

The suggestion that the rod of iron and the Liahona represent two different approaches to gospel living is unfortunate.[11] They cannot be dichotomized without seriously impairing both. Scripture is not subject to the individual interpretations of millions of Church members (2 Peter 1:20). When we interpret the word of the Lord in terms of our own predilections, the rod of iron becomes a very unstable, unreliable rubber band.

The Liahona worked "according to the faith and diligence and heed" of the people (1 Nephi 16:28; compare Mosiah 1:16). Can we transform or, worse, let go of the iron rod and still have the requisite faith needed for the Liahona to point the way "we *should* go" rather than the way we *want* to go?

Plainly, the rod of iron and the Liahona are not two contrary ways of looking at the Church or the gospel, but two sources of divine revelation—general and specific, long range and immediate—designed to guide and sustain the Saints under all circumstances. Honoring *both* led Lehi's people to the land of promise (Alma 37:45). Honoring *both* will do the same for us.

The Nephite Kingdom

Twenty-odd years after fleeing Jerusalem, Lehi died (2 Nephi 4:12). The great division that split his family into Nephites and Lamanites followed almost immediately thereafter. Nephi's divine mandate to succeed Lehi was rejected: "We will not have him to be our ruler; for it belongs unto us, who are the elder brethren, to rule over this people" (2 Nephi 5:3; compare 1 Nephi 18:10). His life sought, Nephi fled with his family and supporters a considerable distance to the north to what became known as the land of Nephi where he established the Nephite nation.

Although opposed to a monarchy, Nephi acceded to his people's desire and became the first in a dynasty of kings, all of whom were his descendants and bore his name (2 Nephi 5:18; Jacob 1:9–11; Mosiah 25:13). His dynasty lasted for almost five hundred years—from about 570 to 91 B.C. when it was replaced by a system of judges (Mosiah 25:13; 29:41–47). At least four Book of Mormon prophets and an unknown number of kings were called Nephi.

Since Nephi served as both spiritual and temporal leader, his government was essentially theocratic in nature. He held the Melchizedek Priesthood and consecrated his younger brothers, Jacob and Joseph, priests and teachers. He also built the first Nephite temple, patterned after that of Solomon (2 Nephi 5:16).

The life of Nephi vindicated his divine appointment and exposed the falsity of the charge that he sought power over the people. He sought their salvation, not their subservience. Nephi forged a righteous and industrious nation which he led with spiritual intelligence and practical skill.

Nephi was about seventy years old when he passed away. He left behind a treasure of truth written upon plates of gold that neither time nor circumstance can tarnish, a treasure which will enrich the lives of countless millions in the dispensation of the fulness of times.

The Psalm of Nephi

Nephi attributed his every virtue to God; he never took glory unto himself. Nowhere is his heart better revealed or his life better summarized than in the prayerful psalm he wrote in his middle years (2 Nephi 4:16–35).

Before quoting extracts from it, may I suggest a caveat. As with Joseph Smith in his account of the First Vision, Nephi's references to personal sins should not be taken to imply any serious moral transgression on his part. No man could have seen and known God as he did who was not pure in heart.

Rather, he is almost surely alluding to the negative emotions of anger, impatience, and frustration he must have felt at times in dealing with his enemies, his own family, and others who lacked his singleness of purpose in carrying out the Lord's will. We know little of his later years and the trials they brought him. Jacob describes him as the "great protector" of his people, "having wielded the sword of Laban in their defence, and having labored in all his days for their welfare" (Jacob 1:10).

He was keenly sensitive to the negative feelings his enemies, especially the devil, engendered in his soul. It is paradoxical that the more godly a man becomes, the more he is prepared to excuse the sins of others, and the less he is prepared to excuse his own.[12] Tolerance for any imperfection diminishes as we approach the character of that God who "cannot look upon sin with the least degree of allowance" (Alma 45:16; D&C 1:31). Now the psalm.

Behold, my soul delighteth in the things of the Lord; and my heart pondereth continually upon the things which I have seen and heard. Nevertheless . . . my heart exclaimeth: O wretched man that I am! Yea, my heart sorroweth because of my flesh; my soul grieveth because of mine iniquities. I am encompassed about, because of the temptations and the sins which do so easily beset me. And when I desire to rejoice, my heart groaneth because of my sins; nevertheless, I know in whom I have trusted. My God . . . hath filled me with his love, even unto the consuming of my flesh . . . upon the wings of his Spirit hath my body been carried away upon exceedingly high mountains. And mine eyes have beheld great things, yea, even too great for man. . . . O then . . . why should my heart weep and my soul linger in the valley of sorrow. . . . Why am I angry because of mine enemy? Awake, my soul! . . . Rejoice, O my heart. . . . May the gates of hell be shut continually before me, because that my heart is broken and my spirit is contrite! . . . O Lord, I have trusted in thee, and I will trust in thee forever. . . . Yea, I know that God will give liberally to him that asketh. . . . Behold, my voice shall forever ascend up unto thee, my rock and mine everlasting God. (2 Nephi 4:16–35.)

The Prophet Joseph Smith was the first to utter these words in modern times. How congenial are these two prophets! How

Joseph's heart must have resonated to the words of Nephi! For the prayer of Nephi is the prayer of every righteous soul who, conscious of the frailties of the flesh, looks to God in faith and gratitude for the strength to overcome.

Conclusion

The closing testimony of Nephi rings with the fervor of a pure heart:

> I glory in plainness; I glory in truth; I glory in my Jesus, for he hath redeemed my soul from hell. . . . I have charity for the Jew. . . . I also have charity for the Gentiles. But behold, for none of these can I hope except they shall be reconciled unto Christ, and enter into the narrow gate, and walk in the strait path which leads to life, and continue in the path until the end of the day of probation. (2 Nephi 33:6–9.)

There is not a soul anywhere who does not, or will not, know that Nephi spoke the solemn truth. For he has sealed that truth upon us (2 Nephi 33:15). Each of us will respond to it in our own way. And how we respond will make all the difference.

A thoughtful observer of our times asked:

> Who are our heroes, and how can they make us happier? Heroes are a fading memory in our times, but we can still recall a little about them. We know, at least, that what sets the hero apart is some extraordinary achievement. Whatever this feat, it is such as to be recognized at once by everyone as a good thing; and somehow, the achieving of it seems larger than life. The hero, furthermore, overcomes the ordinary and attains greatness by serving some great good. His example very nearly rebukes us; telling us that we fail, not by aiming too high in life, but by aiming far too low. Moreover, it tells us we are mistaken in supposing that happiness is a right or an end in itself. The hero seeks not happiness but goodness and his fulfillment lies in achieving it.[13]

He has described Nephi. How grateful we should be for the heroes God has given us! How grateful we should be for such men as Nephi! How worthy they are of emulation! May we, and especially our youth, aspire to their immortal company.

Nephi and You

If you ask me to speak of courage,
I'll tell you of Nephi's fame.

If you ask me to speak of honor,
My answer is Nephi's name.

If you bid me read of a boundless faith
Born of virtue and truth from on high,
I'll turn from the worldly journals of men
To the writings of ancient Nephi.

There are his words as he wrote them;
There in those sacred pages
Is the story of one man's greatness
Writ in the dust of the ages.

Up from the dust of the ages,
A challenge hurled by the past,
A gauntlet flung by the prophet of God
To those who were summoned the last.

What will you do, will you drop it?
Let it slip from your hand to the earth?
Shrink from the call like a craven,
Pretending the prize has no worth?

What then's the meaning of birthright,
What then, the gospel plan,
If you'll turn from the duty before you,
Forsaking what others began?

Will you answer the challenge of Nephi?
Will you catch the gauntlet he's thrown?
Will you meet the world with its taunting doubts
With a shining faith of your own?

Then follow the pathway he followed,
Make his life a guide for your soul,
Set your hands to the present work to be done,
Put your heart on its heavenly goal.

And someday when others are speaking
Of those who were valiant and true,
Someone will tell them of Nephi,
And someone will tell them of you.

(Rodney Turner)

NOTES AND REFERENCES

1. Conference Report, October 1983, p. 107.

2. At least two of their forebears, missing from the Old Testament, were Zenock and Zenos (3 Nephi 10:16). They are quoted in 1 Nephi 19:10–17 concerning the death and resurrection of Christ, and the scattering and eventual redemption of the Jews. The complex allegory of Zenos (Jacob 5) treats the overall history of Israel vis-á-vis the Gentiles. Neum (1 Nephi 19:10) and Ezias (Helaman 8:20) may also have been ancestors of Lehi.

3. Although Lehi seems to have had a home in or near Jerusalem, his wealth was located elsewhere in a place his sons called "the land of our inheritance" (1 Nephi 3:22).

4. The fact remains that Jacob 4:5 and D&C 132:36 support the Genesis 22 account.

5. *Teachings of the Prophet Joseph Smith*, comp. Joseph Fielding Smith (Salt Lake City: Deseret Book Co., 1976), p. 391; hereafter *TPJS*.

6. Ibid., p. 320.

7. Ibid., p. 256.

8. Nephi briefly summarized his father's Jerusalem experiences in 1 Nephi 1 and 2, having abridged Lehi's own record on the large plates (1 Nephi 1:17; 6:1). The first book on the large plates was called the Book of Lehi. It covered the period from about 585 to 150 B.C. and constitutes the 116 pages of manuscript lost by Martin Harris in 1828.

9. The revelation or apocalypse of John is primarily concerned with those events which will transpire in the time of the seventh seal and beyond. See D&C 77:6–7.

10. Unlike the Doctrine and Covenants, the Book of Mormon does not distinguish between the three heavens or degrees of glory comprising the eternal kingdom of God. As used by the angel, the term "church of the Lamb of God" is relative. It necessarily includes, but is not limited to, The Church of Jesus Christ of Latter-day Saints.

11. Referring to this tendency on the part of some members of the Church, President Harold B. Lee said: "There are many who profess to be religious and speak of themselves as Christians, and, according to one such, 'as accepting the scriptures only as sources of inspiration and moral truth,' and then ask in their smugness: 'Do the revelations of God give us a handrail to the kingdom of God, as the Lord's messenger told Lehi, or merely a compass?' Unfortunately, some are among us who claim to be Church members but are somewhat like the scoffers in Lehi's vision—standing aloof and seemingly inclined to hold in derision the faithful who choose to accept Church authorities as God's special

witnesses of the gospel and his agents in directing the affairs of the Church"
(Conference Report, April 1971, p. 91).

12. See *TPJS*, p. 241.

13. George Roche, "A World Without Heroes," *Imprimis* (Hillsdale,
Mich.: Hillsdale College, August, 1986).

7

THE BOOK OF MORMON PLATES

Rex C. Reeve, Jr.

On 22 September 1823, after receiving repeated instruction from the angel Moroni, Joseph Smith went to a large hill convenient to his father's home.

> On the west side of this hill, not far from the top, under a stone of considerable size, lay the plates, deposited in a stone box. . . .
>
> Having removed the earth, I obtained a lever, which I got fixed under the edge of the stone, and with a little exertion raised it up. I looked in, and there indeed did I behold the plates, the Urim and Thummim, and the breastplate, as stated by the messenger. (Joseph Smith—History 1:51–52.)

Four years later Joseph Smith was allowed to take these plates into his possession with a strict charge to preserve them until the messenger should call for them. He translated the plates by the gift and power of God, and then published his translation as the Book of Mormon in March of 1830. After accomplishing

Rex C. Reeve, Jr., is Assistant Professor of Ancient Scripture at Brigham Young University.

that which was required of him, Joseph said, "according to arrangements, the messenger called for [the plates], I delivered them up to him; and he has them in his charge until this day" (Joseph Smith—History 1:60).

By opening that stone box Joseph Smith opened to the world a flood of knowledge that will eventually fill the whole earth. That sacred event brought into reality the plan of the Lord which had been in preparation for many years. Before young Joseph completed his work, the world would have the Book of Mormon, Another Testament of Jesus Christ, which stands unequaled in bringing men, worldwide, to Christ, and also the Doctrine and Covenants, the Pearl of Great Price, and the Joseph Smith Translation of the Bible.

In 1827 when Joseph Smith received the gold plates, he found that much of the record was an abridgment of many other records written by ancient kings and prophets living in the Americas. The plates he held referred to several other sets of plates and records, an understanding of which is necessary to understand the Book of Mormon. The purpose of this paper is to analyze the plates of Mormon translated by Joseph Smith and show how the other Nephite records were used to produce the Book of Mormon.

The Plates of Mormon

The plates that Joseph Smith received had been personally made by the hand of Mormon, and were called the plates of Mormon. He said, "And behold, I do make the record on plates which I have made with mine own hands" (3 Nephi 5:11). When Joseph Smith received the plates of Mormon, they contained (1) an abridgment of the large plates of Nephi (of Lehi's family history); (2) an unabridged set of small plates made by Nephi and his successors; (3) an abridgment of the record of the Jaredites made by Moroni; and (4) the writings of Moroni. There was also a sealed portion that was not translated by Joseph Smith.

The Role of Mormon

About the year A.D. 320, the prophet Ammaron, "being constrained by the Holy Ghost, did hide up the records which were sacred . . . which had been handed down from generation to generation" (4 Nephi 1:48). Mormon said,

And about the time that Ammaron hid up the records unto the Lord, he came unto me, (I being about ten years of age, and I began to be learned somewhat after the manner of the learning of my people) and Ammaron said unto me: I perceive that thou art a sober child, and art quick to observe;

Therefore, when ye are about twenty and four years old I would that ye should remember the things that ye have observed concerning this people; and when ye are of that age go to the land Antum, unto a hill which shall be called Shim; and there have I deposited unto the Lord all the sacred engravings concerning this people.

And behold, ye shall take the plates of Nephi unto yourself, and the remainder shall ye leave in the place where they are; and ye shall engrave on the plates of Nephi all the things that ye have observed concerning this people. (Mormon 1:2–4.)

As a young man, Mormon remembered and followed the instructions of the prophet Ammaron and recorded a complete and detailed record of his people upon the large plates of Nephi. "And behold I had gone according to the word of Ammaron, and taken the plates of Nephi, and did make a record according to the words of Ammaron. And upon the plates of Nephi I did make a full account of all the wickedness and abominations." (Mormon 2:17–18.)

In addition to engraving his own personal record upon the large plates of Nephi, Mormon, years later, near the end of his life, was instructed to make a smaller record of his people, an abridgment of the larger records. He said,

And it hath become expedient that I, according to the will of God, that the prayers of those who have gone hence, who were the holy ones, should be fulfilled according to their faith, should make a record of these things which have been done—

Yea, a small record of that which hath taken place from the time that Lehi left Jerusalem, even down until the present time.

Therefore I do make my record from the accounts which have been given by those who were before me, until the commencement of my day. (3 Nephi 5:14–16.)

. . . therefore I write a small abridgment, daring not to give a full account of the things which I have seen (Mormon 5:9).

He also included in his record the unabridged small plates of Nephi. His son Moroni completed the record and hid up the plates. These then are what are known as the plates of Mormon and are the ones from which Joseph translated the Book of Mormon.

What Do We Know About the Plates of Mormon?

1. The plates were about 6 x 8 x 6 inches and were skillfully made by the hand of Mormon.[1]

2. They had the appearance of gold leaves and were not quite as thick as common tin.

3. They were engraved in reformed Egyptian (Mormon 9:32).

4. They contained an abridgment from the large plates of Nephi including an abridgment by Mormon of his own more complete record (3 Nephi 5:10) which he had written on those large plates (Mormon 2:18).

5. They contained even less than a one-hundredth part of the history of the seed of Lehi (Jacob 3:13; Words of Mormon 1:5; Helaman 3:14; 3 Nephi 5:8; 26:6; Ether 15:33).

6. They included the small plates of Nephi unabridged (Words of Mormon 1:1−8).

7. A portion was sealed and was not translated by Joseph Smith (Ether 5:1).

8. These are the plates from which Joseph Smith translated the Book of Mormon by the gift and power of God.

9. The plates were returned to Moroni (Joseph Smith—History 1:60).

In translating the plates of Mormon, Joseph Smith learned that many other records and plates were kept and preserved by the family of Lehi. The history and doctrine from these other records weave in and out of the text of the plates of Mormon and combine together into a harmonious testament of Jesus Christ. Elder Boyd K. Packer said, "As the influence of that message is traced from generation to generation, more than twenty writers record the fate of individuals and of civilizations who accepted or rejected that testament."[2]

The Brass Plates

The first set of other plates Mormon refers to is the plates of brass, which Nephi and his brothers returned to Jerusalem to obtain. Nephi said:

> And behold, it is wisdom in God that we should obtain these records, that we may preserve unto our children the language of our fathers;
> And also that we may preserve unto them the words which have been spoken by the mouth of all the holy prophets, which have been delivered unto them by the Spirit and power of God, since the world began, even down unto this present time. (1 Nephi 3:19–20.)

The brass plates contained:

> The five books of Moses, which gave an account of the creation of the world, and also of Adam and Eve, who were our first parents (1 Nephi 5:11);
> And also a record of the Jews from the beginning, even down to the commencement of the reign of Zedekiah, king of Judah (1 Nephi 5:12);
> And . . . the words . . . of all the holy prophets, which have been delivered unto them by the Spirit and power of God (1 Nephi 3:20; see also 1 Nephi 5:13);
> And . . . a genealogy of [Lehi's] fathers (1 Nephi 5:14).

The brass plates were comparable to, but more complete than, our current Old Testament down to about 600 B.C. (1 Nephi 13:23). They proved to be of supreme importance to the family of Lehi by preserving their language and spiritual heritage. About 130 B.C. King Benjamin explained to his sons that "were it not for these [brass] plates, which contain these records and these commandments, we must have suffered in ignorance, even at this present time, not knowing the mysteries of God" (Mosiah 1:3).

Alma later explained to his son Helaman that the brass plates "have enlarged the memory of this people, yea, and convinced many of the error of their ways, and brought them to the knowledge of their God unto the salvation of their souls" (Alma 37:8).

Mormon did not abridge the brass plates or include them with his record. He did, however, include quotes from them which support and elucidate many Bible events and doctrines. In addition, the plates of brass may have set the pattern for the Nephite practice of preserving their writings on metal and may have established the language which would be used in other records.

The Large Plates of Nephi

Even though they were armed with the scriptures recorded on the plates of brass, as his family journeyed toward the promised land, Lehi began keeping a record which would eventually become the foundation record for a major part of the Book of Mormon. "He kept something of a secular account of their journeys, interspersed with his revelations and teachings and spiritual experiences. Nephi succeeded his father, Lehi, as keeper of the record, which became known as the large plates of Nephi."[3]

It is not clear from the Book of Mormon just when Lehi began keeping his written record. Nephi seems to have started his large plates about 590 B.C., soon after arriving in the promised land. When Nephi started writing, he included the record of his father. Perhaps Lehi began his record soon after he was commanded to leave Jerusalem, but this cannot be affirmed. In the small plates written about twenty years later, Nephi said that he abridged the record of his father (1 Nephi 1:17), but there is no statement concerning when Lehi began his account.

In explaining the record of the large plates, Nephi wrote:

> And it came to pass that the Lord commanded me, wherefore I did make plates of ore that I might engraven upon them the record of my people. And upon the plates which I made I did engraven the record of my father, and also our journeyings in the wilderness, and the prophecies of my father; and also many of mine own prophecies have I engraven upon them.
>
> Wherefore, I, Nephi, did make a record upon the other plates [the large plates of Nephi], which gives an account, or which gives a greater account of the wars and contentions and destructions of my people. And this have I done, and commanded my people what they should do after I was gone; and that these plates should be handed down from one generation to another. (1 Nephi 19:1, 4.)

Shortly after Nephi began his small plates, he wrote, "Upon the other plates [the large plates of Nephi] should be engraven an account of the reign of the kings, and the wars and contentions of my people" (1 Nephi 9:4).

The large plates became the official historical record of the people of Nephi. Pursuant to Nephi's instructions, these plates were enlarged and handed down from generation to generation, thus becoming a large and detailed record. For over four hundred years, down to the reign of King Benjamin, the large plates were mostly historical and kept by the kings (Words of Mormon 1:10) or by those appointed by the kings to record their history.

Jarom said,

> And I, Jarom, do not write more, for the plates are small. But behold, my brethren, ye can go to the other plates of Nephi [large plates]; for behold, upon them the records of our wars are engraven, according to the writings of the kings, or those which they caused to be written. (Jarom 1:14.)

The large plates were kept by the kings down to the reign of King Benjamin, about 130 B.C. Following this time period, the plates were apparently the responsibility of the prophets (Alma 37:1; 45:2; 50:38; 63:1).

The Small Plates of Nephi

In order to understand clearly the significance of the changes that occur at the time of King Benjamin, we must return to the days of Nephi. About thirty years after leaving Jerusalem and about twenty years after having begun his large record, Nephi was commanded of the Lord to make a second record for a "wise purpose" (1 Nephi 9:5). Nephi clearly recorded his intent in writing yet another record.

> And thirty years had passed away from the time we left Jerusalem. And I, Nephi, had kept the records upon my plates, which I had made, of my people thus far [large plates].
> And it came to pass that the Lord God said unto me: Make other plates [small plates]; and thou shalt engraven many things upon them which are good in my sight, for the profit of thy people.
> Wherefore, I, Nephi, to be obedient to the commandments of the Lord, went and made these plates [small plates] upon which I have engraven these things.
> And I engraved that which is pleasing unto God. And if my people are pleased with the things of God they will be pleased with mine engravings which are upon these plates [small plates].
> And if my people desire to know the more particular part of

the history of my people they must search mine other [large] plates. (2 Nephi 5:28–33.)

And upon these [small plates] I write the things of my soul, and many of the scriptures which are engraven upon the plates of brass. For my soul delighteth in the scriptures, and my heart pondereth them, and writeth them for the learning and profit of my children. (2 Nephi 4:15.)

Jacob, Nephi's younger brother, further explained the purpose of the small plates:

And he gave me, Jacob, a commandment that I should write upon these [small] plates a few of the things which I considered to be most precious; that I should not touch, save it were lightly, concerning the history of this people. . . .

For he said that the history of his people should be engraven upon his other [large] plates, and that I should preserve these [small] plates and hand them down unto my seed, from generation to generation.

And if there were preaching which was sacred, or revelation which was great, or prophesying, that I should engraven . . . them upon these [small] plates, and touch upon them as much as it were possible, for Christ's sake, and for the sake of our people. (Jacob 1:2–4.)

Nephi said:

It mattereth not to me that I am particular to give a full account of all the things of my father . . . for I desire the room that I may write of the things of God.

For the fulness of mine intent is that I may persuade men to come unto the God of Abraham, and the God of Isaac, and the God of Jacob, and be saved.

Wherefore, I shall give commandment unto my seed, that they shall not occupy these [small] plates with things which are not of worth unto the children of men. (1 Nephi 6:3–4, 6.)

This I do that the more sacred things may be kept for the knowledge of my people. . . . I do not write anything upon plates save it be that I think it be sacred. (1 Nephi 19:5–6.)

I have received a commandment of the Lord that I should make these [small] plates, for the special purpose that there should be an account engraven of the ministry of my people (1 Nephi 9:3).

It appears the large plates of Nephi were kept and expanded by the kings, but the small plates of Nephi were kept by the prophets, and were not expanded. The last writer on the small plates, Amaleki, merely comes to the end of the last plate with the abrupt announcement that "these plates are full. And I make an end of my speaking." (Omni 1:30.)

Nephi provided a dual set of records, one basically historical and the other predominantly spiritual, kept by kings or by prophets down to the reign of King Benjamin.

The first important change that took place at the time of King Benjamin was that the small plates of Nephi became full, and this separate spiritual record was given to King Benjamin for safekeeping (Omni 1:25). Thereafter the small plates remained, unaltered, among the large plates of Nephi.

A second important change during the time of King Benjamin was that the large plates of Nephi were now used to record both secular and spiritual events. There was no longer a separate spiritual record being kept; therefore preachings, visions, and prophecies, etc., were included in the large plates.

A third important change affecting the record was that beginning with King Benjamin all of the records, including the large plates of Nephi, were kept by righteous men, most of whom were prophets as well as political or military leaders.

The combining of secular and spiritual records in the hands of the prophets produced a more balanced account. It was from this portion of the record that Mormon was able to abridge a major part of the Book of Mormon and include a powerful mixture of historical and spiritual writings.

When Mormon finally received the records the prophet Ammaron had hidden up, he added to the large plates of Nephi an account of his people and the events that occurred during his lifetime (Mormon 2:18). He later abridged this complete record for the final latter-day account (Mormon 5:9). In a final effort to preserve the records and the sacred treasures of his people, Mormon hid them all up in the hill Cumorah and gave only a few of the plates to his son Moroni.

> I, Mormon, began to be old; and knowing it to be the last struggle of my people, and having been commanded of the Lord that I should not suffer the records which had been handed down by our fathers, which were sacred, to fall into the hands of the Lamanites, (for the Lamanites would destroy them) therefore I made this record out of the plates of Nephi, and hid up in the hill Cumorah all the records which had been entrusted to me by the hand of the Lord, save it were these few plates which I gave unto my son Moroni (Mormon 6:6).

Near the end of his life, Mormon wrote a letter to his son Moroni. "I trust that I may see thee soon; for I have sacred records that I would deliver up unto thee" (Moroni 9:24). Mormon's desire was granted. He was able to preserve all the sacred records of his people and give "these few plates" unto Moroni (Mormon 6:6).

From the record and from his original response, it seems that the plates of Mormon which Moroni received were small and almost full. Moroni, writing soon after the final destruction of his people in A.D. 385, said,

> Behold I, Moroni, do finish the record of my father, Mormon. Behold, I have but few things to write, which things I have been commanded by my father.
> And my father also was killed by them, and I even remain alone to write the sad tale of the destruction of my people. But behold, they are gone, and I fulfil the commandment of my father. And whether they will slay me, I know not.
> Behold, my father hath made this record, and he hath written the intent thereof. And behold, I would write it also if I had room upon the plates, but I have not; and ore I have none, for I am alone. My father hath been slain in battle, and all my kinsfolk, and I have not friends nor whither to go; and how long the Lord will suffer that I may live I know not. (Mormon 8:1, 3, 5.)

About fifteen years later, in A.D. 400, Moroni returned to the record and added eight verses and closed by saying,

> And whoso receiveth this record, and shall not condemn it because of the imperfections which are in it, the same shall know of greater things than these. Behold, I am Moroni; and were it possible, I would make all things known unto you.
> Behold, I make an end of speaking concerning this people. I am the son of Mormon, and my father was a descendant of Nephi. (Mormon 8:12–13.)

Even after fifteen years, it seems that Moroni was still without additional plates as his comments are brief as he bids farewell.

The third time Moroni came back to the records something had changed. He did not give the new date, but room on the plates no longer seemed to be a problem. Moroni finished the record of his father (Mormon 8 and 9), abridged the twenty-four gold plates of Ether, wrote his own book, wrote part of the title page, and added a large amount which was sealed and not translated by Joseph Smith.

The Twenty-Four Gold Plates

When space was no longer a problem, Moroni abridged the record of the Jaredites, which he took from the twenty-four gold plates found by the people of Limhi in the days of King Mosiah. He started his abridgment by saying,

> And now I, Moroni, proceed to give an account of those ancient inhabitants who were destroyed by the hand of the Lord upon the face of this north country.
>
> And I take mine account from the twenty and four plates which were found by the people of Limhi, which is called the Book of Ether. (Ether 1:1–2.)

The Jaredites were a separate people from the family of Lehi. They came to this land many hundreds of years before Lehi, at the time the languages were confounded at the Tower of Babel. Their records were translated with the help of "interpreters" prepared by the Lord for that very purpose.

Ether was the last prophet of the Jaredites. He was rejected, and hid himself in caves, and recorded the complete destruction of his people (Ether 13:13–14).

The Sealed Portion of the Plates of Mormon

Moroni wrote in great detail the visions and teachings of the brother of Jared. He said,

> Behold, I have written upon these plates [plates of Mormon] the very things which the brother of Jared saw; and there never were greater things made manifest than those which were made manifest unto the brother of Jared.
>
> Wherefore the Lord hath commanded me to write them; and I have written them. And he commanded me that I should seal them up. (Ether 4:4–5; see 2 Nephi 27:7.)

Moroni sealed up this portion of his record with instructions to the future translator, "And I have told you the things which I have sealed up; therefore touch them not in order that ye may translate; for that thing is forbidden you, except by and by it shall be wisdom in God" (Ether 5:1).

We do not know exactly how large a portion of the plates of Mormon is sealed. Estimates range from one-third to two-thirds. Joseph Smith simply recorded: "a part of which was sealed."[4] Whatever the portion, Moroni's sealed writings were extensive and very important and will yet be brought forth.

Elder Bruce R. McConkie, commenting on the contents of the sealed plates, said,

> When, during the Millennium, the sealed portion of the Book of Mormon is translated, it will give an account of life in the premortal existence; of the creation of all things; of the Fall and the Atonement and the Second Coming; of temple ordinances, in their fulness; of the ministry and mission of translated beings; of life in the spirit world, in both paradise and hell; of the kingdoms of glory to be inhabited by resurrected beings; and many such like things.
>
> As of now, the world is not ready to receive these truths.[5]

In A.D. 421, Moroni finished his record and buried the plates of Mormon, along with other sacred treasures, where they remained until he personally delivered them to Joseph Smith in 1827.

The Records of the Book of Mormon

Through more than nine hundred years, the records and sacred things of the family of Lehi had become very extensive. For generations, the Lord had been preparing the background materials from which he would draw together the most powerful testament of Jesus Christ ever written. The records of prophets, peoples, blessings, destructions, visions, covenants, and promises were now in place. By revelation, the prophet Ammaron hid these valuable records up and charged a ten-year-old boy to remember them and add to them when he became twenty-four years old. Mormon faithfully protected the sacred records and diligently recorded his observations concerning his people.

After a lifetime of obedience and service, Mormon in his old age was prepared, and the time was right for him to compile what would become known as the Book of Mormon, Another Testament of Jesus Christ. The command was given, and Mormon began a labor of love that would bless future generations.

With the publication of the Book of Mormon in March 1830, Joseph Smith made available to the world that portion of the record selected by the Lord to stand as another testament of Jesus Christ. The book contains the promise and the warning that this small record is a test. For those who receive the Book of Mormon and believe it, "then shall the greater things be made manifest unto them." For those who reject it, "then shall the greater things be withheld from them, unto their condemnation." (3 Nephi 26:9–10.)

NOTES AND REFERENCES

1. See the Wentworth letter, *HC* 4:537, for verification of items 1 and 2.

2. Conference Report, April 1986, p. 74.

3. Boyd K. Packer, *Ensign*, May 1986, p. 59.

4. *HC* 4:537.

5. Bruce R. McConkie, "The Bible, a Sealed Book," address given at CES Symposium, August 1984, p. 1.

8

"BEHOLD, I HAVE DREAMED A DREAM"

Susan Easton Black

Lehi was a prophet of God and a patriarch to his family. We join this prophetic patriarch in the valley of Lemuel, to learn from and to live by his words of counsel.

Preceding our entrance into his realm, Lehi heard the Lord's command "that [Lehi's] sons should take daughters to wife, that they might raise up seed unto the Lord" (1 Nephi 7:1). And immediately following, the family "gathered together all manner of seeds of every kind, both of grain . . . and . . . of fruit" (1 Nephi 8:1). The two parallel themes involve seeds: one the seed of posterity and the other the plant seeds of life substances needed to preserve Lehi's family.

It appears that these two related themes may have preoccupied Lehi immediately preceding the tree of life dream (1 Nephi 8:1–4). He anguished over the bitter contention among his sons (1 Nephi 7:16). Two sons desired righteousness and two murmured against truth (1 Nephi 2:16–17 and 1 Nephi 2:11–12).

Susan Easton Black is Associate Professor of Church History and Doctrine at Brigham Young University.

What hopes did Lehi have for a continuation of his seed as his sons united with the daughters of Ishmael? Perhaps hopes and fears for his own seed were heightened by the concurrent gathering of the plant seeds needed to sustain life. Would these grain and fruit seeds survive the tempest to save and to sustain generations of his family? Would his own posterity survive the storms of jealousy (1 Nephi 3:6), doubt (1 Nephi 2:12−13), envy (1 Nephi 2:22), and hate (1 Nephi 2:24) to save and to bless their brethren? (1 Nephi 7:6).

Perhaps as this loving father pondered the outcome of his seed, the Lord revealed the eternal plan of salvation in a family epic dream. In this familial vision Lehi learned of the critical choices available to his family. These choices, when made by his descendants, would ultimately determine their eternal destinies.

Announcement: I Have Dreamed a Dream

"Behold, I have dreamed a dream; or, in other words, I have seen a vision," announced Lehi (1 Nephi 8:2).[1] What were the hopes and fears of his family as they heard this prophetic announcement?

Previous visionary dreams given to Lehi had resulted in loss of fortune (1 Nephi 2:4), home (1 Nephi 2:2), and comfort (1 Nephi 2:6). One dream caused the family to tent in the wilderness rather than continue in the comfort of the prophetically doomed Jerusalem (1 Nephi 2:15). Another dream had caused the boys in the family to risk their lives and even to take a life in order to obtain family genealogy and scripture (1 Nephi 3, 4).

Lehi's dreams and the family's reaction to those dreams dominate the first chapters of the Book of Mormon. It is obvious that these dreams were not greeted with unified acceptance. Nephi's mother, Sariah, "complained against my father, telling him that he was a visionary man" (1 Nephi 5:2). To which Lehi exclaimed, "I know that I am a visionary man" (1 Nephi 5:4). Lehi knew that he was receiving divine messages from the Lord in dreams. The verbal description of these dreams, while vivid visual experiences to Lehi, were not quickly visualized or appreciated by most of his family. As Sariah complained (1 Nephi 5:2), Nephi pondered (1 Nephi 11:1), and Laman and Lemuel disputed (1 Nephi 15:2).

What of this new dream? Was this dream to signal wealth or poverty? Would it lead the family to safety or annihilation?

Would it result in peaceful coexistence or warlike confrontation? Would it result in feelings of humiliation and subjugation for the rebellious Laman and Lemuel? Would new challenges or opportunities be revealed for the righteous Nephi and Sam? What dangers would this additional dream herald for Sariah and her divided family?

Lehi Told the Outcome of the Dream

Prior to relating the dream to his family, Lehi told the expected outcome of the dream to them. Lehi began with what to his patriarchal role was the bottom line, "I have reason to rejoice in the Lord because of Nephi and also of Sam" (1 Nephi 8:3). And why does he rejoice? Because "they, and also many of their seed, will be saved" (1 Nephi 8:3). This to a patriarch father is an assured hope that he will have an enduring, eternal posterity through Nephi and Sam.[2] If Nephi, Sam, and their posterity continued to choose the path they chose in the vision, they would merit eternal lives.

For Lehi the dream also evoked a contrasting reaction of exceeding fear. What was the source of this great fear? Lehi was not seized with fear for his own life but for the lives of his two wandering sons "lest they should be cast off from the presence of the Lord" (1 Nephi 8:36).[3] Lehi despairs as he receives prophetic glimpses that two of his sons will not merit eternal life.

Could words of counsel make a difference for Laman and Lemuel? Lehi seems to think so. Darkened, forbidden paths had already attracted them from righteous pursuits. Perhaps a warning repetition of the dream would make the difference needed by these sons.

Earlier Lehi had tangibly gathered the seeds that would preserve their physical life. He now seeks to gather in spiritually his far less tractable seed—his wayward sons.

Lehi Relates the Dream to His Family

Lehi explained why he had cause to rejoice and yet to fear. He recalled his dream in a detailed, coherent, orderly manner.[4] The dream for Lehi unfolded line upon line and step by step. Let us learn from this symbolic dream why Lehi had mixed emotional reactions.

Dark and Dreary Wilderness

Lehi saw himself and perhaps all mankind beginning in the "dark and dreary wilderness" (1 Nephi 8:4). Indeed, we are in a darkened world, a world filled with doubts, uncertainties, and error. The veil of forgetfulness has closed so that God's continuing presence is no longer with us. Lehi knew that for his own salvation he must find his way back to the light and life of Christ, and escape the loneliness of the dark. Like Lehi, we also need to discover this unalterable truth.

Man Dressed in White

A man dressed in contrasting white "came and stood before [Lehi]" (1 Nephi 8:5). It is not known all that he spoke to Lehi but we do know he "bade [Lehi to] follow him" (1 Nephi 8:6). There was no hesitation or equivocation on Lehi's part, for he had eyes that saw, ears that heard, and feet that were quick to follow the Lord. This man, whether a messenger from the throne of God, the Holy Ghost, or Jesus the Christ,[5] led father Lehi through the dark and dreary waste. His words were a symbolic representation of Christ's words, to "follow me" (Matthew 4:19 and 2 Nephi 31:10). These words chart a course of hope for all mankind amidst darkened surroundings.

Lehi Prays

Though Lehi followed his guide obediently, with childlike faith and love, he began to yearn for greater light. He began to pray for mercy. "I began to pray unto the Lord that he would have mercy on me, according to the multitude of his tender mercies" (1 Nephi 8:8).[6] He was now ready to move from a simple, obedient faith to the more challenging choices that would determine his eternal worth.

The choices leading to exaltation demand more than the clear choice Lehi had previously experienced between the brilliant white robe of the loving guide and the dreary darkness everywhere else (1 Nephi 8:5, 7). These more demanding choices are between the true light of Christ and the pseudo, tinseled "lights" of Lucifer.

Large and Spacious Field

Lehi now views the "large and spacious field" (1 Nephi 8:9). A relief from the darkness; yet, was it really? A later and closer look at this field would eventually reveal its deceptive, luciferous perils. However, at this point in his dream Lehi's "mind [was so] swallowed up in other things" that Lucifer's seductive lights, snares, and traps went unnoticed (1 Nephi 15:27).

His gaze, his being, was immediately riveted upon a tree, the tree of life.[7] This tree yields fruit to cure every ill, to extend love to all, and to signal the ultimate destination of the eternal pathway to godhood (1 Nephi 8:11).[8] The continual partaking of its life-giving properties means eternal life to Lehi, a life full of the enjoyment of the love of God.

Here we hearken back to the gathering concept. The family had been gathering seeds so they could continue on their appointed journey. Lehi sees the culmination of the seed: the tree, the fruit. As he observes this tree, he finds that its "fruit was desirable to make one happy" (1 Nephi 8:10). This is a different seed and a different kind of fruit than that which the family had been laboring to obtain. Lehi went "forth and [partook] of the fruit." By partaking he discovered a fruit that "was most sweet, above all that [he had] ever before tasted," "white, to exceed all the whiteness that [he] had ever seen." (1 Nephi 8:11.) His soul was open to the sweetness of the illuminating light of glorified truth. His joy was indescribable. He had found the purpose for traversing the dark, avoiding false beacons, in his taste of the pearl of great price.

This pearl is the love of God. "For God so loved the world, that he gave his only begotten Son, that whosoever believeth in him should not perish, but have everlasting life" (John 3:16).

Filled with the love of God, this noble patriarch "began to be desirous that [his] family should partake of it also" (1 Nephi 8:12),[9] that each family member should follow the path he had first taken in childlike obedience, that each one might desire through personal revelation to ignore the enticing carnality and embrace the pearl—God's love.

Lehi cast his eyes about in hopes that he might discover his family (1 Nephi 8:13). So filled with the love of God was Lehi that even though he now saw (apparently for the first time) the perilous waters that endangered all who strayed from the strait way he did not note their filth (1 Nephi 15:27). His only thought appears to have been to find his precious family and have them partake of the life-giving tree. Where were they?

River of Water

Sariah, his most beloved companion and mother of his family, was the first one he saw. She had only the last, but surely the darkest and most dangerous, steps ahead to reach the tree. To Lehi's eyes, opened by God's mercy, the difference between life and death was clear and unmistakable. But Sariah, joined by Sam and Nephi, hesitated (1 Nephi 8:14).[10] His wife and his children must obey their patriarch's lead to avoid the snares of Lucifer in the river of water.[11] Would she be tempted to ignore his call and rely on her own wisdom? She and her obedient children "stood as if they knew not whither they should go" (1 Nephi 8:14).[12]

Lehi did not hesitate, for he had tasted of the fruit. He knew the course towards great joy. He could not and would not force them. They were already close, but still in great danger from the river of filthy water (1 Nephi 12:16). He beckoned them with a loud voice, calling them to come unto him and partake of the fruit (1 Nephi 8:15). The result of his sure voice was that Sariah, Sam, and Nephi came to him and partook of the most desirable fruit (1 Nephi 8:16).[13]

Empty places remained in his family circle. Where were Laman and Lemuel? Each one in the family was loved. Each empty place left multitudes of posterity outside the gathering at the tree. They had murmured (1 Nephi 2:11). They had not understood (1 Nephi 2:12). They had rebelled (1 Nephi 2:21). Yet they had arrived at the "head of the river" (1 Nephi 8:17). Now they must choose between the tree of life and Lucifer's brilliant but deceptive perils in the spacious field.

Lehi states of Laman and Lemuel, "I saw them, but they would not come unto me and partake of the fruit" (1 Nephi 8:18). No wonder father Lehi had such a mixed reaction to his dream. "I have reason to rejoice in the Lord because of Nephi and also of Sam" (1 Nephi 8:3), but "I fear exceedingly because of [Laman and Lemuel]" (1 Nephi 8:4).

Rod of Iron

From his vantage point at the tree, it appears that Lehi looked for aids to guide his wayward sons to the tree. The first aid he saw was the word of God symbolically represented as a rod of iron.[14] It was not out in the field but it "extended along the bank of the river, and led to the tree" (1 Nephi 8:19). It followed each turn, guided over each stumbling rock, and beckoned around each precipice of the deadly river. It led with secured, enduring strength through the spacious field to the tree.

Strait and Narrow Path

The strait and narrow path can only be the gospel way to eternal life.[15] Yet it appears that it leads not only to the tree of life but also perilously by the nearby "head of the fountain, unto a large and spacious field" (1 Nephi 8:20). This constricted, hazardous, narrow path is located by the rod of iron along the precipice at the edge of the river where a misstep would plunge a traveler into the river of death.

As Lehi viewed the path, his scene shifted to a future people. He saw numerous concourses of people, many of whom may have been his posterity. They struggled to find and follow the narrow path. Some found the path but seemed to have only a tenuous hold, if any, on the iron rod. Because the path extended to differing places, the traveler on the path needed to cling to the rod in order to reach the tree (1 Nephi 8:21–23).

Mist of Darkness

In the midst of dark perils, if the travelers were walking without constant guidance on the path they missed the pearl of great price. A few turns in the strait and narrow path without the sure guidance of the iron rod and they were lost. "There arose a mist of darkness; yea, even an exceedingly great mist of darkness, insomuch that they who had commenced in the path did lose their way, that they wandered off and were lost" (1 Nephi 8:23).

The mist of darkness is the temptations of Satan.[16] These temptations include sin, vice, prideful exaltation of the human mind, and harmful pleasures. These satanic devices blur the perspective ability of the traveler. They dull his sense of human dignity, erode integrity, and obscure the vision of the rod.

In greatest sorrow Lehi saw multitudes of the people, who initially desired the greatest blessings demonstrated by their struggle to find the narrow path, lose their way, their eternal potential, because they did not hold onto the iron rod (1 Nephi 8:23).

In contrast, Lehi saw many others that found the narrow path, "caught hold of the end of the rod of iron; and they did press forward through the mist of darkness, clinging to the rod of iron, even until they did come forth and partake of the fruit of the tree" (1 Nephi 8:24). Yet, after partaking of the glorious fruit they "cast their eyes about as if they were ashamed" (1 Nephi 8:25).[17]

Lehi must have wondered what caused these travelers to be ashamed of the eternal tree of life. What enticement from the spacious field could have dominion over once godly persons to cause them to choose a carnal attitude and be ashamed of past godly attributes?

Great and Spacious Building

"A great and spacious building; and it stood as it were in the air, high above the earth" (1 Nephi 8:26). This building without foundation and without God's light was symbolic of the pride and vain imaginations of the world. Misguided and deceived multitudes, "both old and young, both male and female . . . [pointed] their fingers towards those who had come at and were partaking of the fruit" (1 Nephi 8:27).[18] Such public merriment over a sacred partaking is an affront to the Saints as well as the God of heaven.

Satan will not uphold his own in their folly when confounded by the servants of God. His building and his host of subjugated followers will surely fall. Nephi saw the end of this building without a sure support. The building "fell, and the fall thereof was exceedingly great" (1 Nephi 11:36). This symbolic fall was a foreshadowing of the destruction of nations, kindreds, tongues, and people that fight against the twelve apostles of the Lamb (1 Nephi 12:18 and 1 Nephi 11:35).

Nephi Summarizes the Remainder of Lehi's Dream

In his dream, Lehi saw other multitudes, some partaking of the fruit while others felt their way towards the great and spacious building (1 Nephi 8:30–31). He saw the fountain engulf in its quagmire those that lost their way to the tree (1 Nephi 8:32). Many were lost from Lehi's view while others wandered on strange roads (1 Nephi 8:32). Great was the multitude which he saw entering the strange building and then pointing the finger of scorn (1 Nephi 8:33).[20] But amidst all this multitude and variety of satanic choices available, Lehi remarked, "We heeded them not" (1 Nephi 8:33).

In his final statement Lehi despaired. The reason was that among the multitude moving toward the tree he did not see the two people for whom he had most diligently searched. His last statement was this: "Laman and Lemuel partook not of the fruit" (1 Nephi 8:35). They came not to their Savior to partake of his love.

Lehi Exceedingly Fears

Lehi shared this most sacred, visionary, symbolic dream with his family. How would his family react? Perhaps Lehi hoped the vision of the multitude's partaking and rejoicing would cause life patterns within his family to improve. He may have wanted the family to remember the joy of those who caught hold and continually held fast to the rod of iron.[21]

What would the family learn of envisioned deceptions? The deceptions seemed so clear to Lehi. Would these same deceptions appear logical and attractive to his wayward sons? Had he made it vivid enough for them to see that the death of the spirit results from the life of surface wealth, surface power, and surface gratification? Did his sons see that death awaited them in the spacious building? Could they now see that Satan's falsely "lighted temple" was approached by carnal feeling, not godly vision? Could they see that the death of the spirit began as the carnal became immersed and saturated in the fountain of filthiness?

Might Lehi have wondered what he could do to change what he had seen? This dream was more overarching than the taking to wife the daughters of Ishmael, the leaving of Jerusalem, or the acquiring of sacred plates. This dream showed Lehi the loss of half of his immediate posterity and eventually the loss of far more. Lehi knew the mercy of the Lord. Could the Lord's mercy be so great that his vision of the spiritual deaths of Laman and Lemuel might be merely a warning and not a final reality? Could there be a miracle that would break the barrier between father and sons as revealed in the vision?

"With all the feeling of a tender parent," Lehi exhorted, preached, prophesied, and "bade them to keep the commandments of the Lord" (1 Nephi 8:37–38).[22] His choice words to these sons are not known. I take the literary license to express what I think must have been his feelings at this moment.

Oh sons, hear my voice.
Oh Lord, extend thy great mercy.
Oh sons, come follow me.
Oh Lord, my heart is broken.
Oh sons, I love you, grasp hold.
Oh Lord, soften their hearts that they might see.
Oh sons, find life, not death.
Oh Lord, be merciful to them, to me.

Conclusion

Lehi's last recorded dream teaches the pattern of the eternal family. It teaches how a godly patriarch can guide and devote his life through Christ to the salvation of himself and his family. He gathers his family together, finds the Lord and follows him, hoping that his family will also follow him. He obeys without hesitation. He sacrifices all he has to endure the trials of life and be the exemplar needed for his family. He prays for mercy so that the atoning blood of Christ can be efficacious in his life and the lives of his loved ones. The darkness of life clears and he briefly notes the world but ignores its distractions, for his heart and soul are fully riveted on the true light of Christ—the tree of life. He pushes forward to the tree, partakes of its glorious fruit, and is filled with supreme joy, not partaking in self-indulgence but partaking with the conviction that this fruit is what he most wishes to share with his family.

He first sees and reaches out to his wife. She comes to him to join him in the love of God. He then reaches out to his children who need his loving call to make a final right choice. He then looks further to find his lost family members. His love wells up as he calls, but they being agents unto themselves do not respond. He searches to understand the world and its follies so that he might warn them of the imminent dangers that await their perilous choice. When they continue not to respond, he persists in faith, in love, praying that someday in God's mercy they will hear, and reach for the rod—the word of God—to lead them to eternal life (Alma 37:43–44).

NOTES AND REFERENCES

1. Dreams and visions are often mentioned together in this verse, indicating their close relationship, although differing in important ways. See George Reynolds and Janne M. Sjodahl, *Commentary on the Book of Mormon* (Salt Lake City: Deseret News Press, 1955), vol. 1, p. 60.

2. It is significant that three of his family members partook of the fruit. These three were Nephi, Sam, and Sariah. Why did Lehi not say that he rejoiced because Sariah partook? It could be because the symbolism of the dream was the seeds—his continuing posterity.

3. One of the objects of this dream was to acquaint Lehi with the condition of his sons, in order that he might warn them, and bring them to repentance. Reynolds and Sjodahl, *Commentary on the Book of Mormon*, p. 61.

4. His vividly reported dream is in direct contrast to the total forgetfulness of the dream by Nebuchadnezzar (Daniel 2:1–5).

5. Who was the messenger that appeared to Lehi? A messenger, whom Nephi calls the Spirit, appeared also to him in a later vision. One school of thought says that it was the Holy Ghost; another indicates that it was Jesus Christ. Elder James E. Talmage of the Quorum of the Twelve takes the position that it was the Holy Ghost. Whether it was the Holy Ghost or Jesus Christ who was the messenger, the important concept to remember is the message which was delivered. See Sidney B. Sperry, *Answers to Book of Mormon Questions* (Salt Lake City: Bookcraft, 1964), pp. 29–30, and James E. Talmage, *Articles of Faith*, 30th Edition, p. 32.

6. "The fundamental and soul-satisfying step in our eternal quest is to come in a day when each does know, for himself, that God answers his prayers. This will come only after 'our soul hungers,' and after mighty prayer and supplication." Harold B. Lee, Conference Report, April 1969, p. 133.

7. It is interesting to note that the tree of life is mentioned sixteen times in the Book of Mormon, six times in the Old Testament, and three times in the New Testament. See James Strong, *Exhaustive Concordance of the Bible* (New York: Abingdon Press, 1894), pp. 1074–75; and George Reynolds, *Concordance of the Book of Mormon* (Salt Lake City: N.p., 1900), p. 419.

The *tree of life* is connected with the *cross*, the two having somewhat the same significance. Both relate to the resurrection, eternal life, the Lord, and the "love of God." The symbolism may be summarized by saying that the tree of life is representative of eternal life, to be obtained by those who love God. Before the crucifixion of Christ, the *tree of life* symbol was used extensively. After the crucifixion the cross seems to have replaced it to a degree. (Milton R. Hunter and Thomas Stuart Ferguson, *Ancient America and the Book of Mormon* [Oakland, California: Kolob Book Co., 1950], p. 213.)

8. "The tree laden with fruit was a representation of the love of God which he sheds forth among all the children of men. The Master himself, later in his earthly ministry, explained to Nicodemus how that great love was manifested. Said he: 'For God so loved the world, that he gave his only begotten Son, that whosoever believeth in him should not perish, but have everlasting life'; and then the Master added: 'For God sent not his Son into the world to condemn the world; but that the world through him might be saved' (John 3:16–17)." Harold B. Lee, Conference Report, April 1971, p. 90.

9. The sweet, white fruit made even more clear that "[his] work and [his] glory" was to share his joy with his posterity (Moses 1:39).

10. Sariah and Lehi were building together for eternities. Nephi and Sam were righteous examples to the unborn posterity of Lehi. Notice that those family members who gathered with Lehi were not perfect. Sariah had complained that her husband was a visionary man. Nephi had his heart softened. Sam had to be taught by Nephi the truths of heaven. In other words, each one at the tree had received of God's mercy in order to partake of the fruit.

11. See 1 Nephi 15:27 and 1 Nephi 12:16.

12. "To me, our leaders are true watchmen on the towers of Zion, and those who follow their counsel are exercising their agency just as freely as would be the man in the forest." Marion G. Romney, Conference Report, April 1942, p. 20.

13. Note that Lehi did not see his oldest sons first, even though through birth they entered into the dark and dreary world prior to Sam and Nephi. Could it be because others of his family had progressed closer to the tree?

14. See John 4:14.

15. Notice the spelling is *strait* not *straight*, and means a narrow passage of water connecting two large bodies of water, or narrow and strict. Examples are the Straits of Gibraltar and Straits of Magellan. These "straits" are not "straight."

16. See Matthew 13:4, 19. "And the mists of darkness are the temptations of the devil, which blindeth the eyes, and hardeneth the hearts of the children of men, and leadeth them away into broad roads, that they perish and are lost" (1 Nephi 12:17).

17. See Matthew 13:5, 6. "How can one be unfaltering? First, be alert enough to know that the challenge when it comes is individual." Boyd K. Packer, "Shall the Youth of Zion Falter?" *BYU Speeches of the Year*, 12 April 1966, pp. 7–8.

18. See 2 Kings 2:23–24; Psalm 1:1; Galatians 6:7.

19. This dream, seen in similarity by three (Lehi, Nephi, and Joseph Smith, Sr.), is only recorded in full with all of its symbols by father Lehi. For example, Nephi records the following symbols which he saw: (1) the tree and the fruit, (2) rod of iron, (3) great and spacious building, (4) mist of darkness, and (5) river of water. In other words, Nephi does not record seeing the strait and narrow path. When Laman and Lemuel began to ask Nephi questions, they only asked the interpretation of three parts of the dream. One is the tree, one is the rod of iron, and the other is the river of water. They do not ask for an understanding of the great and spacious building, the mist of darkness, or the strait and narrow path. Joseph Smith, Sr., saw the dark world, narrow path, stream of water, rope (rod of iron), pleasant valley, tree, fruit, spacious building, and the family joining him at the tree (see Lucy Mack Smith, *History of Joseph Smith* [Salt Lake City: Bookcraft, 1956], pp. 48–50).

20. See Matthew 13:7, 22.

21. Hold to the rod, the iron rod;
'Tis strong, and bright, and true.
The iron rod is the word of God;
'Twill safely guide us through.
Hymns of The Church of Jesus Christ of Latter-day Saints, 1985, No. 274.

22. This approach to Laman and Lemuel continued throughout the rest of Lehi's life. Even his last blessing to them was a plea to stop their unrighteousness and unite with family and with God (2 Nephi 1).

9

STELA 5, IZAPA: A LAYMAN'S CONSIDERATION OF THE TREE OF LIFE STONE

Alan K. Parrish

The Book of Mormon is a testimony of Jesus Christ, who is introduced in the twin visions of the tree of life given to the book's leading characters, Lehi and Nephi. Following their visions they taught their families about the life and ministry of Christ, who would come in the meridian of time, about his redeeming sacrifice, and his mission as the Savior of the world. Lehi saw a large tree "whose fruit was desirable to make one happy." Eating the fruit of the tree filled his soul with "exceedingly great joy," and he declared, "I knew that it was desirable above all other fruit" (1 Nephi 8:10–12).

Nephi's account of the same vision is much more detailed than Lehi's, and it includes a personal visitation of the Lord and a lengthy discussion with an angel of God. The two accounts extend over sixteen of the fifty-two pages of 1 Nephi (31 percent). Knowing the intent of Nephi's writing, "to persuade them [his father's descendants] that they would remember the Lord their

---

Alan K. Parrish is Assistant Professor of Ancient Scripture at Brigham Young University.

Redeemer'' (1 Nephi 19:18), one would expect the tree of life to be a preeminent symbol in the teachings of his seed. This investigation will examine the question of whether Stela 5, Izapa could be a depiction fulfilling that expectation.

Background on Izapa

Izapa is of the preclassic period, approximately 300 B.C.— A.D. 300.[1] It was inhabited between the times of the Olmec and the Mayan civilizations. Writing about the Olmec civilization and the Mexico-Guatemala border region, Jacques Soustelle described the importance of Izapa:

> The most important site is that of Izapa, to the east of Tapachula (Chiapas), in Mexican territory at a distance of several kilometers from the Rio Suchiate. What is spectacular at Izapa is the stone sculpture: 22 Stelae and 19 altars, plus other monuments, all covered with bas-reliefs. The style of these representations is extraordinarily dynamic and "baroque." The scenes depicted refer to a mythology that we know nothing of and that appears to be very different from that of the Olmecs. . . .
> The tentative conclusion that may be drawn on the basis of what we know today, is that this border zone between Mexico and Central America saw a period of intense cultural activity in the last centuries of the first millennium B.C. and at the beginning of the pre-classic and proto-classic eras, between the Olmecs and the Mayas. Various local styles emerged, spread, and changed. Like that of Izapa, like that of the colossal sculptures, they are neither Olmec nor Maya; rather, they sometimes bear traces of the influence and the heritage of the past, and sometimes foreshadow the future.[2]

Gyles and Sayer described Izapa as a huge ceremonial complex containing monuments that display their gods and show busy scenes of daily life.[3] Gallenkamp adds that Izapan art is a warehouse of Olmec themes from which the later Maya culture drew.[4]

Bernal noted that Izapa was one of the first ceremonial centers that introduced priesthood and a formalized religion. These represented distinct advances in scientific, astronomical, and mathematical knowledge.[5] He also noted that the custom of placing stelae and altars in front of buildings, so prominent in Maya times, began in an earlier period at Izapa and similar sites.[6]

Hunter wrote, "The most important stylistic influence on the Pacific Slope in the Late Preclassic Period came from Izapa" and described many original characteristics including "deities descending from the sky, winged figures, U-shaped symbols, and the long-lipped god."[7] He also noted the Izapan influence on Maya monuments, and the rarity of dates, or glyphs.

Badner reported connections between Izapan and Chavin (Andean) art of northern Peru. He viewed Izapa as the direct connecting link between the Olmec and the Mayan civilizations, with numerous cultural and religious connections.[8] Coe described Izapa as "crucial to the problem of how higher culture came about among the Maya."[9] He also found it to be the connecting link between the Olmec and the Maya.

Smith found Izapan art to be highly specialized. "Far from being a connecting link in time and space between the earlier Olmec civilization and the Classic Maya art styles, the Izapa style is unique."[10]

Interpretation and Analysis of Izapa, Stela 5

While many have praised the quality and significance of Izapa and its monuments, few have tried to interpret its art. Stela 5 is recognized as the most complex stela, bearing the most important message. Some brief interpretations give an indication of the difficulty of determining its message.

Keeler, writing on surviving tree of life customs, drew a reconstruction of the scene and gave the following interpretation of Stela 5 (see Figure 1):

> This elaborate monument shows the Tree of Life beside the Earthmother's Genitals (zig-zag and slit). The Water of Life gushes forth to form the Oceans of the World (wave symbol). The "Two Headed Sungod" stands to the right of the Tree of Life with his Sacred Flute. The Two Headed Snake frames the picture. The Fish are symbols of the Earthmother. The Jaguar nose and teeth symbols represent the Physical Power of God. Chief Ikaniklipippi says that the bearded figure at the lower left is a Merman (Ansu), and that before him is a new Tree of Life. At the lower right is a monkey that sometimes symbolizes the Placenta Dragon. He holds a parasol which would be taken by the Cunas to be the Umbilical Cord and the Foetal Membranes of the child.[11]

Figure 1. A drawing of Stela 5, Izapa, as part of an interpretation
by Clyde E. Keeler.

Miles carried out extensive study of the sculpture of the
Guatemala-Chiapas region. An interpretation and drawing of
Stela 5 (see Figure 2) follows:

> Izapa Stela 5 presents a fantastic visual myth. A nine-
> branched tree whose origins are in a subterranean dragon variant
> divides the scenes. On the left bottom two men, seated opposite
> each other over an incensario that is like Kaminaljuyu Stela 11,
> wear peaked caps. The larger figure has a secondary man behind
> him who supports a short post with a bare alveolum dragon. At
> the back of the smaller figure a little man with a long lock of hair
> has some business with the tree roots. Directly above his head a
> small helmeted man seems to present two ring-tail fish to a larger
> figure wearing a cape and having birds on his left shoulder and on
> top of his head. On the right side, bottom, again two men sit in
> consultation, the larger having a flunky with an umbrella behind
> him. This large man appears to be a sculptor with a small slab at
> his knee and a chisel in his left hand. He gestures toward the child
> in front of his small companion. Above is another large man

whose face is erased with an enormous headdress. At his back a smaller figure carries a child on his shoulders. The whole is framed by great dragon heads, one quite serpentine, with enormous scroll hats, set on posts. Two ring-tail fish hang from the signature at the left while at the right birds (one looks like a vulture) contemplate the tree.[12]

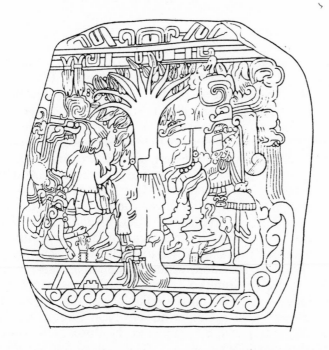

Figure 2. A drawing of Stela 5, Izapa, as part of an interpretation by S. W. Miles.

Miller, a professor of history of art with specialized training in the numerous art forms of ancient Mesoamerica, gave this interpretation:

Stela 5 depicts a mythic origin from a central tree. Representation of natural flora are rare in Olmec and Maya art—the two traditions most clearly related to Izapa—and the tree of Stela 5 is a supernatural one, from which human forms flow, as if released by the large figure to the right, who uses his nose to drill an opening into the trunk. The scene may be designed for oral reading, with components recorded as if in simultaneous narrative. The old couple at lower left who divine with kernels may be the ancestral couple (referred to in later Aztec sources) from whom all subsequent human beings descend.[13]

Two noted LDS researchers, M. Wells Jakeman and V. Garth Norman, have given Stela 5 exhaustive analysis. Their findings are the major focus of this investigation.

The Jakeman Study

In 1946, M. Wells Jakeman filled a newly created BYU Chair of Archaeology at the recommendation of Elder John A. Widtsoe of the Council of Twelve Apostles. That December he was made chairman of the new Department of Archaeology at BYU. Dr. Jakeman received a Ph.D. from the University of California at Berkeley in 1938 in the field of ancient history and Near Eastern archaeology. His dissertation was entitled *The Maya States of Yucatan, 1441–1545.* He had received his MA in history with an emphasis on ancient and Near Eastern history—biblical archaeology at the University of Southern California and his BA in history from the University of Utah, magna cum laude.[14]

The newly discovered Stela 5 captured the curiosity of Dr. Jakeman through its similarities to both the ancient Near East and the Book of Mormon. After considerable research he was prepared to present some courageous possibilities. Much of what he concluded was based on the reliability of the connections he found between Stela 5, similar ancient Near Eastern representations, and the tree of life accounts in the Book of Mormon. He published two significant reports. The first, addressed primarily to Church peers, was a consideration of Stela 5's being an actual portrayal of the tree of life visions of Lehi and Nephi.[15] The second was to professionals in archaeology.[16]

In the first report he noted twenty-three correspondences between the Izapa carving and ancient Near Eastern representations of the tree of life or related art conventions.[17] Having found these similarities, he stated:

> What should we conclude from these several specific and close Near Eastern similarities presented by the Izapa sculpture? Certainly the arbitrary nature of most of the corresponding features seems to rule out the possibility of the ancient priest-artists of Izapa having hit upon them independently of the Near Eastern representations. . . . In other words, the Tree of Life symbol of

ancient America, especially as portrayed on the Izapa monument called Stela 5, must be considered definite evidence of a connection between the ancient civilizations of America and those of the Near East in the Old World.[18]

Dr. Alfred L. Kroeber, "a leading authority on anthropological theory and method," postulated that

a complex device used in two or more parts of the world suggests a connection between them in very proportion to its complexity. A combination of *two* or even three elements might conceivably have been repeated independently. [But] a combination of *five* or *ten* parts serving an identical purpose in an identical manner must necessarily appeal as impossible of having been hit upon more than once. *One thinks almost under compulsion, in such a case, of historical connection.*[19]

Jakeman based his proof of historical connection between Stela 5 and ancient Near Eastern cultures on the principles established by Kroeber. With a valid connection to the Old World religious art, interpretation of Stela 5 was greatly enhanced.

He found numerous connections between Stela 5 and the written accounts of the tree of life visions in 1 Nephi. He cited 22 correspondences, but in all but 2 of these he found several "points of agreement" from which he estimated the degree of correspondence ranging from "extreme" (as many as 38 points of agreement) to "rather close" (only 3–4 points of agreement). In all he identified 114 points of agreement in the 22 correspondences between the Book of Mormon account and Stela 5.

In addition to the correspondences, Dr. Jakeman noted:

Also significant, as tending to rule out accident, is the fact that there is nothing in the Izapa carving that cannot be explained in the light of the Lehi story (or in the light of Near Eastern art conventions probably known to the Lehi people of the Book of Mormon), or that *conflicts* with this story (e.g. an otherwise corresponding feature in the wrong place in the composition in relation to the representation of the Tree of Life).[20]

As to the composition of Stela 5, he noted some important aspects.

Now it is not likely that such a formally patterned composition would have *accidentally* included so many correspondences to the Book of Mormon Tree-of-Life story—especially in their correct directional or spatial relationships—as actually occur in the Izapa carving. Very careful planning, in fact, would obviously have been necessary to achieve such a remarkable combination of formal design elements with special subject features. This, consequently, makes it even more certain that *intention*, and not accident, is the reason for the resemblance.[21]

All of the evidence confirmed his impression of a relationship between Stela 5 and the Book of Mormon, so strongly, in fact, that he boldly stated the "main conclusion" of his study:

By all the rules of correlation, the resemblances of the Izapa carving to the ancient Near Eastern symbolism of the Tree of Life . . . found in the Book of Mormon cannot be the result of accident, but must be due to historical connection; and that consequently *this carving is definitely a portrayal of the Lehi story*— i.e. the episode of the Book of Mormon prophet Lehi's gathering his family around him and narrating to them the vision he had had of the Tree of Life, also as many of the features of that vision itself as possible, and the discussion and recording of Lehi's account by his son Nephi.[22]

Jakeman's Interpretation of Stela 5

Under the direction of Matthew W. Stirling, exploration of Izapa sponsored by the Smithsonian Institution and the National Geographic Society began in April of 1941. The National Geographic photograph is the oldest known photograph of Stela 5 and is the one Dr. Jakeman used to study the stone. From careful examination of both the Stela and the photograph, Dr. Jakeman made a drawing of Stela 5 (see Figure 3) from which we can review some of his interpretations.[23]

Feature 1: Dr. Jakeman indicated that this is obviously the principal person in the event depicted. The artist had endeavored to indicate that he was a religious leader teaching about the tree which had sacred religious meaning. "This person corresponds, in both character and role, to Lehi of the Book of Mormon Tree-of-Life episode."[24]

Feature 2: Another of the six persons involved in teaching or learning about the tree appears to speak with the old man and to be in attendance upon him. The ear pendants, long-horned tiara, and age association suggest that this is a woman and probably his wife, an obvious correspondence to Sariah.

Figure 3. A drawing of Stela 5, Izapa, as part of an interpretation
by M. Wells Jakeman.

Feature 3: Shown larger than others in front of the old man, this person appears to have considerable importance. A small beard seen through a magnifying glass indicates he is a young man. In his left hand is what appears to be a stylus or writing instrument used, as it appears, to record the teachings of the old man. This person corresponds well to Nephi.

Feature 4: This appears to be a young man holding a parasol over Person 3 and to be in attendance upon him. His actions identify Person 3 as a ruler whom he follows. This person corresponds well to Sam, third of the four sons of Lehi.

Feature 5 and 6: These also appear to be young men being instructed about the tree. Their mouths and hands show they are conversing with Persons 1 and 3 (Lehi and Nephi). Seated with their backs turned to the tree may indicate their rejection of the tree and the message it symbolized. These correspond well to Laman and Lemuel.

Dr. Jakeman found virtually all of the elements that Lehi and Nephi described in their twin visions. Beyond the specific items they described, Dr. Jakeman found some apparent glyphs identifying some of the chief persons.

Feature 9 held above Person 1 (Lehi) by Person 2 (Sariah) appears to be a hieroglyph recording the name of the old man so prominent in the scene. Dr. Jakeman identified this glyph as the cipactli (see-packt-lee) or "crocodile" symbol of ancient Mesoamerican hieroglyphics. It was used as a rebus hieroglyph for the name of a certain old man who in Aztec legends was said to have invented the calendar with the help of his wife. The symbol thus represented an old couple. After reviewing all of the possibilities of a couple in ancient Mesoamerican iconography, Jakeman concluded that this glyph identified the old couple of the Popol Vuh:

> We are left, then, with the identification of the "Cipactónal" and "Oxomoco" of the Izapa carving with the *second* old couple of ancient Mesoamerican tradition—the "great father" and "great mother" reported to have been the ancestors of the ancient inhabitants of the Guatemala Quiché region after "the flood," i.e. the old man "Cipactónal" or "Ixpiyacoc" and old woman "Oxomoco" or "Ixmucané" also called "Zaqui-Nim-Ac" and "Zaqui-Nimá-Tziís," the immediate parents of two sons who became the first warrior heroes of the ancient Quiché Mayan people of highland Guatemala.[25]

This interpretation matches Lehi and Sariah whose two warrior sons Laman and Lemuel were very much like the two warrior sons of the old couple of the Popol Vuh.

More astonishing is the possibility that the glyph symbolizes the actual name of the famed old man.

> This in fact is found to be the case. For the meaning of the name Lehi is the jaws[26]—especially the upper jaw—in side view, i.e. "cheek." And we have already noted that Feature 9, the *cipactli* glyph held above the old bearded man, mainly depicts a pair of huge jaws (those of the crocodile)—especially the upper jaw—in side view, i.e. a great cheek! That is, this glyph is essentially a portrayal of what the name Lehi means. It therefore constitutes—*whether intended or not*—a symbolic recording of that name. . . .[27]
>
> That Feature 9 is an *intentional* glyph-recording of the name Lehi appears, however, to be the only possible conclusion. For the coincidence of symbol and meaning occurring here seems much

too peculiar to be accidental. (The changes of such a symbol as a cheek being associated accidentally, i.e. without reason, with a figure identifiable on other grounds as a person whose name had this same peculiar meaning, must be extremely remote.) It should also be pointed out that the simplest, most direct symbolization of the name Lehi by ancient artists would, of course, have been the depiction of a cheek.[28]

The headdress on Person 2, like a name glyph of Person 1, may be a means of identifying her as Sariah of the Book of Mormon. The headdress is unusual in early Mesoamerican art, but is very much like Egyptian representations of a queen or princess.

> (*Sariah*, "Princess of Yahweh"). In other words, this crown can be considered as actually a kind of name-glyph (*derived from an Egyptian symbol*, just as expected), giving the name of the person wearing it as the Book of Mormon name Sariah.[29]

Having found evidence for the names of Lehi and Sariah in the Stela 5 scene, Dr. Jakeman indicated that he would expect something similar to identify Person 3, likewise a key person in the story depicted. From a consideration of various possibilities from which the name *Nephi* may have come, he found one in the Egyptian pantheon of gods with the very same pronunciation.

A close examination of the 1941 photograph of Stela 5 reveals that the headdress worn by Person 3 (Nephi) contains markings that tie it to Egyptian nomenclature.[30] There is a serpent projecting out from his forehead; behind the serpent is a human face with a plant rising above and leaves flowing from it down the young man's back. Having considered the possible connection, Dr. Jakeman concluded:

> Now the reader has doubtless already observed that this peculiar headdress worn by the person with the stylus—very probably a young man's face in profile with a maize (i.e. Indian corn or *grain*) plant rising above it as a headdress or growing out of it . . . essentially duplicates the representations of the ancient Egyptian grain god, Nepri or Nepi (latter form, as we have shown, young man's figure with the face in profile and ears of wheat or barley [i.e. grain] rising above it as a headdress or growing out of it. In other words, this headdress is in fact the name-glyph we were expecting to find!—a symbol connected with the figure of the young man with the stylus and identifiable with the Egyptian grain-god symbol, thereby indicating that his name was that of the

Egyptian grain god, Nepri or Nepi (latter form, as we have shown, probably pronounced with the *p* aspirated), i.e. that he was the corresponding young man Nephi of the Book of Mormon.[31]

The result of these many correlations and the absence of alternative ones led Dr. Jakeman to identify a number of important consequences, some of which I include to indicate his convictions and the dynamic possibilities of Stela 5 (numbers in the original).

    1. The first, of course, is that Izapa Stela 5 is thus the first ancient monument to be discovered as actually recording a *specifically Book of Mormon* event. The significance of this conclusion will be immediately apparent to the reader.
    2. The second is that the particular identification we have given of the various features of the Izapa carving in the light of the Book of Mormon account, as warranted by the correspondences considered *separately*, now becomes (with the above identification of that carving as definitely a portrayal of the Book of Mormon account) even more certain or probable, as the case may be. For example, Feature 1 must surely now be considered *very definitely* a portrayal of the ancient Israelite prophet Lehi of the Book of Mormon. . . .
    4. It is at this point that the extreme importance of the Izapa monument appears. For we have seen that the *second* resemblance of the carving on this monument, its very close and arbitrary resemblance to the special Lehi story of the Tree of Life in the Book of Mormon, *forces us to the conclusion that this carving is an actual portrayal of that story*. And this in turn necessarily establishes a connection between the ancient people of Izapa and the Lehi people of the Book of Mormon. Indeed, the accurate and detailed knowledge of the Lehi story (and of many Near Eastern art conventions) displayed by the ancient Izapans who produced the carving on Stela 5, can be explained only by their identification as an actual group of the Lehi people of the Book of Mormon.[32]

The Norman Study

In 1965, V. Garth Norman began professional archaeological work as a research associate with the New World Archaeological Foundation (NWAF). His interest in the cultural history and religion of pre-Mayan times led him to study the Izapan ruins. His association with the NWAF culminated in a two-volume monograph entitled *Izapa Sculpture*.

Figure 4. A photograph of Stela 5, Izapa, with tracing and labels
as part of the interpretation by V. Garth Norman.

Having considered previous interpretations of Stela 5,
Norman saw the need to give the monuments and altars of Izapa
the closest possible scrutiny and interpretation.

> Adequate illustrations have been lacking, and even under first-
> hand observation many significant features have remained unde-
> tected due to difficulties resulting from extreme weathering of
> some parts of all the carved monuments. Consequently, incom-
> plete or inaccurate observations have rendered invalid parts or all
> of most existing descriptions and interpretations of the Izapa
> carved monuments.[33]

To achieve these ends, Norman carefully cleaned each
monument. Every possible detail that remained was exposed to
the critical lenses of Graphic View Cameras that produced large,
high-quality negatives. The larger negatives gave greater clarity to
enlargements from which he produced a superimposed drawing
of Stela 5 (see Figure 4). This drawing contains the details from
which his interpretation proceeded. Photographs were taken

under a variety of lighting conditions. Water was sprayed onto badly damaged portions to reveal every trace of the original work.

All of the motifs of Stela 5 were then classified and considered with similar examples on other Izapan pieces. Careful study of each of the motifs in the whole Izapan library gave Norman a broader base from which to consider their appearance on Stela 5. In his report he called Stela 5 the "Supernarrative" and the "Grandiose Stela."[34] So thorough was his work that today he is considered the authority on pre-Mayan iconography of the region of Izapa and is a regular participant in symposia and seminars that bring together the most noted scholars of Mayan and pre-Mayan antiquity.

Norman's Interpretation of Stela 5

General considerations that Norman took into account were relationships between the human figures in the scene and the movement patterns that seem to indicate the overall meaning in the events depicted. Relationship is shown in "gesture indicated interactions," direct contact between figures, the same height, and interassociated motifs and positions.[35] The central and most overpowering image is the tree, but the bird-masked deities on either side of the tree are also focal points. Norman points out that almost every feature on either side of the tree is somehow connected to one of the bird-masked deity impersonators and thus "appear generally to relate to the tree through them."[36] As all of the persons in the scene tie into the deity representative on either side, interpretation of the side scene should precede discussion of prominent persons in the scene.

The Right-Hand Scene

The right-hand scene is dominated by a complicated head of the U Serpent or Sky Serpent, labeled number 9 in the drawing. This serpent was a double-headed U Serpent. The other head is labelled number 15 and dominates the left-hand scene.

> The basic symbolic function of the double-headed raised earth serpent is that of divine or supernatural power *bridging the sky barrier in transferring elements between the heavenly and earthly realms* with the two heads relating to the two-way movement.

The right-hand serpent figure undoubtedly characterizes the bringing of rains to the earth and the dual functions of rain in connection with earth life.[37]

Several parallels were identified between the two heads of the U Serpent though with the movement reversed.

We will see abundant evidence throughout the course of our investigation that the motifs in this parallelism relate to various aspects of the beginning (right) and ending (left) stages of man's life cycle.[38]

Person 2 in Norman's analysis is a priest representative of Deity A. This is indicated by the parasol held over his head by his attendant and by the Jaguar Snout headdress he is wearing. His connection to Deity A is also indicated by the contact of interconnecting objects in his headdress and his speech glyph with Deity A. Such a person was an intermediary between God and man. This priest representative role is also indicated by the hand glyphs of Persons 2 and 6.

Instructionally, as seems to be the Stela 5 usage, this hand sign could mean that the word or act in progesss is in effect an irrevocable command or the unalterable conclusion of whatever is transpiring in regard to the instructed person seated opposite. . . . As a gesture perhaps climaxing the instructions, it might be interpreted as, "so be it,"—the last unalterable word of authority.[39]

Person 1 appears to be an attendant linked to Person 2. The unique thing about this person is the fact that he is seated beyond the ground panel, to suggest that he originated "from beyond the ground panel."[40] He is closely linked to Symbol 8.

Person 1 and Symbol 8 have been seen to have some correspondence with the beginning stages of mortal man through comparative evidence of corresponding figures on other stelae and through the symbolism of the right-hand earth serpent and its rain-cycle correspondence to man's life-cycle beginning at birth.[41]

Persons 10 and 11 are extensions of Person 1 and relate to his journey through life. Of this relationship Norman wrote:

I believe the sundry interpretive correspondences of Person 10 with Person 11, the child, traveler's staff, and surrounding symbolical connections, all give evidence of functional aspects of humanity in general as opposed to the representation of specific individuals. It appears that this complex reveals various aspects of the nature of man's journey toward the Tree of Life including the postmortal phase.[42]

Deity A. Each person in the right-hand scene is connected to the scene through Deity A, a bird-masked, anthropomorphic, deity representative standing next to and facing the tree. His headdress and mask indicate the deity he is impersonating. In its most complete sense, Deity A represents Quetzalcoatl in a variety of his aspects or representations. The bird-serpent aspects connect to the Quetzalcoatl deity (Maya-Itzamna), the upturned snout and rain bands on the headdress mask signify a rain deity, while the long bill on the bird mask resembles a form of Quetzalcoatl, Ehecatl (eh-kot-ol). The Quetzalcoatl deity pervaded all aspects of life. In addition to being their creator, he controlled two important requisites to life, the right rains at the right times, and fertile soil.

Similar to the role of the anthropomorphic deity to the left in delivering the fruit of the Tree of Life, it appears that Deity A is holding supposed fruit or medicine bags, and that with his bird beak, forward bag, and forward foot touching the tree, he undoubtedly controls and directs what I feel to be a journey to the Tree of Life in this right-hand side. (Both deities might actually represent a paternal deified couple who preside over the sacred tree; see Deity B).[43]

Another important aspect of Deity A is his connection to Person 13. A line dissecting the tree extends from his bird beak to Person 13, whom Norman considers to be an immortal person.

The Ehecatl form of Quetzalcoatl seems most comparable to Deity A. This deity was for the Aztecs *master of the winds which normally precede rain.* The sign of Ehecatl-Quetzalcoatl is a bird mask with a great bill which "transforms the human, masculine figure into the deity." . . . The bird seems to signify wind sweeping across the sky bringing the rain-filled clouds, and the bill suggests the mouth as the source of the wind (breath of god).[44]

Persons 3 and 4, like 10 and 11, represent "significant aspects of the nature of a man's journey toward the Tree of

Life."[45] Norman suggested that these represent "a beginning or intermediate stage in the 'journey' toward the Tree of Life."[46] Pursuing the similarities in these and migration myths led Norman to the mythical journeyings of Quetzalcoatl in Nahuatl theology, which he felt corresponded well with the right-hand scene. These myths seem related to the life cycle of man.

> As in the Quetzalcoatl and Popol Vuh myths he is required to pass through a mortal probation in a "blinded" condition which includes torments and suffering before he is able to rise as a god (apparently after death) to the highest heaven. . . . Man is brought to "his lord" and apparently to the Tree of Life through responding to the guidance of deity representatives.
>
> Potential correspondences to Stela 5 from this myth are rather striking. Although the details differ, the general conception is the same, and it is easy to see a common origin with the Stela 5 scene.[47]

Norman considered the features of the Sky Panel, the Ground Panel, the Water Panel, and the Tree. He looked at the movement lines and the triangles to understand every possible meaning and association in the scene. Further correlation in the tree, its trunk, roots, and branches suggests even closer connection with migration myths in the Boturini Codex[48] and the Popol Vuh.[49]

> Evidence has mounted to indicate that the Popol Vuh and Boturini Codex migration traditions are closely related and have a common more ancient origin as portrayed in the Stela 5 narration. . . .
>
> The "Tamoanchan/Tulan" tree on Stela 5 is a symbol of human transition, a representation of the ancestral tree (land of birth) from which man originated, and at once a symbol of the underworld land of death and the post-mortal heavenly paradise into which he can be reborn, as well as a symbol of his earthly Mesoamerican garden paradise. . . .
>
> We can only speculate at this time that some historical facts are recorded on Stela 5 which have been carried up in recorded or oral traditions to survive in a few documents of the historical period.
>
> Certain parallels between the Popol Vuh account and Izapa Stela 5 tend to push some elements of the Popol Vuh origin tradition back another thousand plus years. Stela 5 is not necessarily a record of any Popol Vuh migration account, but it does appear that parallels are too close to be entirely coincidental.[50]

The Left-Hand Scene

Person 13 is a key in understanding Norman's interpretation. As noted above, he represents the arrival point in the journey depicted in the right-hand scene. He appears to have become a branch of the tree, being connected to it at the branch stub. He has some of the fruit of the tree in his hand and is being waited upon by Deity B. He is the opposite extreme of Person 1 and the representative of Persons 3 and 4, different mortal stages of the journey to the tree.

Deity B appears to be receiving the fruit of the tree, as represented in the mouths of the fish in contact with the deity's arms, and by the detached pieces, above the deity mask yet within the large scrolls that emanate either as smoke from the incense burner or speech from the deity impersonator. The deity appears to face Person 13 and is giving the fruit to him from the fringed bag in his/her hand.

Associated with Deity B are several fertility and feminine symbols, including the conch shell, the head masks, and the bird beak face masks. Another indication is suggested in the manner in which Person 13 receives fruit from Deity B, suggestive of a rebirth into a postmortal heavenly state.

Deity B correlates well with Mesoamerican goddess traditions as a goddess consort of Deity A. She corresponds well with Ix Chebel Yax, wife of Itzamna and as the moon goddess and wife of the sun. These representations are common in the codices of ancient Mesoamerica.

Persons 5 and 6. Person 6 is portrayed as an elderly man (ancestor) of prominence and probably royalty (indicated by the eye element of a profile deity on his cushion or throne). In character and action he is much like Person 2 considered above. His left arm and forefinger are outstretched in a directive gesture as discussed under Person 2. A piece of fruit from the tree appears to be touching his chin. His aged appearance suggests that he is near the end of his earthly journey.

Person 5 is closely associated with Person 6 and seems to be instructed or administered to by him. His hand gestures indicate receptivity to the instructions and offering on the incense burner emanating from Person 6. The smoke ring from the offering on the incense burner blown into the face of Person 5 indicates the prayer offering is in his behalf and that its benefit is for him. The suggestion is that Person 5 is advancing toward the blessings of the tree in sustaining his life or his eventual partaking of the precious fruit.

The fruit before the mouth of the "skull" in Person 2's headdress, like that at the chin (approaching the mouth?) of the priestly Person 6, suggests that the fruit is *achieved in mortality but actually partaken of after death*. The aged Person 6 is logically in the final stage of his mortal journey and I suppose that in death he will actually partake of the symbolic fruit.[51]

In addition to these relationships of Persons 5 and 6, Norman observed that the right to left movement and the interconnecting alignments of the triangles in the base panel indicate that Person 5 is being drawn toward Person 6. "It can be reasoned that Person 5 is being instructed in the pathway of Person 6 in order to reach the heavenly goal."[52]

Person 7 is positioned as to be assisting or attending Person 6. The bent back (like Person 6) suggests old age and the headdress, beaded necklace, and ear ornament suggest female identity. These features combine as if to indicate that Person 7 is a female attendant, probably the wife of Person 6. In her left hand there appears to be an obsidian or flint knife, while in her right hand is a decapitated ring-tail fish. These, with her headdress, indicate that she is making an offering. The deity mask (#14) connecting her to Deity B, her upturned face and eye focus on Deity B, and the feathered headdress suggest that she is making an offering to Deity B and is therefore a priestess of Deity B.

Norman agrees with Jakeman in the suggestion that Persons 6 and 7 qualify "as parents of original tribal chiefs who are evidently represented symbolically in the tree roots and possibly in figures of the right-hand scene."[53] Person 7 in association with the deity mask 14 complex is in "the very final stage of the mortal journey toward the heavenly destiny."[54]

The U Serpent 15 complex is the opposite representation of the Serpent 9 complex and the opposite end of the two-way communication with heaven. As the Serpent 9 complex described above signifies downward movement through rain from heaven, the Serpent 15 complex signifies the upward movement of the moisture toward heaven through evaporation symbols. Likewise, man's journey from heaven to this mortal world (Person 1) ends with his upward movement from this world toward heaven (Persons 7 and 13).

Norman's Conclusion

From his comprehensive study of the art of Izapa, Norman arrived at the most detailed understanding we yet have of the many symbols in the scene on Stela 5. Having applied the best skills of the science of epigraphy, for which he has gained international recognition, he brought to his study a great deal of confidence. His conclusion is that *it is a portrayal of the road from man's beginning to man's ultimate life in an exalted realm with the Great God.*

While various sculptures give detail to specific phases, only Stela 5 reveals the full life cycle. This message is rather remarkably recreated in the central prominent tree on Stela 5; the tree symbolizing both the supreme God and his heavenly realm is the ultimate goal achievable by man, signified by partaking of the tree's fruit. Man's origin and earth life leading to that goal may be expressed symbolically in the tree roots and trunk markings with associated symbols:

> The eternal tree—the human allegory—
> Spanning the course of mortal destiny,
> Marks the changing seasons of human events:
> The beginning;
> The struggle;
> The end;
> The beyond . . .

As an example of the way in which we might be able to eventually interpret verbally the "writing" on various Izapan sculptures, I have written *an imaginary ritual instruction passing from Person 6 to Person 5* on Stela 5; this verbalization is based on the interrelationships pointed out in the Stela 5 discussion:

"As your hands are open in supplication to God through this burned offering, as his priest I perform this offering in your behalf and in so doing point the way to everlasting life in the heavenly Tamoanchan paradise. Through your observance of sacred statutes in life's journey, you can reach this goal and partake of the fruit of the Tree of Life as I partake. The incense smoke rises heavenward before your face, blinding your eyes as with a mist of darkness, but it can carry your prayers heavenward through your inner faith returning the blessings of God upon your head as the dews from heaven [fish water symbol overhead]; and the water of life and the fruit of the Tree of Life will be bestowed upon you from above."[55]

Since 1976

Since his publication of *Izapa Sculpture* in 1976, Norman has written further of his interpretation of Izapa and especially Stela 5. In March, 1984, he wrote of the relationship of both studies (Jakeman and Norman) to the Book of Mormon. While mentioning that much more data on Izapa and the vicinity is needed to prove the validity of Dr. Jakeman's conclusions, no one yet has successfully refuted them and his own study tended more to sustain than invalidate them.

In my opinion, due to limited data, the TLE [tree of life episode] hypothesis has been neither validated nor invalidated following the Jakeman studies. In order to verify a specific detailed Book of Mormon textual inscription, such as Stela 5, we would have had to reach for the whole picture of both Book of Mormon and Mesoamerican historical reconstruction. . . .

A major accomplishment set forth in my *Izapa Sculpture* was the high level of success in deciphering and accurately illustrating weathered and damaged details, by means of cataloguing and comparing all motifs on all the sculptures. Only in the course of this analytical process did the presence and significance of many details become evident. While some prior interpretations of Stela 5 were invalidated, most motifs previously analyzed were confirmed and elucidated. For instance *the cipactli glyph, a bared jawbone and possible name glyph for "Lehi" (meaning "jawbone" in Hebrew), was sustained*, in spite of decipherment of significant new details. The "Nephi" name glyph, however, is in serious doubt.

While it is true that the many new details that emerged in my study of Stela 5 require changes in earlier interpretations, these differences by no means invalidate the central TLE hypothesis; rather, they have considerably deepened its meaning. For instance, two of the more pointed meanings that have emerged, corresponding to the Book of Mormon account, are (1) a *"dark mists"* glyph, and (2) *the immortality theme.*[56]

Responding in the *Ensign* to the question "What is the current status of research concerning the 'Tree of Life' carving from Chiapas, Mexico?" Norman supported the work of Dr. Jakeman and made an important statement about the contributions of his own study to Book of Mormon doctrine.

The years of research since Dr. Jakeman's first study have neither proved nor disproved his thesis. As yet, published data has been inconclusive, and will continue to be until we have a more complete picture of Izapan culture. In the 1970s I published an interpretive study of Izapa monuments, including Stela 5. . . . The study shows that Stela 5 occupies a central position, conceptually speaking, in relation to the other carvings discovered in Izapa, which display, among other concepts, the following: (1) There is an anthropomorphic god whose prime symbol is the sun and who dwells in the heavens and on mountains. (2) He is god of the Tree of Life, which relates to life after death. (3) At death, the human spirit rises into heaven from the body. (4) A physical resurrection is implied. (5) Worship involves sacrifice and a divine sacrificial atonement. And (6) the spirit of an unborn child originates in the heavens.[57]

Norman wrote of the importance of Book of Mormon archaeology giving some direction that pertains to the interest of all of us.

It seems that a major challenge has been to discover some solid ground from which straightforward, non-apologetic research can proceed. Once that gulf is bridged, Book of Mormon archaeology can come into its own with the same intensity and objectivity that have characterized much archaeological research in the biblical field. This can certainly result if research has succeeded in identifying a major artifact within a New World archaeological-cultural context, such as Izapa Stela 5, that can be unequivocally linked to a unique Book of Mormon text. This is one continuing interest in Stela 5 and the TLE hypothesis that potentially embraces ruins of the whole Izapan culture period. *This extremely difficult task demands a long-range scholarly commitment that should be second to none if we hope to succeed.*[58]

Conclusion

Izapa, especially Stela 5, is widely recognized for the valuable religious inscriptions on its monuments. Izapa also appears to coincide with both Book of Mormon dating and location, and therefore has drawn the attention of Church members with an interest in archaeological evidences of the Book of Mormon.

We should expect that discoveries of ancient American art will contain Book of Mormon themes. Most prominent will be the symbols embodied in the tree of life visions of Lehi and Nephi because of the importance of the message and its origin with the culture's founding ancestors.

The pioneering work of M. Wells Jakeman opened many eyes to the possibilities of a connection between known artifacts and Book of Mormon accounts. Further work by V. Garth Norman has provided substantial documentation supporting Jakeman's basic claims and increased evidence of a connection. From the solid base established by these investigators and related advances in other Mesoamerican research, there is good justification for increased excitement about external evidences relating to the Book of Mormon.

NOTES AND REFERENCES

1. Jacques Soustelle, *The Olmecs: The Oldest Civilization in Mexico,* translated by Helen R. Lane (Garden City, N.Y.: Doubleday & Company, Inc., 1984) pp. 19, 137; see also Ignacio Bernal, *The Mexican National Museum of Anthropology,* translated by Carolyn B. Czitrom (Mexico: Panorama Editorial, S.A., 1984), p. 34; Mary Ellen Miller, *The Art of Mesoamerica from Olmec to Aztec* (London: Thames and Hudson Inc., 1986), pp. 6, 59–61.

2. Soustelle, pp. 134–35, 136.

3. Anna Benson Gyles and Chloe Sayer, *Of Gods and Men, The Heritage of Ancient Mexico* (New York: Harper & Row, Publishers, 1980), p. 124.

4. Charles Gallenkamp, *Maya: The Riddle and Rediscovery of a Lost Civilization* (New York: Viking Penguin Inc., 1985), pp. 69–70.

5. Bernal, p. 34.

6. *Ibid.,* pp. 132–33.

7. Bruce Hunter, *A Guide to Ancient Maya Ruins* (Norman, Oklahoma: University of Oklahoma Press, 1986), pp. 32–37.

8. Mino Badner, *A Possible Focus of Andean Artistic Influence in Mesoamerica* (Washington, D.C.: Dumbarton Oaks, 1972), pp. 7, 23.

9. Michael D. Coe, *The Maya* (New York: Thames and Hudson Inc., 1984), p. 47; see also *Mexico,* by the same author (New York: Thames and Hudson Inc., 1986), pp. 85–86.

10. Virginia G. Smith, *Izapa Relief Carving* (Washington, D.C.: Dumbarton Oaks Research Library and Collection, 1984), p. 48.

11. Clyde E. Keller, "The Cuna Indian Tree of Life," in *Bulletin of the Georgia Academy of Science,* vol. 15, no. 1 (1957), p. 32.

12. S. W. Miles, "Sculpture of the Guatemala-Chiapas Highlands and Pacific Slopes, and Associated Hieroglyphs," in *Handbook of Middle American Indians,* vol. 2, ed. Robert Wauchope (London: University of Texas Press, Ltd., 1965), pp. 258–59.

13. Miller, p. 64.

14. "The Pioneer Work of M. Wells Jakeman: An Editorial," *S.E.H.A. Newsletter,* #116, ed. Ross T. Christensen, 20 Oct. 1969, pp. 2–3.

15. M. Wells Jakeman, *Stela 5, Izapa, Chiapas, Mexico: A Major Archaeological Discovery of the New World* (Provo, Utah: Brigham Young University, 1958); hereafter cited as *Stela 5.*

16. M. Wells Jakeman, *The Complex "Tree of Life" Carving on Izapa Stela 5: A Reanalysis and Partial Interpretation* (Provo, Utah: Brigham Young University, 1958).

17. *Stela 5,* p. 71.

18. Ibid., p. 7.

19. A. L. Kroeber, *Anthropology* (New York, 1923), p. 216, as quoted in Jakeman, *Stela 5,* pp. 76–77; italics on last sentence added.

20. Jakeman, *Stela 5,* p. 83.

21. Ibid.

22. Ibid., pp. 83–84; italics added.

23. Dr. Jakeman's interpretation has been severely criticized by some who allege that it reflects too strong a bias toward proving the Book of Mormon connection. Most of the criticism has been directed at Dr. Jakeman's interpretations and his qualifications to make the assertions he does. The critical assessments have been left out of the paper because the focus was upon Dr. Jakeman, not Stela 5. The most prominent of these critiques are: An unpublished manuscript by Hugh W. Nibley; John L. Sorenson, "Some Voices from the Dust," *Dialogue: A Journal of Mormon Thought,* vol. I, no. 1, Spring 1966, pp. 144–48; Dee F. Green, "Book of Mormon Archaeology: The Myths and the Alternatives," *Dialogue: A Journal of Mormon Thought,* vol. IV, no. 2, Summer 1969, pp. 71–80.

24. *Stela 5,* p. 16.

25. Ibid., p. 23.

26. Ibid., p. 32, n.49; see also *Interpreter's Dictionary of the Bible,* 5 vols. (Nashville, Tennessee: Parthenon Press, 1962), v. 3, pp. 110–11.

27. The cipactli figure or pictoglyph, so common and prominent in later times, was in the period of Izapa simply a personal name glyph. "In other words, it here quite surely records the personal name of the old man as the name for what it depicts in the unknown (not necessarily Mayan) language of the ancient people of Izapa." *Newsletter and Proceedings of the S.E.H.A.,* Dec. 1982, p. 4; italics added.

28. *Stela 5,* pp. 32–33.

29. Ibid., p. 37; italics added.

30. A detailed discussion of an Egyptian connection and identification of this headdress pictoglyph as a name glyph of Nephi is contained in *Newsletter and Proceedings of the S.E.H.A.* #151, Dec. 1982. This headdress is a well-known motif of Aztec and Mayan art and was called Centeotl (maize god) by the Aztecs. "The name of the grain spirit or grain god [Jakeman continues] which

148

was thus quite surely the name of the large young man or similar thereto, was, however, not the name of that spirit or divinity in the language of the Aztecs, *Centeotl*, since there is strong evidence that Nahuan (Toltec-Aztec) was not a language of Mesoamerica until long after the period of Izapa Stela 5."

What its meaning was in the period of Izapa is a more difficult question. Drawing upon Near Eastern connections, Dr. Jakeman has suggested an answer: "Consequently (returning to the crucial problem in its interpretation), the figure on the head of the large young man in the tree-of-life carving on that monument—quite surely a representation of the spirit of growing grain or young grain god of the Mesoamericans—*may well be a Mesopotamian or Egyptian iconographic motif.* . . .

"It has been concluded that the function of this figure in the Izapa carving is that of a phonetic *name glyph*; i.e., a pictograph recording the name of the large young man. That is, it records his name as that of (or at least as *like* that of) the grain spirit or grain god, in the language or one of the languages of the ancient people of Izapa."

31. *Stela 5*, pp. 43–44.

32. Ibid., pp. 84–85; last italics added.

33. V. Garth Norman, *Izapa Sculpture*, part 2 (Provo, Utah: Brigham Young University Printing Service, 1976), pp. 6–7; italics added.

34. Ibid., pp. 165, 329.

35. Ibid., pp. 167–68.

36. Ibid., p. 168.

37. Ibid., p. 171; italics added.

38. Ibid., p. 172.

39. Ibid., p. 174.

40. Ibid.

41. Ibid., p. 179.

42. Ibid., p. 186.

43. Ibid., p. 188.

44. Ibid; italics added.

45. Ibid., p. 190.

46. Ibid., p. 191.

47. Ibid., p. 192.

48. "The Codex Boturini is an example of the type of book the Spaniards used to reconstruct Aztec history. It was painted after the conquest, but may be a copy of a preconquest work. It is a very long roll (7 ½ inches by 15 feet), probably painted in Tenochititlan, and it tells the story of the migration of the Mexica before the foundation of Tenochititlan." Esther Pasztory, *Aztec Art* (New York: Harry A. Abrams, Inc.), pp. 200–202.

49. "The Popol Vuh is the most important single text in the native languages of the Americas. It is unique among the books produced by ancient civilizations, whether Old World or New, in balancing myth and history . . .

The original Popol Vuh was in Mayan hieroglyphs, but it was rewritten in a Latin alphabet adaption of the Quiche language in the sixteenth century." Dennis Tedlock, *Popol Vuh* (New York: Simon and Schuster, 1985), inside front cover.

50. Norman, pp. 213–14.

51. Ibid., pp. 222–23; italics added.

52. Ibid., p. 223.

53. Ibid., p. 228.

54. Ibid.

55. Ibid., pp. 329–30; italics added.

56. *Newsletter and Proceedings of the S.E.H.A.*, March 1984, pp. 7–9; italics added.

57. "I Have a Question," *Ensign*, June 1985, p. 54.

58. *Newsletter and Proceedings of the S.E.H.A.*, March 1984, p. 7; italics added.

10

THE MYSTERIES OF GOD REVEALED BY THE POWER OF THE HOLY GHOST

Gerald N. Lund

In what must surely rank as one of the great visionary experiences in all of scriptural literature, the young prophet Nephi, very possibly still in his teenage years, had unfolded for him the grand vistas of the future (see 1 Nephi 2:16). The time was six hundred years before the coming of Christ. The place—at least the place where it began—was three days' journey south of the northern tip of the Gulf of Aqaba on the Red Sea, alongside the eastern shoreline. Today the location would be part of the territory of Jordan. Lehi simply called it the valley of Lemuel (1 Nephi 10:16).

The Vision of Nephi

Whether Nephi wrote an account of the vision at the time it happened is not clear. We do know that he kept a record, from which he then wrote upon what we call the small plates of Nephi,

---

Gerald N. Lund is Director of the Curriculum and Instruction Division in the LDS Church Educational System.

some thirty years after the colony left Jerusalem (2 Nephi 5:28–31). This is worthy of note, because with that perspective of time, he chose to introduce his account of the vision with some very interesting commentary.

The purpose of this paper is to examine the seven verses of commentary that Nephi chose to give us as prelude to his record of the vision he had. Let us examine the verses, placing alongside each of them the salient points he seemed to be making.

But the Lord knoweth all things from the beginning; wherefore, he prepareth a way to accomplish all his works among the children of men; for behold, he hath all power unto the fulfilling of all his words. And thus it is. Amen. (1 Nephi 9:6.)	1. The Lord knows all things. 2. He accomplishes all his works. 3. He has all power.

Though these three concepts are not specifically mentioned in the vision, they become pivotal in our understanding of (1) how Nephi could be shown what he saw; and (2) what he saw. We shall say more about these important concepts later in the paper.

And it came to pass after I, Nephi, having heard all the words of my father, concerning the things which he saw in a vision, and also the things which he spake by the power of the Holy Ghost, which power he received by faith on the Son of God— and the Son of God was the Messiah who should come— I, Nephi, was desirous also that I might see, and hear, and know of these things, by the power of the Holy Ghost, which is the gift of God unto all those who diligently seek him, as well	4. Lehi saw and spake marvelous things by the power of the Holy Ghost. 5. He received that power by faith. 6. Nephi wanted to *see* and *hear* and *know* the same things by the same power. 7. This power is the gift of God unto all men who diligently seek him.

in times of old as in the time
that he should manifest
himself unto the children of
men (1 Nephi 10:17).

This seems to be Nephi's way of disclaiming any unique or privileged status from his having seen the vision. He recognized (1) that it came from God; (2) that it came because of faith; and (3) that others of faith can have the same thing.

Nephi's expressed desire "that [he] might *see*, and *hear*, and *know*, of these things" (verse 17; italics added) was literally fulfilled. As we look at the language of the vision, the sensory reality of the experience is dramatically underscored. For example, Nephi was commanded to "Look" or "Behold" approximately forty times in the course of the vision. The pattern wherein the angel or the Spirit says, "Look!" and Nephi then says, "I looked and beheld," is repeated no less than sixteen times (1 Nephi 11:8, 24, 26–27, 32). Nephi uses the phrase "I saw" or "I beheld" almost a hundred times as he recounts the vision, and he used some form of *see, look,* or *behold* over 175 times in the four chapters or, on the average, 1.33 times per verse.

The Prophetic Experience

It may be of interest to analyze briefly exactly what it was Nephi "saw" or experienced. At least three major kinds of things can be identified:

1. He saw things outside the real world, things whose primary meaning is symbolic. These would include things such as the tree of life (11:8); the rod of iron (11:25); the river of water (12:16) or the great and spacious building (11:35).

2. He saw future events unfolding in a linear fashion, that is, one major item at a time. For example, he saw Mary and the birth of the Savior (11:13–20); the ministry, trial, and crucifixion of Jesus (11:31–33); the Savior's visit to the Nephites (12:6); and many other events that were yet future to Nephi.

3. He saw future events unfolding in a grand sweep; numerous things were happening simultaneously. Good examples of this type of experience would include his seeing "many gen-

erations pass away, . . . and . . . many cities'' (12:3). In another place he said he beheld "many nations and kingdoms" (13:2). This kind of experience seems analogous to that of Moses when he "discerned" every particle and inhabitant of the earth by the Spirit of God (see Moses 1:27–28).

For he is the same yesterday, to-day, and forever; and the way is prepared for all men from the foundation of the world, if it so be that they repent and come unto him.

8. God never changes.

9. The mysteries of God will be revealed to those who seek them.

For he that diligently seeketh shall find; and the mysteries of God shall be unfolded unto them, by the power of the Holy Ghost, as well in these times as in times of old, and as well in times of old as in times to come; wherefore, the course of the Lord is one eternal round.

10. This will be done by the power of the Holy Ghost.

11. No unclean thing can dwell in God's presence.

Therefore remember, O man, for all thy doings thou shalt be brought into judgment.

12. God has prepared a way for men to return to him.

Wherefore, if ye have sought to do wickedly in the days of your probation, then ye are found unclean before the judgment-seat of God; and no unclean thing can dwell with God; wherefore, ye must be cast off forever. (1 Nephi 10:18–21.)

13. These promises hold true in all ages.

How We Get the Mysteries of God and Why

As we compare the points made in these last verses with those made in verse 17, we see several reiterations. And when we tie them to the major premises laid down in 1 Nephi 9:6, we see that Nephi set up an interesting sequence of God's operation. Diagrammed, it could look something like this:

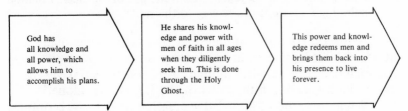

God has all knowledge and all power, which allows him to accomplish his plans.

He shares his knowledge and power with men of faith in all ages when they diligently seek him. This is done through the Holy Ghost.

This power and knowledge redeems men and brings them back into his presence to live forever.

Nephi then concluded his introduction of these principles by bearing testimony: "And the Holy Ghost giveth authority that I should speak these things, and deny them not" (1 Nephi 10:22).

Once a person accepts these premises (or this chain of reasoning, if you will), the vision which follows becomes a logical sequence of what Nephi said. In other words, not only is the vision of Nephi itself proof that God knows all things and will reveal his knowledge to men, but the content of the vision likewise validates that God is working and will continue to work his plan of redemption—through the ministry of the Savior, through the establishment of America, through the coming forth of the Book of Mormon, and so on—so that all who seek him can return to his presence.

Some Challenging Questions

Nephi's logical chain is simple but powerful, and yet it raises numerous questions—not questions of doubt, but questions which seek understanding. To say that God has all power and all knowledge is a staggering concept to the finite mind, especially in our generation, when we are starting to grasp the vastness of the universe around us. When Nephi says the Lord knows all things, does that truly imply that He has all knowledge in the universe?

An article some years ago in *National Geographic* used a graphic example to help us better conceptualize the vastness of the space that surrounds us.

How can the human mind deal with the knowledge that the farthest object we can see in the universe is perhaps ten billion light-years away? Imagine that the thickness of this page represents the distance from earth to sun (93,000,000 miles, or about eight light-minutes). Then the distance to the nearest star (4-⅓ light-years) is a 71-foot-high sheaf of paper. And the diameter of our own galaxy (100,000 light-years) is a 310-mile stack, while the edge of the known universe is not reached until the pile of paper is 31 million miles high—a third of the way to the sun![1]

Astronomers now estimate that there may be as many as a hundred billion galaxies in the known universe. With the huge 200-inch telescope on Mt. Palomar, astronomers can see as many as a million galaxies in the bowl of the Big Dipper alone.[2]

While this kind of knowledge greatly supports the scriptural concept of a God who has created innumerable worlds (see, for example, Moses 1:33, 37), it also raises some challenging questions about how God manages to oversee all of his dominions. Even if he is capable of traveling at the speed of light, it still leaves insurmountable time problems.

Let us illustrate with just one example. Abraham told us by means of the Urim and Thummim that the star nearest to the throne of God is called Kolob (Abraham 3:3). Assuming for a moment that Kolob was in our own Milky Way Galaxy, it still leaves a staggering time question, since our own solar system is approximately thirty thousand light years out from the hub of the Milky Way in one of the spiral arms.[3] Even if we assume Kolob is somewhere near the center of our own galaxy, it would still take a being moving at the speed of light thirty thousand years to travel from Kolob to earth! In other words, if God were moving at the speed of light, he would have had to leave Kolob twenty-four thousand years before the fall of Adam in order to appear to Joseph Smith in the Sacred Grove in the spring of 1820!

The same kinds of time questions surface with prayer. How can a prayer, even if it moves at the speed of light, cross the mind-boggling immensity of space to be heard by our Heavenly Father?

Equally difficult is the question of God's knowledge of the future. Nephi said that God knows everything. Does that include the future? Obviously! He has foretold many events, sometimes millennia before they actually occur. The Savior taught that his Father knows what we need even *before* we ask it in prayer (see Matthew 6:8). One might assume from that that in some cases he might know what we need before *we* even know it! And therein is the difficult question. If God knows whether a person will marry in the temple (or be baptized, or sin, or whatever) before he does it, how can that person be free to exercise agency?

One final question raised by these concepts is how does the Lord *show* (that is, allow them to see) prophets like Nephi something that hasn't happened yet?

A Question of Time

With a little thought, we see that all of these questions are questions of time. How does God go so far so fast, really means how does he do so in so little time? Things happening in the future really means they happen in a time that has still not happened to us.

There are several scriptures that suggest that God may not be bound by the same system of time as we are. For that matter, these scriptures suggest he may actually *perceive* time differently than we do. For example, Alma told his son Corianton that "all is as one day with God, and time only is measured unto men" (Alma 40:8). In the Doctrine and Covenants, the Lord revealed that "all things are present before mine eyes" (D&C 38:2). There are two definitions of the word *present*. One is geographical. To be present is to be *here*. The other is temporal. To be present is to be *now*. In which sense does the Lord mean "all things are present before mine eyes"? Does he mean all things are *here* before me, or all things are *now* before me? We shall examine some evidence that suggests that both are correct.

Another scripture in the Doctrine and Covenants suggests that past, present, and future are "continually before the Lord" (D&C 130:7). Lael Woodbury, using that scripture as a springboard, speculates that all of these questions on time that trouble us may be due to the fact that our perception of time is restricted.

You and I don't yet have that facility of viewing time as an essence. But we will. That is part of what it must mean to be exalted. Right now we perceive . . . time as a blind man perceives form in space—sequentially. He explores with his fingers, noting form, texture, contours, rhythms. He holds each perception in his mind, one by one, carefully adding one to the other, until he synthesizes this concept of what that space object must be like. You and I don't do that. We perceive a space object immediately. We simply look at it, and to a certain degree we "know" it. We do not go through a one-by-one, sequential, additive process. We perceive that it is, and we are able to distinguish it from any other object. I'm suggesting that God perceives time as instantaneously as we perceive space. For us, time is difficult. Lacking higher facility, we are as blind about time as a sightless man is about space. We perceive time in the same way that we perceive music— sequentially.[4]

A Question of Relativity

There is something in the human psyche that rebels at seeing the future, something that hasn't happened yet, as happening now. Every logical fiber of our being rejects it, for every experience we have had contradicts it. But again, just in our generation, some scientific theories of space and time have been widely accepted that seem just as strange to our experience. One such theory is Albert Einstein's theory of relativity. It has some fascinating implications for our understanding of the attributes and nature of God.

It will be left to those more qualified than I to explain this theory. Suffice it to say that the unexpectedness of the ideas about time and space that were merely introduced by Einstein and others makes clear that the universe is very different from our naive notions. God's ability to see and know the future and how he was and is able to show his prophets future events such as those described in Nephi's visions may well be explained by properties of time and space that are even more surprising than those proposed by Einstein.

Modern scripture supports the idea that *time* is relative, that is, there is no absolute standard of time that exists throughout the entire universe. Abraham was told that one revolution (or day) on Kolob equals a thousand of our years (Abraham 3:4). If one were to carry the ratio down to smaller units of time we see some interesting implications.

Kolob Time	Earth Time
1 day	1,000 years
1 hour	41.67 years
1 minute	253 days
1 second	4.22 days
.25 second	1.1 days
.01 second	1 hour

Think of the implications of that. While a person on Kolob takes a two-hour nap, a person on Earth is born, lives to the age of eighty, and dies before the other awakens. One blink on the part of a Kolobian and he misses one whole day of ours.

That God's power is limitless is made clear in the scriptures. This is the incredibly awesome power that allows him to say, "I . . . spake, and the world was made" (D&C 38:3; see also Genesis 1:3). It is the power that can move a mountain or take note of even a sparrow's fall (see Ether 12:30; Matthew 10:29–31).

This concept gives added significance to Nephi's basic premise, which could now be turned around to read: God "prepareth a way to accomplish all his works among the children of men" precisely and specifically because (1) he "knoweth all things from the beginning" and (2) "he hath all power" (1 Nephi 9:6). That is a marvelous summary of God's attributes, but equally miraculous to Nephi is the fact that God willingly shares that knowledge and power with faithful men of all ages. As Nephi so powerfully bore witness:

> For he that diligently seeketh shall find; and the mysteries of God shall be unfolded unto them, by the power of the Holy Ghost, as well in these times as in times of old, and as well in times of old as in times to come; wherefore, the course of the Lord is one eternal round (1 Nephi 10:19).

NOTES AND REFERENCES

1. Kenneth F. Weaver, "The Incredible Universe," *National Geographic*, vol. 145, no. 5, May 1974, p. 592.

2. Ibid.

3. This is only an assumption for purposes of illustration. The scriptures give no clue as to the actual location of Kolob. It could just as easily be in a galaxy millions of light years from our own.

4. Lael J. Woodbury, "Continually Before the Lord," Commissioner's Lecture Series, 1974, pp. 5–6.

11

ANOTHER TESTAMENT OF JESUS CHRIST

Robert L. Millet

The Prophet Joseph Smith stated in 1841 that a man could get "nearer to God by abiding by" the precepts of the Book of Mormon "than by any other book."[1] Those who have made the Book of Mormon more than casual reading know of the truthfulness of the Prophet's declaration; they can testify with President Ezra Taft Benson that the serious study of this sacred volume can bring "spiritual and intellectual unity to [one's] whole life."[2] The Book of Mormon has been preserved and prepared with our day in mind. Prophets and noble men who wrote on the plates knew of our day, sensed and saw our challenges, and were fully aware of the sublime strength that the Nephite/Jaredite record could be in a troubled and uncertain world (see Mormon 8:35; 9:30). The Book of Mormon has been given to bring men and women to Christ—to point them toward the reality of his existence, to bear witness of his divine Sonship, and to demonstrate how the peace which comes through a remis-

---

Robert L. Millet is Assistant Professor of Ancient Scripture at Brigham Young University.

sion of sins here and the ultimate peace through salvation hereafter are to be had through calling on his holy name, and in no other way. The Book of Mormon brings men to Christ because it is a masterful revelation of him, an additional witness (with the New Testament) that he "hath abolished death, and hath brought life and immortality to light through the gospel" (2 Timothy 1:10). It is indeed "another testament of Jesus Christ."[3]

The Need for Another Testament

In a revelation given at the time of the organization of the restored Church, the Lord explained that the Book of Mormon had been given for the purpose of "proving to the world that the holy scriptures are true" (D&C 20:11). Presumably the expression *the holy scriptures* refers to the Bible. That is to say, the Nephite record has been delivered to this final dispensation to establish the truthfulness of the biblical record, or, in the words of Mormon, "this [the Book of Mormon] is written for the intent that [we] might believe that [the Bible]" (Mormon 7:9). The Book of Mormon establishes clearly that the Bible is the "book of the Lamb of God" (1 Nephi 13:28); that Old and New Testament characters like Adam and Eve, Noah, Abraham, Moses, David, Solomon, John the Baptist, and John the Beloved were real persons through whom God fulfilled his purposes; that the miracles and wonders described in the Bible (for example, crossing the Red Sea, healings through looking upon the brazen serpent, displacing the Canaanites from the promised land) are genuine manifestations of divine power.

Most important, the Book of Mormon attests that Jehovah, the God of ancient Israel, truly became the Son of the Highest; that Jesus of Nazareth came to earth through birth and took upon himself a physical body; that he submitted to the throes and pains of mortality; and that he lived a sinless life, took upon him the sins of all mankind on conditions of repentance, was crucified, died, and rose again three days later into glorious immortality. In other words, the Book of Mormon is another testament of the *gospel*, the glad tidings that deliverance from death and hell and endless torment is available through the infinite atonement and by obedience to the laws and ordinances of the gospel. (See 3 Nephi 27:13–21.)

In a time when men are eager to acknowledge Jesus of Nazareth as a great teacher, as a model of morality and decency, and as the prototype of purity and peaceful living—but who in the same breath deny his divinity—the prophets of the Book of Mormon boldly declare that Jesus is the Christ, the Eternal God; that he has power to forgive sins, power over life and death, and that as the Holy One of Israel he is the "keeper of the gate," the Eternal Judge of both quick and dead. It has become fashionable among some biblical scholars during the last century to undertake the "quest for the historical Jesus," seeking through form-critical methods to peel away the traditions of the centuries concerning the God-Man until they would arrive, as some suppose, at a simple picture of the lowly Nazarene. However, in the words of F. F. Bruce: "Perhaps the most important result to which Form Criticism points is that, no matter how far back we may press our researches into the roots of the gospel story, no matter how we classify the gospel material, we never arrive at a non-supernatural Jesus."[4] The Book of Mormon saves us "the quest." It attests that Jesus was God before he came to earth and the promised Messiah and Savior on earth.

Lehi and Nephi: A Remarkable Vision

Some time after Nephi and his brothers had returned from their journey to Jerusalem to get Ishmael and his family, Lehi announced: "I have dreamed a dream; or, in other words, I have seen a vision" (1 Nephi 8:2). In the words of a modern Apostle, "All inspired dreams are visions, but all visions are not dreams. Visions are received in hours of wakefulness or of sleep and in some cases when the recipient has passed into a trance; it is only when the vision occurs during sleep that it is termed a dream."[5] Lehi, a visionary man and designated prophet of God, declared that he had been the recipient of a prophetic revelation. The dream, which most Latter-day Saints have read numerous times, is a literary masterpiece and a doctrinal gem. In a personal way, the dream provided Lehi with a forum for family instruction: the great patriarch expressed deep concern that his elder sons, Laman and Lemuel, would not pay the price sufficient to press forward on the strait and narrow path which led to the tree of life, and thus would never know of the consummate joys associated with full participation in the plan of the Father (1 Nephi 8:3–4, 12–18).

In a more general way, the dream provided a vivid description of four main groups of people, types and representations of all walks of life, persons with varying spiritual aptitudes and diverse degrees of sensitivity toward things of righteousness. This part of the dream (1 Nephi 8:21–33) might well be called the parable of the path. It has fascinating similarities to the parable of the soils in the New Testament (Matthew 13:3–8, 18–23), and stresses the differences in spiritual receptivity. According to Lehi's vision, to navigate the path and arrive securely at the tree of life, one was required to hold tenaciously to the rod (word of God), pass safely through the mists of darkness (temptations of the devil), avoid detours from the path which might lead to the waters of filthiness (depths of hell) beneath the path,[6] and ignore the taunting voices of ridicule of those situated in the great and spacious building (the pride and wisdom of the world).

Nephi explained that he was desirous to "see, and hear, and know" of the same things which his father had experienced in vision. Knowing full well that God was no respecter of persons, that the Almighty constantly reveals the things of eternity to those who seek him in faithfulness and in truth, and, in his own words, "believing that the Lord was able to make them known unto me, as I sat pondering in mine heart I was caught away in the Spirit of the Lord, yea, into an exceedingly high mountain, which I never had before seen, and upon which I never had before set my foot." (1 Nephi 10:17–11:1.) Mountains are frequently the meetingplaces between God and men; they serve as nature's temples, the point of intersection between the finite and the infinite. As is so often the case, Nephi's meditation upon the things of the Spirit resulted in a heavenly manifestation (cf. D&C 76:11–19; 138:1–11); he received the same vision his father had received.

Nephi's rendition of his vision, given to us in 1 Nephi 11–14, is obviously a much more extensive account than that which Lehi delivered in 1 Nephi 8. It is a vision not only of the tree of life, but also a glimpse of the future destiny of the world, a vision not unlike that given to the brother of Jared, Enoch, Moses, and John the Revelator. And yet, Nephi himself explained to us later: "I, Nephi, am forbidden that I should write the remainder of the things which I saw and heard; wherefore the things which I have written sufficeth me; and I have written but a small part of the things which I saw. And *I bear record that I saw the things which my father saw*, and the angel of the Lord did make them known unto me." (1 Nephi 14:28–29, italics added.) Nephi's words, spoken here at the end of the vision, seem to imply not simply that his vision comprehended or circumscribed that of his father's (and thus he had seen what his father saw *and much more*), but rather that they had beheld the same vision. Let us note here that Nephi had earlier observed (1 Nephi 1:16–17) that the opening chapters of the small plates would be devoted to an abridgment of some of his father's experiences (now chapters 1–8), while he would soon come to devote the remainder of his record to an account of his own life (see, for example, 1 Nephi 10:1). Lehi spoke "all the words of his dream or vision" to his family, "which," Nephi hastened to add, *"were many"* (1 Nephi 8:36; italics added). In 1 Nephi 8, therefore, we are introduced to the vision of the tree of life, an obvious abridgment of Lehi's much lengthier spiritual experience. We turn, however, to subsequent chapters—chapters 11, 12, and 15—for Nephi's commentary and explanation of the vision and the specific symbolism involved.

Nephi's Guides in the Vision

Having been caught away to a high mountain for instruction, Nephi was asked by a personage whom he calls "the Spirit": "What desirest thou?" Nephi answered promptly: "I desire to behold the things which my father saw." (1 Nephi 11:1–3.) Then followed a series of questions, answers, and visual explanations to the young Nephite seer. Having been shown the vision of the tree, the same which Lehi had beheld, Nephi was asked, "What desirest thou?" to which he responded, "To know the interpretation thereof—for I spake unto him as a man speaketh; for *I beheld that he was in the form of a man;* yet nevertheless, *I knew that it was the Spirit of the Lord*; and he spake unto me as a man speaketh with another" (1 Nephi 11:9–11, italics added). One is faced right away with an interesting theological question: is Nephi's guide, designated by him as "the Spirit of the Lord," the premortal Christ (the individual spirit personage who became Jesus Christ in mortality) or the Holy Ghost?

If this is a personal appearance of the Holy Ghost to a man, it is indeed a singular occasion, so far as our scriptural accounts are concerned.[7] In addressing this issue some years ago, Sidney B. Sperry suggested the latter alternative—that the "Spirit of the Lord" was the Holy Ghost—based upon the following textual evidence.[8] First, we read of Nephi's desires (in the preceding chapter) to "see, and hear, and know of these things, *by the power of the Holy Ghost.*" He further testified that the Holy Ghost gave authority for his words. (See 1 Nephi 10:17–22, italics added.) Second, Nephi used phrases like "the Spirit said," "the Spirit cried," and "I said unto the Spirit" (verses 2, 4, 6, 8, 9), all of which sound very much like reference to the Holy Ghost rather than Jehovah. Third, Nephi never spoke of the Lord Jesus Christ as the "Spirit of the Lord" when the Master appeared to him on other occasions (1 Nephi 2:16; 2 Nephi 11:2–3). Fourth, the phrase *Spirit of the Lord* occurs some forty times in the Book of Mormon, and in every case reference seems to be to either the Holy Ghost or the Light of Christ. Examples of this would be 1 Nephi 1:12, where Lehi, having read from the book delivered to him, was filled with the "Spirit of the Lord"; 1 Nephi 13:15, where the "Spirit of the Lord" was poured out upon the Gentiles in preparation for the establishment of the American nation; Mosiah 4:3, where the "Spirit of the Lord" came upon the people of King Benjamin and they experienced a remission of sins and its subsequent joy; and, of course, those references wherein the expression *Spirit of the Lord* is used after the mortal ministry of Jesus Christ, places where these words could only mean the Holy Ghost (for example, Mormon 2:26; 5:16; Moroni 9:4). "The Holy Ghost undoubtedly possesses personal powers and affections," Elder James E. Talmage has written. "These attributes exist in Him in perfection. . . . That the Spirit of the Lord is capable of manifesting Himself in the form and figure of man," Elder Talmage continued, "is indicated by the wonderful interview between the Spirit and Nephi, in which He revealed Himself to the prophet, questioned him concerning his desires and belief, instructed him in the things of God, speaking face to face with the man."[9]

After explaining to the Holy Ghost that he sought the meaning behind the representation of the tree of life, Nephi "looked as if to look upon " the Spirit, "and [he] saw him not; for he had gone from before [his] presence" (1 Nephi 11:12). Nephi was then caught away into vision again, this time beholding many of the cities of the Holy Land, specifically Nazareth of Galilee. The heavens were opened to Nephi and "an angel came down and stood before" him. This angel, whose identity is not given, became Nephi's guide and instructor throughout the remainder of his panoramic vision, providing both prophetic sight and doctrinal insight into such future matters as the coming of Jesus Christ to both hemispheres; the formation of the great and abominable church; the journey of Columbus and the establishment of the American nation under divine direction; the plain and precious truths taken away and kept back from the Bible; the spread of the great and abominable church and the church of the Lamb to all nations of the earth; and the winding up scenes preparatory to the coming of the Lord in glory.

The Condescension of God

Nephi's attention was drawn specifically to Nazareth of Galilee. There he "beheld a virgin, and she was exceedingly fair and white."[10] The angel then asked Nephi a penetrating question: "Knowest thou the condescension of God?" (1 Nephi 11:13–16.) To condescend is literally to "go down with" or to "go down among." It is "the act of descending to a lower and less dignified state; or waiving the privileges of one's rank and status; of bestowing honors and favors upon one of lesser stature or status."[11] The angel's question might be restated thus: "Nephi, do you fathom the majesty of it all? Can your mortal mind comprehend the infinite wonder and grandeur of the marvelous love made manifest by the Father and the Son?" Nephi answered: "I know that he loveth his children; nevertheless, I do not know the meaning of all things" (1 Nephi 11:17). One of the remarkable discoveries of those who come to know him who is Eternal is that God's infinity as the Almighty does not preclude either his immediacy or his intimacy as a loving Father of spirits. Enoch learned this precious lesson during his ministry (see Moses 7:28–32), and Nephi evidenced his knowledge of the same principles.

The "condescension of God" described in 1 Nephi 11 seems to be twofold: the condescension of God the Father (verses 16–23) and the condescension of God the Son (verses 24–36). "Without overstepping the bounds of propriety by saying more than is appropriate," Elder Bruce R. McConkie has written, "let us say this: God the Almighty; the Maker and Preserver and Upholder of all things; the Omnipotent One . . . elects, in his fathomless wisdom, to beget a Son, an Only Son, the Only Begotten in the flesh. God, who is infinite and immortal, condescends to step down from his throne, to join with one who is finite and mortal in bringing forth, 'after the manner of the flesh,' the Mortal Messiah."[12] In the words of President Ezra Taft Benson, "The Church of Jesus Christ of Latter-day Saints proclaims that Jesus Christ is the Son of God in the most literal sense. The body in which He performed His mission in the flesh was sired by that same Holy Being we worship as God, our Eternal Father. Jesus was not the son of Joseph, nor was He begotten by the Holy Ghost. He is the Son of the Eternal Father!"[13]

The condescension of God the Son consists in the coming to earth of the great Jehovah, the Lord God Omnipotent, the God of the ancients. The 1830 edition of the Book of Mormon contains the following words from the angel to Nephi: "Behold, the virgin whom thou seest is the *mother of God*, after the manner of the flesh" (1 Nephi 11:18; italics added). The angel later said unto Nephi regarding the vision of the Christ child: "Behold the Lamb of God, yea, *the Eternal Father*!" (1 Nephi 11:21; italics added; cf. 1 Nephi 13:40, 1830 edition). Later in the same vision of the ministry of Christ, the angel spoke, saying: "Look! And I looked," Nephi added, "and beheld the Lamb of God, that he was taken by the people; yea, *the everlasting God* was judged of the world; and I saw and bear record" (1 Nephi 11:32; italics added). In the 1837 edition of the Book of Mormon, Joseph Smith the Prophet changed these verses to read "the mother of *the Son of* God," "the *Son of the* Eternal Father," and "the *Son of the* everlasting God," respectively. It would appear that the Prophet made these textual alterations to assist the Latter-day Saints in fully understanding the meaning of the expressions.[14]

Critics of the Church or myopic historians are eager to point up these changes as illustrative of Joseph Smith's changing views on the doctrine of the Godhead, an example of pre- and post-1835 theology; some would suppose that Joseph was tied to a type of "trinitarianism" before his theology "developed" over time, and would thus place (inappropriately) the Book of Mormon within that developmental process. Such a conclusion is both unwarranted and incorrect. For one thing, the Book of Mormon writers make scores of references to the distinct identities of Jesus Christ and his Father.[15] One need only read Nephi's words in 2 Nephi 25, regarding the necessity of the Jews believing in Christ and worshiping the Father in his name (verse 16) to appreciate the distinctness of the members of the Godhead in the minds of Nephite prophets. In addition, in 2 Nephi 31 we note the constant reference to the "words of the Father" as opposed to the "words of the Son." In our chapter now under consideration (1 Nephi 11), we read in verse 24 (italics added) these words: "And I looked, and I beheld *the Son of God* going forth among the children of men; and I saw many fall down at his feet and worship him" (see also verse 7; Alma 5:50). The Prophet Joseph Smith's alterations in previous verses—mother of *the Son of* God and the *Son of the* Eternal Father—are perfectly consistent with the description of Christ in verse 24.[16]

Mary was indeed the "mother of God," and Jesus Christ was the "Eternal Father," the "everlasting God" (cf. Mosiah 15:4; 16:15; Alma 11:38–39). The condescension of God the Son thus consists in the fact that the Eternal One would "descend from his throne divine" (*Hymns*, 1985, no. 193), be born in the most humble of circumstances, become among the most helpless of all creation—a human infant—and submit to the refining influences of mortal life. An angel further explained the condescension of God the Son to King Benjamin: "The time cometh, and is not far distant," he prophesied, "that with power, the Lord Omnipotent who reigneth, who was, and is from all eternity to all eternity, shall come down from heaven among the children of men, and shall dwell in a tabernacle of clay." Further, Jehovah, the God of creation, "shall suffer temptations, and pain of body, hunger, thirst, and fatigue, even more than man can suffer, except it be unto death." (Mosiah 3:5, 7.) The condescension of the Son—his ministry among the unenlightened, his suffering and death, followed by the persecution and death of his anointed servants—is described by Nephi in 1 Nephi 11:27–36.

Inextricably tied to the concept of the Incarnation, of the condescension of the Great God, is the awful irony of the suffering and atonement of our Lord. He who was sinless was persecuted and put to death by sinners whom he came to save. He who was sinless became, as it were, the great sinner. In Paul's words, God the Father has "made him to be sin for us, who knew no sin" (2 Corinthians 5:21). He who deserved least of all to suffer suffered most—more than mortal mind can fathom. He who had brought light and life—the more abundant life (John 10:10)—was rejected by the powers of darkness and death. As Joseph Smith taught the members of the School of the Prophets in Kirtland, Jesus Christ is called the *Son* of God because he "descended in suffering below that which man can suffer; or, in other words, suffered greater sufferings, and was exposed to more powerful contradictions than any man can be."[17] All this Nephi saw in vision, including the persecution and deaths of the Twelve Apostles after the crucifixion and ascension of the Master (1 Nephi 11:24–36).

The Tree of Life

After Nephi had explained that he desired to see the things his father had seen, the Spirit asked what appears, at first blush, to be a most unusual question: "Believest thou that thy father saw the tree of which he hath spoken?" Nephi answered the query: "Yea, thou knowest that I believe all the words of my father." (1 Nephi 11:3–5.) One wonders about the Spirit's question: why did the angel not ask Nephi if he believed that his father had seen a large and spacious building, or mists of darkness, or a strait and narrow path, or a rod of iron? The fact is, faith is not exercised in trees, and the Spirit of the Lord was not simply inquiring into Nephi's knowledge of a form of plant life. Indeed, it was not a belief in the tree which would qualify Nephi for the manifestation to follow; nor was this the concern of the Spirit. The tree was obviously a doctrinal symbol, a "sign" which pointed beyond itself to an even greater reality. Yet the tree was of marvelous importance, for it was the symbol, even from the time of the Edenic paradise, of the central and saving role of Jesus Christ and the glorified immortality to be enjoyed by the faithful through his atoning sacrifice. Nephi's vision was to be more than an involvement with an abstract concept called the "love of God" (1 Nephi 11:22); it was a messianic message, a poignant prophecy of him toward whom all men press forward on that strait and narrow path which leads to life eternal.

"My soul delighteth in proving unto my people," Nephi would later say, "the truth of the coming of Christ; for, for this end hath the law of Moses been given; and *all things which have been given of God* from the beginning of the world, unto man, *are the typifying of him*" (2 Nephi 11:4; italics added; compare Moses 6:63). In reference to this verse, Elder Bruce R. McConkie has written: "It follows that if we had sufficient insight, we would see in every gospel ordinance, in every rite that is part of revealed religion, in every performance commanded of God, in all things Deity gives his people, something that typifies the eternal ministry of the Eternal Christ."[18] It is just so with the vision enjoyed by Lehi and Nephi: it is Christ-centered and to be fully appreciated only by focusing attention upon him who is the author of salvation. Consider the following:

1. After Nephi had certified his belief in the fact that his father saw the tree, the Spirit "cried with a loud voice, saying:

Hosanna to the Lord, the most high God; for he is God over all the earth, yea, even above all. And *blessed art thou, Nephi, because thou believest in the Son of the most high God*; wherefore, thou shalt behold the things which thou hast desired." (1 Nephi 11:6; italics added.) Note that the angel rejoiced over Nephi's *faith in Christ*, not simply in his belief in a tree.

2. The words of the Spirit continue: "And behold this thing shall be given unto thee for *a sign*, that after thou hast beheld *the tree* which bore the fruit which thy father tasted, thou shalt also behold *a man* descending out of heaven, and him shall ye witness; and after ye have witnessed him ye shall bear record that *it is the Son of God*" (1 Nephi 11:7; italics added). The Spirit here began to unfold the typology to Nephi. The tree has been given, "for a sign," as a symbolic representation of a man, even he whose branches provide sacred shade and shelter from the scorching rays of sin and ignorance.

3. Consider Nephi's description of the tree: "The beauty thereof was far beyond, yea, exceeding of all beauty; and the whiteness thereof did exceed the whiteness of the driven snow" (1 Nephi 11:8). Whiteness generally symbolizes purity. Jesus of Nazareth was the purest of pure, for he lived without spot or blemish, the only mortal to achieve moral perfection through never wandering from the path of righteousness (see 2 Corinthians 5:21; Hebrews 4:15; 1 Peter 2:22).

4. After Nephi had been asked concerning his knowledge of the condescension of God and had then seen Mary "carried away in the Spirit for the space of a time," he "looked and beheld the virgin again, bearing a child in her arms." Nephi's account continues: "And the angel said unto me: Behold the Lamb of God, yea, even the Son of the Eternal Father! *Knowest thou the meaning of the tree which thy father saw?*" That is, while looking at the Christ child, it is as if the angel were summing up, bringing Nephi back to the point where he had begun—the deeper significance of the tree. Essentially Nephi was asked, "Now, Nephi, do you finally understand the meaning of the tree? Now do you

171

understand the message behind the sign?'' And he answered: "Yea, *it is the love of God,* which sheddeth itself abroad in the hearts of the children of men; wherefore, it is the most desirable above all things.'' The angel then added by way of confirmation: "Yea, and the most joyous to the soul.'' (1 Nephi 11:19−23; italics added.) Nephi's answer was perfect: it was an understanding given by the power of the Holy Ghost. Again, the tree represented more than an abstract emotion, more than a vague (albeit divine) sentiment. It was the greatest manifestation of the love of God—the gift of Christ. "For God so loved the world," Jesus explained to Nicodemus, "that he gave his only begotten Son, that whosoever believeth in him should not perish, but have everlasting life" (John 3:16). That love is made manifest and is extended to all men through the atonement—it *"sheddeth* itself abroad in the hearts of the children of men"—through, appropriately, the blood *shed* in Gethsemane and on Golgotha.[19]

There is no ceiling to the number of saved beings, no limit to the love of the Father which can be received by all who qualify for the fulness of salvation. "And again," Moroni spoke to the Savior, "I remember that thou hast said that thou hast loved the world, even unto the laying down of thy life for the world." Continuing, Moroni added, "And now I know that this love which thou hast had for the children of men is charity." (Ether 12:33−34.) Those who partake of the powers of Christ through repentance gain the blessings mentioned in regard to the people of King Benjamin. "O have mercy," they had pleaded in prayer at the conclusion of the king's mighty sermon, "and apply the atoning blood of Christ that we may receive forgiveness of our sins, and our hearts may be purified; for we believe in Jesus Christ, the Son of God." As a result of their sincere petition, "the Spirit of the Lord came upon them, and they were filled with joy, having received a remission of their sins, and having peace of conscience." (Mosiah 4:2−3.)

5. Finally, we attend carefully to Nephi's words regarding the tree: "And it came to pass that I beheld that the rod of iron, which my father had seen, was the word of God, which led to *the fountain of living waters, or to the tree of life;* which

waters are a representation of the love of God; and I also beheld that the tree of life was a representation of the love of God" (1 Nephi 11:25; italics added). The "fountain of living waters" or "waters of life," linked to the tree of life very often in the literature of the ancient Near East (compare Revelation 22:1–2),[20] would seem to symbolize the cooling draft available through Him alone whose words and works are as an oasis in the desert of the world. "Whosoever drinketh of the water that I shall give him shall never thirst," Jesus said to the Samaritan woman; "but the water that I shall give him shall be in him a well of water springing up into everlasting life" (John 4:14). Finally, in dramatizing the sins of Judah in Lehi's day, the Lord Jehovah spoke to Jeremiah: "For my people have committed two evils; they have forsaken *me the fountain of living waters*, and hewed them out cisterns, broken cisterns, that can hold no water" (Jeremiah 2:13; italics added).

Conclusion

It has wisely been observed that what a person thinks of Christ will largely determine what kind of a person he will be. How then could one utilize his time more profitably than by seriously studying the Book of Mormon, a book whose primary purpose is to reveal and testify of Jesus Christ? We learn from its title page that the Book of Mormon has been preserved and delivered through prophets to us in this day for "the convincing of the Jew and Gentile that Jesus is the Christ, the Eternal God, manifesting himself unto all nations" (compare 2 Nephi 26:12). True to its central theme, and with Christocentric consistency, the Nephite prophets talk of him, preach of him, prophesy of him, and rejoice in him, that all of us might know to what source we may look for a remission of our sins (see 2 Nephi 25:26). Salvation is in Christ. Of that central verity the Book of Mormon leaves no doubt. "And my soul delighteth in proving unto my people," Nephi exulted, "that save Christ should come all men must perish. For if there be no Christ there be no God; and if there be no God we are not, for there could have been no creation. *But there is a God*," Nephi boldly proclaimed, "*and he is Christ*." (2 Nephi 11:6–7; italics added.) The witness has been borne and thus the testament is in force.

NOTES AND REFERENCES

1. *Teachings of the Prophet Joseph Smith,* comp. Joseph Fielding Smith (Salt Lake City: Deseret Book Co., 1976), p. 194.

2. Conference Report, April 1975, p. 97.

3. This appropriate subtitle for the Book of Mormon was announced to the Church by Boyd K. Packer in the 152nd Semiannual General Conference of the Church. See Conference Report, October 1982, p. 75.

4. F. F. Bruce, *The New Testament Documents: Are They Reliable?* (Grand Rapids, Mich.: Eerdmans, 1974), p. 33.

5. Bruce R. McConkie, *Mormon Doctrine,* 2nd ed. (Salt Lake City: Bookcraft, 1966), p. 208.

6. For a discussion of the "gulf" which separated the righteous in paradise from the wicked in hell (see 1 Nephi 12:18; 15:28; 2 Nephi 1:13; Helaman 3:29), see Robert L. Millet and Joseph Fielding McConkie, *The Life Beyond* (Salt Lake City: Bookcraft, 1986), pp. 21–24, 179.

7. It may be that the Holy Ghost appeared in person at the baptism of Jesus, but there is no reference to him conversing with anyone. See Matthew 3:13–17; *Teachings of the Prophet Joseph Smith,* pp. 275–76.

8. Sidney B. Sperry, *Answers to Book of Mormon Questions* (Salt Lake City: Bookcraft, 1967), pp. 27–30; see also Sperry's *Book of Mormon Compendium* (Salt Lake City: Bookcraft, 1968), pp. 116–18.

9. James E. Talmage, *The Articles of Faith* (Salt Lake City: Deseret Book Co., 1975), pp. 159–60. See also Marion G. Romney, Conference Report, April 1974, p. 131.

10. "Can we speak too highly of her whom the Lord has blessed above all women? There was only one Christ, and there is only one Mary. Each was noble and great in preexistence, and each was foreordained to the ministry he or she performed. We cannot but think that the Father would choose the greatest female spirit to be the mother of his Son, even as he chose the male spirit like unto him to be the Savior." (Bruce R. McConkie, *The Mortal Messiah: From Bethlehem to Calvary,* 4 vols. [Salt Lake City: Deseret Book Co., 1979–81], 1:326–27, n.4.)

11. Bruce R. McConkie, "Knowest Thou the Condescension of God?" *Brigham Young University Speeches of the Year,* 16 December 1969 (Provo, Utah: Brigham Young University Press, 1969), pp. 3–4.

12. Bruce R. McConkie, *The Mortal Messiah,* 1:314–15.

13. Ezra Taft Benson, *Come Unto Christ* (Salt Lake City: Deseret Book Co., 1983), p. 4.

14. It may also be that Joseph Smith altered these verses to make certain that no reader—member or nonmember—would confuse the Latter-day Saint understanding of the Father and the Son with that of other Christian

denominations, particularly the Roman Catholic Church. See an article by Oliver Cowdery, "Trouble in the West," in *Latter Day Saints' Messenger and Advocate*, I (April 1835), p. 105.

15. For a more detailed discussion on the roles of both members of the Godhead, see my paper at the First Annual Book of Mormon Symposium (1985), "The Ministry of the Father and the Son," *The Book of Mormon: The Keystone Scripture* (Salt Lake City: Bookcraft, 1987).

16. Joseph Smith spoke the following just eleven days before his death: "I have always declared God to be a distinct personage, Jesus Christ a separate and distinct personage from God the Father, and that the Holy Ghost was a distinct personage and a Spirit: and these three constitute three distinct personages and three Gods." (*Teachings of the Prophet Joseph Smith*, p. 370.)

17. *Lectures on Faith* (Salt Lake City: Deseret Book Co., 1985), 5:2.

18. Bruce R. McConkie, *The Promised Messiah: The First Coming of Christ* (Salt Lake City: Deseret Book Co., 1978), p. 378.

19. It is instructive to consider the language used in this verse: the love of God which *"sheddeth* itself abroad," instead of *"spreadeth* itself abroad," as we might expect Nephi to have said.

20. See John M. Lundquist, "The Common Temple Ideology of the Ancient Near East," in *The Temple in Antiquity*, ed. Truman G. Madsen (Provo, Utah: Religious Studies Center, Brigham Young University, 1984), pp. 53–76.

12

EARLY CHRISTIANITY AND 1 NEPHI 13–14

Stephen E. Robinson

In chapters 13 and 14 of 1 Nephi, the prophet Nephi describes the vision in which he saw the future of the world and its kingdoms as it related to his posterity. Nephi's vision is the type of revelation known in biblical literature as apocalyptic, and it is represented in the New Testament most fully by the Revelation of John. The revelations of Nephi and of John have more in common, however, than merely the apocalyptic form, for Nephi's vision (1 Nephi 14:19–28) anticipates that of John. The two are complementary, centering in part on the same characters and themes: the Lamb and his Church, the Apostasy, the great and abominable church of the devil, and the restoration of the gospel in the latter days. The purpose of this inquiry is to see whether the descriptions given by Nephi, specifically those of the Apostasy and of the great and abominable church, when added to the information of John and other pertinent scriptures, help us draw some historical conclusions about the nature of the Apostasy and the identity of the great and abominable church.

Stephen E. Robinson is Associate Professor of Ancient Scripture at Brigham Young University.

Before proceeding, however, we must define our terms. The Greek word *apostasia* (apostasy) means "rebellion" or "revolution." It conveys the sense of an internal takeover within an organization or institution by factions hostile to the intentions of its previous leaders. I personally prefer the translation "mutiny" for *apostasia*, as it calls up the image of a ship being commandeered by those who are not authorized to do so and being taken in a direction the ship was not intended to go. Since early Christians often thought of the Church as a ship, I think "mutiny" conveys exactly the right sense of what Paul and others meant by the term *apostasy*.

We must also analyze and define the component parts of the phrase *great and abominable church*. The word *great* in this context is an adjective of size rather than of quality and (like the Hebrew *gadol* or the Greek *megas*) informs us of the great size of the abominable entity. Secondary meanings might refer to great wealth or power.[1] The term *abominable* is used in the Old Testament to describe that which God hates, which cannot fail to arouse his wrath. In the book of Daniel the abomination of desolation is that thing which is so hateful to God that its presence in the temple causes the divine presence to depart, leaving the sanctuary desolate. (See Daniel 11:31; 12:11; Matthew 24:15; Joseph Smith—Matthew 1:12-20.) In the Old Testament the terms translated into English as abominable or abomination (Hebrew roots *shiqqutz, ta'ab, piggul*; Greek Septuagint and New Testament *bdelugma*) are usually associated with one of two practices: idolatrous worship or gross sexual immorality.[2]

The term *church* (Hebrew *qahal* or *edah*; Greek *ekklesia*) had a slightly broader meaning anciently than it does now and referred to an assembly, congregation, or association of people which bonded them together and commanded their loyalties. Thus the term was not necessarily restricted to religious associations and, in fact, at Athens was used to denote the legislative assembly of government.[3] When we put all this together it appears that the phrase *great and abominable church* means an immense assembly or association of people bound together by their loyalty to that which God hates. Most likely this will be a religious association involved specifically in sexual immorality and/or idolatry (that is, false worship—abandoning the God of Israel and worshipping anything else).

While the revelation of John does not use the exact term *great and abominable church*, the entity so described by Nephi is clearly the harlot described by John in Revelation 17-18, since the identical terms *mother of abominations, mother of harlots,* and *the whore who sitteth upon many waters* are used by both prophets (see 1 Nephi 14:10–12, 16 and Revelation 17:1, 5). Major characteristics of the great and abominable church in 1 Nephi may be listed as follows:

1. It persecutes, tortures, and slays the Saints of God (13:5).

2. It seeks wealth and luxury (13:7).

3. It is characterized by sexual immorality (13:7).

4. It has excised plain and precious things from the scriptures (13:26–29).

5. It has dominion over all the earth, among all nations, kindreds, tongues, and people (14:11).

6. Its fate is to be consumed by a world war, in which the nations it incited against the Saints turn to war among themselves until they destroy the great and abominable church itself (22:13–14).

These same characteristics are also attributed to the whore (Babylon) in the Revelation of John:

1. She is drunk with the blood of the Saints and with the blood of the martyrs of Jesus and of the prophets (17:6, 18:24).

2. She is characterized by the enjoyment of great wealth and luxury (17:4; 18:3, 11–16).

3. She (naturally) is characterized by sexual immorality (17:1, 2, 5).

4. She has dominion over all nations (17:15, 18; 18:3, 23–24).

5. Her fate is to be consumed by the very kings who have made war on the Lamb under the influence of her deceptions (17:14–16; 18:23).

It should be noted that one characteristic not common to both prophetic descriptions is Nephi's statement that the great and abominable church has held back important parts of the canon of scripture. But since John's record is one of the very scriptures Nephi refers to (14:20–23), this omission in John's account is not surprising.

It must also be noted that in John's Revelation the whore cannot be equated with the two beasts; they do not represent the same things. The whore and the beasts are motivated by the same evil genius, Satan. The one beast supports the whore (Revelation 17:3), but the beast and the whore are separate entities with separate functions in the evil empire. The whore of Revelation 17–18 is specifically the satanic counterpart of the woman in chapter 12 who symbolizes the Church of Jesus Christ which was forced into the wilderness (that is, became inaccessible to human beings). Symbolizing the great and abominable church (the counterfeit) as a whore underscores the nature of her evil: she is physically and spiritually unfaithful, that is, she represents both sexual immorality and idolatry, the twin abominations of the Old Testament. Thus she is the "mother of abominations." It seems that in John's Revelation the symbol of the whore is used narrowly to represent false religion, while the beasts, the image of the beast, and the horns of the beast serve to represent other aspects of the kingdom of the devil. Moreover, if the symbol of the virtuous woman of Revelation 12 is intended to represent specifically the true Church of Jesus Christ (and the crown of Twelve Apostles and her being driven into the wilderness so indicate)[4], it follows that the whore, her counterpart, represents specifically false and counterfeit religion. Satan has more than one institution at his disposal, but the whore is false religion. The whore cannot represent kingdoms or governments—the beast and its horns do that (Revelation 17:12).[5] But she can represent the false beliefs and ideologies that often capture or motivate governments. The whore provides the theory; government provides the muscle. When the false religion represented by the whore is joined to the civil governments (the kings of the earth) represented by the horns of the beast with whom she fornicates, then the wine of their fornication (the results of the union of church and state, or of ideology and police power) plunders the resources of the earth and makes all the world drunk. That is, the power of the state church, or of the church state, seeks to dominate the economy of nations and destroys the spiritual equilibrium and discernment of human beings (Revelation 17:2; 18:3).

Moreover, since the great and abominable church from 1 Nephi is identified in every aspect with the whore, while the beast is never even mentioned in Nephi's vision, it follows that when we discuss *the* great and abominable church, we must not confuse the whore which Nephi saw and described with the beast which he didn't. There are no references to the beasts of Revelation in Nephi's vision of the great and abominable church. As both John and Nephi make clear, the nations outlast the whore, and they eventually destroy her. Both beast and whore are component parts of the kingdom of the devil, but they are *separate* parts even though they sometimes work together.

Perhaps the greatest difficulty in Nephi's description of the great and abominable church is an apparent contradiction between chapters 13 and 14. In 1 Nephi 13 the great and abominable church is one specific church among many. Indeed, Nephi's description of it as "most abominable above all other churches" (verses 5, 26) is nonsense otherwise. Moreover, it has a specific historical description: it is formed among the Gentiles *after* the Bible has been transmitted in its purity to the Gentiles by the Jews (verse 26), and it is the specific historical agent responsible for excising plain and precious truths from the scriptural record. It would appear that in chapter 13 Nephi is describing a specific historical institution as the great and abominable church. To this we must add the information given in Doctrine and Covenants 86:1–4, which states that the great and abominable church did its work after the Apostles had fallen asleep, that is, around the end of the first century A.D. Similarly, in the Revelation of John the role of the whore has a historical frame. She comes into the picture after the beasts, upon which she rides and which give her support, and she is eliminated from the picture while they yet continue. Again, the great and abominable church (Babylon) is not a term identical with "the kingdom of the devil," for the whore is only one of the component parts of a larger empire, together with the beasts, the image, the horns, and the false prophet—and also with other false churches. This last idea is clearly brought out in 1 Nephi 22:22–23:

> But it is *the kingdom of the devil,* which shall be built up among the children of men, which kingdom is established among them which are in the flesh—
> For the time speedily shall come that *all churches* which are built up to get gain, and all those who are built up to get power

over the flesh, and those who are built up to become popular in the eyes of the world, and those who seek the lusts of the flesh and the things of the world, and to do all manner of iniquity; yea, in fine, *all those who belong to the kingdom of the devil* are they who need fear, and tremble. (Italics added.)

Indisputably, the full kingdom of the devil is made up of many churches (or denominations) and will be until the end of the world. Taking 1 Nephi 13 and 22 as our starting points, we might be justified in asking just which of all those false denominations is the *actual* great and abominable church of the devil. The apparent contradiction comes in 1 Nephi 14:10 where we are told that there are only *two* churches: "And he said unto me: Behold there are save two churches only; the one is the church of the Lamb of God, and the other is the church of the devil."

How can this be? How can the devil's church or churches be one and many at the same time? The apparent contradiction actually gives us the solution to the larger puzzle and ultimately our identification of the great and abominable church.

The answer is that the term is used in two different ways in these two chapters. In chapter 13 it is used historically and in chapter 14 it is used typologically, or apocalyptically. In apocalyptic literature (remember that both Revelation and Nephi 13−14 are apocalyptic in nature) the seer is caught up in vision and sees things from God's perspective. Time ceases to be an important element. This is why the chronology of John's Revelation at times seems to be scrambled; with God there is no time. Apocalyptic visions are highly symbolic, usually requiring an angelic interpreter for the seer to understand what he sees. But the symbols are inclusive; that is, they stand for archetypical categories into which all specific instances of something can be placed. This is why the whore can be called Nineveh (some of John's language comes from Nahum's description of Nineveh),[6] or Babylon, Sodom, Egypt, Jerusalem, or Rome. It doesn't matter; the names change, but the character—"that great city"—remains the same in every dispensation. To illustrate, let us take the name of the whore, or great and abominable church: Babylon. A literal reading would lead us to believe that some particular city is being described, and we would want to know which city it was. But if we read carefully, we see that Babylon in John's Revelation is not one city but many cities, all of which fall into the larger category of "that great city" which is the antithesis of the city of God, the heavenly Jerusalem or Zion. Just as Zion is wherever the pure in heart dwell (Doctrine and Covenants 97:21), so Babylon is where the whore lives. Since Latter-day Saints understand that Zion is a spiritual category, which may in different contexts mean Salt Lake City, Far West, Jerusalem, or the city of Enoch, why do we have such a hard time understanding Zion's opposite, Babylon, in the same way? It is precisely this variable identity that Jacob teaches to us when he says: "Wherefore, he that fighteth against Zion, both Jew and Gentile, both bond and free, both male and female, shall perish; *for they are they who are the whore of all the earth; for they who are not for me are against me, saith our God* (2 Nephi 10:16; italics added).

In other words Babylon, "the whore of all the earth," is in this context anyone who fights against Zion. In apocalyptic literature the cast of characters is constant in every dispensation; they are these same archetypical categories into which all things can be placed. From the apocalyptic point of view there is only one script, one plot, from the foundation of the world until its end. The characters in the play and the lines they deliver are always the same from dispensation to dispensation, although the individual actors who play the roles and speak the lines may change with time. Therefore, there is always the role of "that great city," though the part might be played at different times in history by Sodom, Egypt, Nineveh, Babylon, Rome, Berlin, Moscow, or Washington, D.C. The important thing is to know what the archetypical patterns are and their identifying characteristics. Then we can orient ourselves in any time or place and know who functions *now* in the role of Babylon and where Zion is located.

Once we understand that the term *great and abominable church* has two extensions, the one open, inclusive, and archetypical, and the other limited and historical, the rest is easy. In chapter 14, Nephi describes the archetypical roles themselves: "There are save two churches only" (that is, Zion and Babylon). But in chapter 13 he is referring to the specific institution (the actor, if you will) who played the role of Babylon in the Roman Empire in the second century A.D. Nevertheless, it won't do us much good in the twentieth century to know who played Babylon in the second. We need to recognize Babylon now, in our time, although the actors have been changed.

Apocalyptic literature is also dualistic. Since it deals with archetypes, it boils everything down to opposing principles: love and hate, good and evil, light and dark. There are no gray areas in apocalyptic scripture. At the very least, everything can be reduced to the opposing categories of A and not-A ("They who are not for me are against me, saith our God" [2 Nephi 10:16]). In the realm of religion there are only two categories: religion that will save and religion that won't. The former is the church of the Lamb, and the latter—no matter how well intentioned—is a counterfeit. Thus, even a "good" church must still be part of the devil's kingdom in the sense used in 1 Nephi 14 ("there are save two churches only"), for it cannot do what it pretends to do. Nevertheless, such a church cannot be called the great and abominable church in the sense used in 1 Nephi 13, for its intentions are good and honorable, and quite often such churches teach people enough truth that they can then recognize the true church when they meet it. These churches do not slay the Saints of God, they do not seek to control civil governments, nor do they pursue wealth, luxury, and sexual immorality. Such churches may belong to the kindom of the devil in the apocalyptic sense, where there are only two categories, A and not-A, but they cannot be called the great and abominable church in the historical sense— the description is just not accurate. Furthermore, individual orientation to the Church of the Lamb or to the great and abominable church is not only by membership but by loyalty. Just as there are those on the records of The Church of Jesus Christ of Latter-day Saints who belong to the great and abominable church by virtue of their loyalty to Satan and his life-style (2 Nephi 10:16), so there are members of other churches who will eventually belong to the Lamb by virtue of their loyalty to him and to his life-style, which will lead to their accepting the saving ordinances. The distinction is based on who has your heart, not on who has your records.

It seems to me that many Latter-day Saints have made one of two errors in trying to identify the great and abominable church. The first is to believe that some specific denomination or other, to the exclusion of all others, has been the great and abominable church since the beginning of time. This is dangerous, for if we understand the great and abominable church to be one specific church, some will want to know which one it is, and an antagonistic relationship with that church or denomination will inevitably follow. It might, for example, be argued that

Judaism was the great and abominable church. After all, the Jewish religious establishment of that day would seem to qualify on several points. They persecuted the Church and spilled the blood of the Saints. They crucified the Messiah, the Savior of the world. They joined religion together with civil government and used the police power to enforce their religious views. Both Pharisees and Sadducees were reproved by Jesus for their pursuit of wealth at the expense of justice. Jesus told the Pharisees that Satan was their father, and John referred to certain Jewish meetinghouses in Asia as "synagogues of Satan." (Revelation 2:9; 3:9). It was precisely this kind of religious argument—that the Jews were the infidels, the beast, the anti-Christ—that contributed to the Holocaust and that still fans the moral insanity of neo-Nazi religious groups. Has Satan's hand ever been more clearly discernible in any human undertaking? Latter-day Saints do not want to indulge in witch-hunting.

But while Jerusalem in A.D. 30 might have been one manifestation of Babylon,[7] Judaism cannot be the great and abominable church described by Nephi and John. First, the Jews did not and clearly will not enjoy dominion over all the nations of the earth. Second, Nephi says that the scriptures were complete when they came forth from the mouth of a Jew, but were excised by the great and abominable church which had its formation among the Gentiles. And finally, according to the scriptures, it does not seem to be the fate of the Jews to be utterly consumed by the nations of the earth; it appears quite the opposite.

More often it has been suggested that the Roman Catholic Church might be the great and abominable church of 1 Nephi 13, but this is also untenable, primarily because Roman Catholicism as we know it did not yet exist when the crimes described by Nephi were being committed. In fact, the term *Roman Catholic* makes sense only after A.D. 1054, when it began to be used to distinguish the Western, Latin-speaking Orthodox church, which followed the bishop of Rome, from the Eastern, Greek-speaking Orthodox church, which followed the bishop of Constantinople (in association with others). Indeed, in the period between Peter and Constantine, there were other Christian churches besides the orthodox: Ebionites, Syrian and Egyptian Christians, Donatists, Gnostics, Marcionites, etc. We don't know very much about how they were related to each other. Even if we were to use the term "Roman" Catholic for the church which Constantine began making his state religion in A.D. 313 (and the other orthodox churches would object to this), still the New Testament as we know it (that is, without the excised plain and precious parts) had already been widely circulated by then. In other words, the work of the great and abominable church in slaying the Apostles and excising the scriptures had already been done. By the time Constantine joined church and state together in the fourth century, the Apostles had been dead for centuries, and the true church and its keys had already been lost. The commonly held notion of shifty-eyed medieval monks rewriting the scriptures as they copied is bigoted and unfair. In fact, we owe those monks a debt of gratitude that anything was saved at all. Besides, in comparison to some of the other Christian groups around, the orthodox Christians had quite a high standard of morality. By this time they had gone to the extremes of asceticism and can hardly be accused (in this period, anyway) of having many harlots and practicing gross immorality. In fact, in some areas of the ancient world, orthodoxy replaced an earlier more corrupt form of Christianity. Finally, during most of the period before 313, the orthodox were hardly in a position to persecute the Saints, as they were being thrown to the lions themselves.

The Catholic (that is, "universal") Church of the fourth century was the result of the Apostasy, its end product—not its cause. To find the real culprits in the case of the excised texts, we need to look at a much earlier period in Christian church history. None of the Presidents of The Church of Jesus Christ of Latter-day Saints has ever identified Roman Catholicism as the great and abominable church. And, in speaking of Catholic and Protestant faiths, the Prophet Joseph Smith said:

> The old Catholic church traditions are worth more than all you have said. Here is a principle of logic that most men have no more sense than to adopt. I will illustrate it by an old apple tree. Here jumps off a branch and says, I am the true tree, and you are corrupt. If the whole tree is corrupt, are not its branches corrupt? If the Catholic religion is a false religion, how can any true religion come out of it? If the Catholic church is bad, how can any good thing come out of it? The character of the old churches have always been slandered by all apostates since the world began.[8]

It was Martin Luther, not Joseph Smith, who identified the Roman Catholic church as Babylon and the Pope as Antichrist.[9] Besides, are we really to believe that Satan had no ministers in the world before there were Roman Catholics? Was there no Babylon to oppose Zion in the days of Cain, Nimrod, Pharaoh, or Herod?

Finally, I would like to submit that no single historical church or denomination known to us can be *the* great and abominable church in an exclusive sense. No single organization meets all the requirements:

1. It must have been formed among the Gentiles and must have controlled the distribution of the New Testament scriptures, which it edited and from which it deleted plain and precious things.

2. It must have slain the Saints of God and killed the Apostles and prophets.

3. It must be in league with civil governments and use their police power to enforce its religious views.

4. It must have dominion over all the earth.

5. It must pursue wealth, luxury, and sexual immorality, and must last until essentially the end of the world.

No one denomination fits the entire description. Neither does world Communism in our own day. The conclusion is inescapable—no *single* entity can be *the* great and abominable church from the beginning of the world to the end. Rather, the role has been played by many different actors in many different times, and the great and abominable church that Nephi described in 1 Nephi 13 is not the same one that crucified Christ or that martyred Joseph and Hyrum.

So the one error, as I see it, is to try to blame some modern denomination for the activities of an ancient great and abominable church described by both Nephi and John. The other error is to go too far the other way and remove the great and abominable church from history altogether. This latter approach does not acknowledge that there ever was or ever will be a historical manifestation of the great and abominable church. It allegorizes the term completely, so that it becomes merely a vague symbol for all the disassociated evil in the world. We cannot accept this in the face of clear and explicit scripture to the contrary, for if we do, we shall not be able to recognize the historical manifestations of the great and abominable church in our own time or in the times to come. On the one hand, we must avoid the temptation to identify the role of the great and abominable church so completely with one particular denomination that we do not recognize the part when it is played by some other organization, but on the other hand we must remember that the role *will* be played by *some* agency. Will we be able to recognize it?

To return to our original topic, can we identify the historical agency that acted as the great and abominable church in earliest Christianity and which Nephi and others describe? I would like to argue that the great and abominable church Nephi describes in chapter 13 had its origins in the second half of the first century and had essentially done its work by the middle of the second century. This period might be called the blind spot of ecclesiastical history, for it is here that the fewest primary historical sources have been preserved. Essentially, what happened is that we have good sources for New Testament Christianity (the New Testament documents themselves); then the lights go out (that is, we have very few historical sources), and in the dark we hear the muffled sounds of a great struggle. When the lights come on again a hundred years or so later, we find that someone has rearranged all the furniture and that Christianity is something very different from what it was in the beginning. That different entity can be accurately described by the term *hellenized Christianity*. The hellenization of Christianity is a phenomenon which has long been recognized by scholars of Christian history, but it is one which Latter-day Saints know better as the Great Apostasy. Hellenization means imposing Greek culture on the native cultures of the East. The result was a synthesis of East and West, with elements of the Greek West predominating, a melting-pot, popular culture which was virtually worldwide.

But in the realm of religion, synthesis means compromise, and when we speak in terms of the gospel, compromise with the popular culture of the world means apostasy from the truth. When Jewish Christianity and Greek culture met head-on in the gentile mission field in the middle of the first century, the Greeks eventually won, and Jewish Christianity was ultimately "revised" to make it more attractive and appealing to a Greek audience. Primary prejudices of the Hellenistic world were the "absolute" nature of God (that is, he cannot be bound or limited by anything) and the impossibility of anything material or physical being eternal. In order to accommodate these ideas and thus appeal to a broader gentile audience, Christianity had to discard the doctrines of an anthropomorphic God and the resurrection of the dead or else "reinterpret" them in a manner that had the same effect.[10] This is precisely what some Greek Christians at Corinth had already done and against which Paul responds with such force in 1 Corinthians 15:12: "Now if Christ be preached that he rose from the dead, how say some among you that there is no resurrection of the dead?"

One assumption necessary to my line of reasoning is that the earliest apostates from the true primitive Church constituted the great and abominable church among the Gentiles. Therefore we need something to link the Apostasy with the great and abominable church, and I think we have such a link in many places, but two will suffice to make my point here. In 2 Thessalonians 2:3, Paul says: "that day shall not come, except there come a falling away [literally, an apostasy] first, and that man of sin be revealed, the son of perdition." This man of sin will sit in the temple of God showing himself that he is God (verse 4). The "mystery of iniquity" was already under way as Paul wrote (verse 7), and you will recall that one of the names of Babylon is "mystery" (Revelation 17:5). This son of perdition, or man of sin, Paul mentions is the counterfeit for the Man of Holiness—he is Satan.[11] And the temple in which he sits is the church, now desolated of the divine presence by the abomination of apostasy and become the church of the devil.[12] The church of the devil is any church that teaches the philosophies of men mingled with scripture, which dethrones God in the church and replaces him with man (2 Thessalonians 2:3f) by denying the principle of revelation and turning instead to human intellect. It is for this reason that creeds which are the product of human intellect are an *abomination* to the Lord[13]—for they are idolatry: men worshipping the creations not of their own hands but of their own minds and knowing all along it is a creation of their intellect that is being worshipped.

Perhaps my point could be made more quickly by citing Doctrine and Covenants 86:3, where the Lord explicitly identifies the whore, Babylon, as the apostate church:

> And after they have fallen asleep the great persecutor of the church, the apostate, the whore, even Babylon, that maketh all nations to drink of her cup, in whose hearts the enemy, even

Satan, sitteth to reign—behold he soweth the tares; wherefore, the tares choke the wheat and drive the church into the wilderness.

Clearly, whatever denominational name we choose to give it, the great and abominable church described by Nephi and John and the earliest apostate church are identical. The fact is that we do not know really what name to give it. I have proposed hellenized Christianity, but that is a description rather than a name. Babylon in the first and second centuries may even have been a collection of different movements. The Jewish Christians could not let go of the law of Moses and so eventually gave up Christ instead. The "orthodox" adopted Greek philosophy. The Gnostics wallowed in the mysteries and in unspeakable practices on the one hand, or in mysteries and a neurotic asceticism on the other. Tatian and Marcion rewrote the scriptures, the latter boldly chopping out anything he did not like, and all of them together forced the virtuous woman, the true church of Jesus Christ, into the wilderness.

NOTES AND REFERENCES

1. See, for example, *gadol* and its cognates in W. L. Holladay, *A Concise Hebrew and Aramaic Lexicon of the Old Testament* (E. J. Brill: Leiden, 1971), pp. 55f.

2. Where the context is given, a large majority of occurrences of *abomination* and its forms refer to immorality or idolatry. Compare R. Young, *Analytical Concordance to the Bible* (Grand Rapids, Mich.: Eerdmans, 1978), pp. 6f.

3. Originally, the term *ekklesia*, from two Greek words meaning "call" and "out," referred to those citizens who were called out or summoned to their public meetings by the heralds. Thus it was an ideal word to represent the body of individuals "called" by God "out" of the world through the Holy Ghost—the Church. The civil dimension of the word can be seen in Acts 19:32, where "assembly" in the Greek text is *ekklesia,* elsewhere translated as "church." However, we must remember that we don't know the original word behind "church" on the plates, but whatever it was, Joseph Smith chose to render it *church* and not *assembly* or something else.

4. This was also the view of the Prophet Joseph Smith. The Joseph Smith Translation of Revelation 12:7 reads: "nor the woman which was the church of God, who had been delivered of her pains, and brought forth the kingdom of our God and his Christ."

5. Compare also the Joseph Smith Translation of Revelation 13:1: "And I saw another sign, in the likeness of the kingdoms of the earth; a beast rise up out of the sea."

6. See Nahum 3.

7. See Revelation 11:8.

8. *History of the Church* 6:478.

9. One of the many instances which might be cited is found in *Table Talk,* No. 4487 (11 April 1539): "I believe the pope is the masked and incarnate devil because he is the Antichrist. As Christ is God incarnate, so the Antichrist is the devil incarnate." See T. Tappert and H. Lehmann (eds.) *Luther's Works* (Philadelphia: Fortress) 54:346.

10. An example might be cited in Acts 17:32–33 where the mere mention to the Greeks of the physical resurrection breaks up Paul's meeting with the Areopagus council.

11. The Joseph Smith Translation makes this identification even more apparent: "for there shall come a falling away first, and that man of sin be revealed, the son of perdition. . . . For the mystery of iniquity doth already work, and he it is who now worketh, and Christ suffereth him to work, until the time is fulfilled that he shall be taken out of the way." (2 Thessalonians 2:3, 7.)

12. For Lucifer as the man of sin, see Bruce R. McConkie, *Doctrinal New Testament Commentary*, 3 vols. (Salt Lake City: Bookcraft, 1973), 3:62–64.

13. Joseph Smith—History 1:19.

13

ESTABLISHING THE TRUTH OF THE BIBLE

Robert J. Matthews

The emphasis in this paper, in keeping with the entire symposium, will be on 1 Nephi. My views are my own—I am speaking for myself, not for the University, but what I am about to say I believe to be correct.

The Book of Mormon is a record like the Bible. It is not designed as a commentary about the Bible, nor is it written to take the place of the Bible. It is a record of people who came from the time and the land and the lineage of the Old Testament and who migrated to America. Through their prophets they produced a record which is in some ways parallel to the Bible and is in some ways superior to it. It does not compete with, but rather it complements the Bible. The Book of Mormon is separate and independent and is not based upon the Bible for its source, yet one who believes the contents of the Book of Mormon will believe in the Bible as well.

Robert J. Matthews is Dean of Religious Education and Professor of Ancient Scripture at Brigham Young University.

.

Furthermore, because of a certain obscurity which surrounds the Bible, no one today—scholar, philosopher, oriental, occidental, Saint, or sinner—can truly understand the doctrinal teachings of the Bible without the aid of the Book of Mormon. That is, the Book of Mormon adds a dimension to understanding the Bible that cannot be obtained in any other way. A scholar may learn much about the Bible, and about the biblical people, through study and exploration, by a knowledge of language, history, culture, archaeology, and religion; but there is a doctrinal dimension and an insight into the dealings of God with his people that escapes all inquirers who search only with the tools of the secular scholar. This dimension, without which no one fully understands the Bible, can be discovered only through the pages of the Book of Mormon and other books of latter-day scripture.

The Book of Mormon repeatedly makes reference to biblical things, both incidentally and deliberately. It boldly announces that one of its own purposes is to establish the truth of the Bible. This it accomplishes in at least four major ways: First, by speaking of the historical verity of specific biblical events and persons. There are literally hundreds of such instances. Second, by quoting extensively from the biblical text, such as from Isaiah or Malachi. Third, by affirming that such things as angels, visions, and miracles are real and that there is a God in heaven who is the father of the human family. And fourth, by giving us a history of the biblical text and also making known and restoring some of the things that have been taken out of the Bible.

The prophet Mormon, addressing the Lamanites of the latter days, said:

[You must] lay hold upon the gospel of Christ, which shall be set before you, not only in this record [the Book of Mormon] but also in the record which shall come unto the Gentiles from the Jews [the Bible], which record shall come from the Gentiles unto you.

For behold, this [the Book of Mormon] is written for the intent that ye may believe that [Bible]; and if ye believe that [Bible] ye will believe this also. (Mormon 7:8–9.)

One purpose of the Book of Mormon is to defend and make known the truth of the Bible. The choice seer (Joseph Smith) was not only to bring forth more of the word of God but was also to convince people of the truth of the word (Bible) already gone forth (2 Nephi 3:11).

The Book of Mormon Cites Specific Biblical Events and Persons

As an example of the first point cited above, I offer a partial list of specific items that are biblical in origin and are confirmed and affirmed in the Book of Mormon record. I have listed 106 specific points in which the Book of Mormon offers confirmation of the biblical record, and many of these are supported by more than one reference. Anyone who examines the list cannot fail to see that the Book of Mormon is a witness for the Bible.

Old Testament

I. *Creation to Abel*

1. Man created in God's image. Mosiah 7:27; Alma 18:34; 22:12; Ether 3:15 (Genesis 1:26–27).
2. Adam and Eve as first parents; and their fall. 1 Nephi 5:11; 2 Nephi 2:19, 20, 22, 25; 9:21; Mosiah 3:11, 16, 19, 26; 4:7; 28:17; Alma 12:22, 23; 18:36; 22:12, 13; 40:18; 42:5 (Genesis chapters 3–4).
3. Adam (and all men) made from dust of earth. Alma 42:2; Mosiah 2:25; Jacob 2:21; Mormon 9:17 (Genesis 2:7; 3:19).
4. Forbidden fruit. 2 Nephi 2:15, 18, 19; Mosiah 3:26; Alma 12:22; Helaman 6:26 (Genesis 2:17; 3:3–6).
5. Serpent tempted Eve. 2 Nephi 2:18; Mosiah 16:3 (Genesis 3).
6. Garden of Eden, man driven from. 2 Nephi 2:19, 22; Alma 12:21; 42:2 (Genesis 3).
7. Flaming sword at east of Eden. Alma 12:21; 42:2, 3 (Genesis 3).
8. Abel, son of Adam, slain by Cain. Helaman 6:27; Ether 8:15 (Genesis 4).

II. *Noah to Babel*

1. Noah (Bible patriarch) and the flood. Alma 10:22; 3 Nephi 22:9; Ether 6:7 (Genesis 6–9).
2. Building of tower, scattering of people, confounding of language. Title page; Omni 22; Mosiah 28:17; Helaman 6:28; Ether 1:3, 5, 33 (Genesis 11).

III. *Abraham to Bondage*

1. Melchizedek as a real person. Alma 13:14–18 (Genesis 14).
2. Abraham, Isaac, Jacob as real persons. 1 Nephi 6:4; 17:40; 19:10; Jacob 4:5; Mosiah 7:19; 23:23; Alma 5:24; 7:25; 29:11; 36:2; Helaman 3:30; 3 Nephi 4:30; Mormon 9:11 (Genesis 12–30).
3. Abraham, God made covenant with. 1 Nephi 15:18; 22:9; 2 Nephi 29:14; 3 Nephi 20:25, 27; Mormon 5:20; Ether 13:11 (Genesis 17).
4. Abraham offering Isaac as sacrifice. Jacob 4:4–6 (Genesis 22).
5. Abraham paid tithes to Melchizedek. Alma 13:15 (Genesis 14).
6. Abraham saw Christ's day. Helaman 8:17 (Genesis 22; John 8:56).
7. Joseph, son of Jacob, taken to Egypt. 1 Nephi 5:14; 2 Nephi 3:4; 4:1; Ether 13:7 (Genesis 37).
8. Joseph sold by his brothers. Alma 10:3 (Genesis 37).
9. Joseph's coat. Alma 46:23–24 (Genesis 37).
10. Manasseh, son of Joseph. Alma 10:3 (Genesis 48).
11. Jacob taken to Egypt by Joseph and died there. Ether 13:7; 1 Nephi 5:14 (Genesis 46–50).

IV. *Moses and Events Connected with Him*

1. Named by prophecy beforehand. 2 Nephi 3:9, 16, 17.
2. Moses to be a writer. 2 Nephi 3:17.
3. Five books of Moses. 1 Nephi 5:11.
4. Books of Moses. 1 Nephi 19:23.
5. Moses not to be great in speaking. 2 Nephi 3:17 (Exodus 4:10–14).
6. Rod of Moses. 2 Nephi 3:17 (Exodus 7:9).
7. Led Israel out of Egypt. 1 Nephi 4:2; 5:15; 19:10; 2 Nephi 3:10; 25:20 (Exodus 14).
8. Moses divided Red Sea. 1 Nephi 4:2; 17:26; Mosiah 7:19; Helaman 8:11 (Exodus 14).
9. Egyptian Army destroyed at Red Sea. 1 Nephi 4:2; 17:27; Helaman 8:11; Alma 36:28 (Genesis 14).
10. Moses received law and commandments at Sinai. Mosiah 12:33–36; 13:12–24 (Exodus 20).

11. Moses' face shone at Sinai. Mosiah 13:5 (Exodus 34:29).
12. Pillar of light for Israel in wilderness. 1 Nephi 17:30 (Exodus 13).
13. Manna in wilderness. 1 Nephi 17:28; Mosiah 7:19 (Exodus 16).
14. Water from the rock. 1 Nephi 17:29; 20:21; 2 Nephi 25:20 (Numbers).
15. Held up brazen serpent for healing. 1 Nephi 17:41; 2 Nephi 25:20; Alma 33:19; 37:46; Helaman 8:13–15 (Numbers).
16. Moses to have a spokesman. 2 Nephi 3:17 (Exodus 4:14–16).
17. Moses prophesied of Christ. 1 Nephi 22:20; Mosiah 13:33; Helaman 8:13; 3 Nephi 20:23 (Deuteronomy 18).
18. Moses' death and burial. Alma 45:19 (Deuteronomy 34:5).
19. Law of Moses, originated in the time of the man Moses. 1 Nephi 4:15–16; 5:11; 2 Nephi 3:17; 25:30; 3 Nephi 15:4–8; 25:4; Ether 12:11.

V. *From Entering Canaan Until Jesus' Time*

1. Israel enters promised land, drove inhabitants out. 1 Nephi 17:32–34, 42 (Joshua 11:6; 24:8).
2. David, king of Israel, had many wives. Jacob 1:15; 2:23–24 (2 Samuel 12:8).
3. Solomon, son of David, had many wives. Jacob 1:15; 2:23–24 (1 Kings 11:1–3).
4. Solomon built temple, very elaborate. 2 Nephi 5:16 (2 Chronicles 3).
5. Zedekiah, king of Judah. 1 Nephi 1:4; 5:12, 13; Omni 1:15 (2 Chronicles 36:11).
6. Sons of Zedekiah. Helaman 6:10; 8:21 (2 Kings 25:7).
7. Jeremiah, Jewish prophet. 1 Nephi 5:13 (Jeremiah 1).
8. Jeremiah's prophecies in record of Jews. 1 Nephi 5:13.
9. Jeremiah cast into prison. 1 Nephi 7:14 (Jeremiah 37:15).
10. Many prophets rejected by Jews at this time. 1 Nephi 1:4; 7:14 (Jeremiah 44:4–6; 2 Chronicles 36:15–16).
11. Jeremiah prophecied of destruction of Jerusalem. Helaman 8:20 (Jeremiah 6).

12. Jeremiah's prophecies fulfilled. Helaman 8:20 (2 Chronicles 36:20–21).
13. Isaiah, Hebrew prophet. Writings on plates of brass. 1 Nephi 19:22–23.
14. Isaiah saw the Lord. 2 Nephi 11:2; 2 Nephi 16:1 (Isaiah 6:1).
15. Babylonian captivity of Jews. 1 Nephi 1:13; 10:3; 17:43; 20:14, 20; 2 Nephi 6:8 (Ezekiel 1).
16. Return from Babylon. 1 Nephi 10:3; 2 Nephi 6:8–9; 2 Nephi 25:10–11 (Ezekiel 1).
17. Samuel, Hebrew prophet. 3 Nephi 20:24 (1 Samuel 1).
18. Elijah, Hebrew prophet. 3 Nephi 25:5 (1 Kings 17:1).
19. Malachi, Hebrew prophet. 3 Nephi 24 and 25 (Malachi 3 and 4).

New Testament

I. *Work of John the Baptist* (Name Not Given)

1. A prophet to prepare way for Christ. 1 Nephi 10:7; 11:27.
2. This prophet to baptize Christ with water. 1 Nephi 10:9–10; 2 Nephi 31:4–8.
3. To bear witness of Christ. 1 Nephi 10:10.
4. Not worthy to unloose Christ's shoe latchet. 1 Nephi 10:8 (John 1:26–27).
5. Place of baptism. 1 Nephi 10:9 (John 1:28).

II. *Jesus Christ* (Named Beforehand by Prophecy, 2 Nephi 10:3; Mosiah 3:8)

1. Jesus, God of Old Testament. 3 Nephi 15:4–5; 1 Nephi 19:7–10; Mosiah 3:5–11; 7:27.
2. Jesus was baptized. 1 Nephi 10:9–10; 11:27; 2 Nephi 31:4–8 (Matthew 3).
3. Received Holy Ghost (form of dove). 1 Nephi 11:27; 2 Nephi 31:8 (Matthew 3).
4. Mocked by people. 1 Nephi 11:28–32; Mosiah 3:7.
5. Jesus sweat blood. Mosiah 3:7 (Luke 22:44).
6. Crucified. 1 Nephi 10:11; 11:33; 2 Nephi 10:3; Mosiah 3:9 (Matthew 27).
7. Buried, rose third day. 2 Nephi 25:13; Mosiah 3:10 (Matthew 28).

8. Jesus the first to rise in resurrection. 2 Nephi 2:8 (Acts 26:23; Colossians 1:18; Revelation 1:5).
9. Chose twelve apostles from the Jews. 1 Nephi 11:29–36; 12:9; 13:24, 26, 39, 40, 41; Mormon 3:18–19 (Luke 6:12–13).
10. Performed many miracles (in Palestine). 1 Nephi 11:31; Mosiah 3:5; 3 Nephi 17:7–8 (John 2).
11. Jesus' apostles performed miracles (in Palestine). Mormon 9:18 (Luke 10; book of Acts).
12. Jesus taught by parable (in Palestine). 3 Nephi 15:14–24 (Matthew 13).
13. Fulfilled law of Moses. 3 Nephi 15:5–8.
14. Cancelled circumcision. Moroni 8:8 (Acts 15).
15. No other name for salvation. 2 Nephi 31:21; Mosiah 3:17; 5:8 (Acts 4:12).
16. Ascended to heaven (from Palestine). 3 Nephi 18:39 (Acts 1:10–11).

III. *Mary, Mother of Jesus* (Named Beforehand by Prophecy, Mosiah 3:8; Alma 7:10)

1. Virgin. 1 Nephi 11:13–20; Alma 7:10 (Matthew 1:23; Luke 1:27).
2. Lived at Nazareth. 1 Nephi 11:13 (Matthew 2:22–23).
3. Mother of the Son of God. 1 Nephi 11:18 (Luke 1:26–27).

IV. *Other*

1. One of the Twelve to be named John. 1 Nephi 14:27 (Matthew 10:2).
2. John to have writings in book of the Jews. 1 Nephi 14:23.
3. John not to taste of death. 3 Nephi 28:6–7 (John 21:21–24).
4. Record of the Jews to consist of the writings of the prophets and also the records of the Twelve Apostles (Old and New Testaments). 1 Nephi 13:38–41.
5. Jerusalem to be destroyed after Christ's ministry. 2 Nephi 25:14; 6:9–10 (Matthew 24).
6. Twelve Apostles to judge Israel. 1 Nephi 12:9; Mormon 3:18–19 (Matthew 19:28).

Experiences Similar to Those Recorded in the Bible

1. Handwriting on wall interpreted. Alma 10:1–2 (Daniel 5).
2. Nephi had power to seal heavens against rain or to call it forth again. Helaman 10:5 to 11:17 (James 5:17–18; 1 Kings 17:1 to 1 Kings 18:46).
3. Three Nephites in furnace and den of beasts. 3 Nephi 28:21–22 (Daniel 3 and 6).
4. Nephi calms storm at sea. 1 Nephi 18:21 (Mark 4:36–39).
5. Food miraculously provided. 3 Nephi 20:6–7 (Mark 7:35–44).
6. Abinadi's face shone, like Moses'. Mosiah 13:5 (Exodus 34:29–35).
7. Mountain moved by faith. Ether 12:30 (Matthew 17:20).
8. Many Saints arise and appear to many after Jesus' resurrection. 3 Nephi 23:9–12; Helaman 14:25–26 (Matthew 27:52–54).
9. Mary, Jesus, John, Moses all named in prophecy before birth, so why not Isaiah able to do this with Cyrus? Mosiah 3:8; Alma 7:10; 2 Nephi 10:3; 1 Nephi 14:27; 2 Nephi 3:9, 16, 17 (Isaiah 44:28; 45:1–5).
10. Alma, Nephi possibly translated. Alma 45:18–19; 3 Nephi 1:3; 2:9 (Deuteronomy 34:5).
11. Person raised from the dead. 3 Nephi 7:19; 19:4 (Mark 5:35–43; Acts 9:36–43).
12. Devils cast out. 3 Nephi 7:19 (Mark 5).

Some Other Similarities

1. Death penalty for murder. Alma 1:13–15 (Genesis 9:5–6).
2. New Jerusalem to come down from heaven. Ether 13:3 (Revelation 3:12; 21:2).
3. Sun stand still. Lengthen out day. Helaman 12:13–15 (Joshua 10:12–14; 2 Kings 20:8–11; Isaiah 38:7–8).
4. Sermon in 3 Nephi similar to Sermon on Mount. 3 Nephi 12; 13; 14 (Matthew 5; 6; 7).

The Book of Mormon Quotes Extensively from the Bible Record

This section illustrates the second way in which the Book of Mormon establishes the truth of the Bible. There are in the Book of Mormon numerous and sometimes lengthy quotations from the Bible. These were chiefly taken from the plates of brass, whose contents are given to us as follows:

> They did contain the five books of Moses, . . .
> And also a record of the Jews from the beginning, even down to the commencement of the reign of Zedekiah, king of Judah;
> And also the prophecies of the holy prophets, from the beginning, even down to the commencement of the reign of Zedekiah; and also many prophecies which have been spoken by the mouth of Jeremiah.
> . . . my father, Lehi, also found upon the plates of brass a genealogy of his fathers. (1 Nephi 5:11–14.)

Since the plates of brass are a different manuscript source than is used by any of the versions of the Old Testament available today, they, as cited in the Book of Mormon, serve as a corroborating witness of the Bible. Chief among the quotations are those from Isaiah, consisting of twenty-one entire chapters and also many isolated passages. A detailed examination of these quotations is outside the scope of this paper, and it is enough to say that one of the consequences of the use of so much of Isaiah from a text that was in existence in 600 B.C. is that it demonstrates the unity and original authorship of the whole book of Isaiah. As you may know, many scholars divide Isaiah into several portions, with multiple authors, most of them later than when the original Isaiah lived, even down to 200 B.C. The Book of Mormon corrects this erroneous view. Likewise, the presence of Malachi chapters 3 and 4 (3 Nephi 24, 25) and the Savior's sermon to the Nephites (similar to the biblical Sermon on the Mount—3 Nephi 12–14) are also witnesses to the biblical text of these chapters.

In its quotations from and references to the Bible, the Book of Mormon makes direct mention of things recorded in Genesis, Exodus, Numbers, Deuteronomy, Joshua, 1 Kings, 1 Chronicles, Isaiah, Jeremiah, Malachi, Matthew, Luke, John, and the book of Revelation. Of special interest is the fact that 1 Nephi and 2

Nephi, by their literary style, have a remarkable affinity for the subject matter and vocabulary of John the Beloved and the book of Isaiah.

The Book of Mormon Affirms the Miraculous Elements of God's Dealing with Mankind

In support of point three, listed above, we find that on almost every page and in nearly every chapter of the Book of Mormon there is repeated reference to such things as God, angels, visions, revelation, miracles, prayer, baptism, Holy Spirit, blessings, divine intervention, cursings, punishments, and numerous items of a similar nature that have to do with revealed religion. That the Book of Mormon supports these kinds of events (which are also characteristic of the Bible) is evident to anyone who has even casually read the book.

The Book of Mormon Foretells the History of the Biblical Text

We now turn our attention to point four. The most extensive statement in all of the scriptures about the history of the Bible is found in chapter 13 of 1 Nephi. It is given to Nephi in vision, with the assistance of an angel as an interpreter—sort of a guided tour accompanying a panoramic view of the Bible through the centuries. This vision, given to Nephi about 600 B.C. shows him what would happen to the biblical text. By heavenly vision Nephi was made aware of the facts *before* they occurred. A vision or inspired prophecy can be more accurate than reading about the matter *after* the fact. Prophecy is history in reverse. When a prophecy is inspired of the Lord, things made known by that prophecy can give a more accurate view than would a historical record written by researchers and scholars who might not write by the Spirit. Today we are able to ascertain by historical search most of the things of Nephi's prophecy, but not all. That there was tampering with the Bible text in the second and third centuries A.D. is evident to many biblical scholars. Marcion and others are known to have done this. But modern textual critics do not realize how extensive the changes really were. It is my belief and faith that, with time and by historical research, every detail of Nephi's prophecy and vision concerning the history of the

Bible text will be proven and verified. Research will someday provide the details of persons, time, and place. If we believe this account in the Book of Mormon, however, we do not have to wait for that future time in order to know the general outline and to understand just what the Bible is and exactly what has happened to the Bible text. We can know it *now* as surely and accurately as we know anything from the scriptures. And we know it because of our faith and confidence in the Book of Mormon. Later discoveries will only confirm what we already knew and were told in the revelations.

The words to which I refer are found in 1 Nephi 13:13–42. Nephi beheld that a people whom he identifies as Gentiles established a government in this land of America and that through the power of God they became politically free and independent of all other nations. We recognize them as the early European colonists in America. He beheld that these Gentiles carried a book with them which they had brought from the nations of Europe (1 Nephi 13:13–20).

> And the angel said unto me: Knowest thou the meaning of the book?
> And I said unto him: I know not.
> And he said: Behold it proceedeth out of the mouth of a Jew. And I, Nephi, beheld it; and he said unto me: The book that thou beholdest is a record of the Jews, which contains the covenants of the Lord, which he hath made unto the house of Israel; and it also containeth many of the prophecies of the holy prophets; and it is a record like unto the engravings which are upon the plates of brass, save there are not so many; nevertheless, they contain the covenants of the Lord, which he hath made unto the house of Israel; wherefore, they are of great worth unto the Gentiles. (1 Nephi 13:21–23.)

We note that the early settlers of America, including the Puritans or Pilgrims, and also early Catholic settlers, brought with them the Bible—the record of the Jews. Those on the Mayflower brought a Geneva Bible, and there is today in the Harvard University library a copy of a Geneva Bible which made its way to America on the Mayflower. This was the same translation that was used by Shakespeare and came before the King James Version was in wide circulation. These were Protestant Bibles. Many of the Catholic immigrants to America brought the English version of the Vulgate, known as the Rheims-Douai version, which was translated into English in 1582, a few years before the King James Version and at about the same time as the other Protestant Bibles were coming into being.

In Nephi's vision the angel describes the Bible as a record of the Jews, noting that it contains (1) the covenants of the Lord to the house of Israel, (2) many of the prophecies of the holy prophets, that (3) it is a record similar to the plates of brass, only smaller, and also (4) is a record of the gospel of the Lord as taught by the Twelve Apostles (1 Nephi 13:23–24).

After establishing beyond question with Nephi that the early American settlers of the seventeenth century had a Bible, the angel then proceeded to explain to him that the Bible he saw in their hands was not the same as when it was originally written by the Jews. The words of the angel are given thus:

> And the angel of the Lord said unto me: Thou hast beheld that the book proceeded forth from the mouth of a Jew; and when it proceeded forth from the mouth of a Jew it contained the fulness of the gospel of the Lord, of whom the twelve apostles bear record; and they bear record according to the truth which is in the Lamb of God.
>
> Wherefore, these things go forth from the Jews in purity unto the Gentiles, according to the truth which is in God.
>
> And after they go forth by the hand of the twelve apostles of the Lamb, from the Jews unto the Gentiles, thou seest the formation of that great and abominable church, which is most abominable above all other churches; for behold, they have taken away from the gospel of the Lamb *many parts which are plain and most precious; and also many covenants of the Lord have they taken away.* (1 Nephi 13:24–26; italics added.)

The angel's words are plain and to the point: When the biblical records were originally written by the Jewish prophets and apostles, they contained the fulness of the gospel. When these records went to the Gentiles, some valuable plain and precious things were taken out of them. That this reduction was *deliberate* and not simply caused by carelessness or by the difficulties encountered by transcription and translation is further emphasized by the angel:

> And all this have they done that they might pervert the right ways of the Lord, that they might blind the eyes and harden the hearts of the children of men.

> Wherefore, thou seest that after the book hath gone forth through the hands of the great and abominable church, that there are many plain and precious things taken away from the book, which is the book of the Lamb of God. (1 Nephi 13:27–28.)

If the foregoing words say anything, they say that the alteration of the text was *deliberate* and intentional and extensive and for unholy and wicked purposes. It is plain also that the corruption of the text was not simply a matter of interpretation, or an awkward rendering of a few passages. It was not simply "lost in the translation." The words of the angel specify that "*many* plain and precious things are taken away" from and "out of" the "book of the Lamb of God" (1 Nephi 13:26, 28, 29, 32, 34). He also said that "*many* covenants of the Lord are taken away." (Italics added.) This explanation gives us to understand why the Bible in its reduced form—the Protestant and Catholic versions of the seventeenth century—is smaller than the plates of brass, as noted in verse 23. This comparative expression by the angel gives us a clue as to just how much has been "taken away" and lost to our present Bible. The plates of brass contained a record beginning with the five books of Moses down to Jeremiah—only a portion of the time period of the Old Testament and none of the New—yet the reduced version of the whole Bible—the Bible with which we are acquainted, containing both the Old and New Testaments—is "not so many" as the record on the plates of brass.

The angel then continues to explain to Nephi the history of the Bible. After many plain and precious things are taken out of the Bible, it then—in its reduced form—goes throughout the nations of the Gentiles (evidently Europe), and eventually to America and then to the Lamanites. Here are the exact words of the prophecy:

> And *after* these plain and precious things were taken away it goeth forth unto all the nations of the Gentiles; and after it goeth forth unto all the nations of the Gentiles, yea, even across the many waters which thou hast seen with the Gentiles which have gone forth out of captivity, thou seest—because of the many plain and precious things which have been taken *out of the book*, which were plain unto the understanding of the children of men, according to the plainness which is in the Lamb of God—because of these things which are taken away out of the gospel of the Lamb,

an exceedingly great many do stumble, yea, insomuch that Satan hath great power over them (1 Nephi 13:29; italics added).

The changes and losses made the Bible not so easy to understand, and thus there are many interpretations and disputations about what is required for salvation.

According to the sequence and the declaration of this prophecy, speaking of things to come as though they had already happened, it is seen that the nations of the Gentiles—the Roman Empire, the Mediterranean world of the early centuries after Christ—never did have a complete Bible, for it was reduced and altered before it was distributed among them. Unfortunately there are no original copies of the Bible manuscripts available today for comparison. The earliest known manuscripts of the New Testament are dated two centuries or more after the time of the Apostles, except for very small fragments. The persecutions against Christianity in the first and second centuries seem to have helped destroy the manuscripts of that time. It appears self-evident from this remarkable vision given to Nephi that the earliest complete New Testament texts available today—among which are the Vaticanus, the Alexandrinus, and Sinaiticus (all fourth century A.D.)—are of such a date that they represent the text in its reduced and altered form, not in its original state. When Constantine made Christianity the state religion of the Empire at about A.D. 313, he ordered Eusebius to prepare fifty copies of the New Testament. The great uncials—Vaticanus, Sinaiticus, etc.—are possibly survivors of this order.

Alteration to the Text Was Early

In order for an alteration to have widespread effect, the text would have to be tampered with early enough that multiple copies were not already extant. In other words, the alteration had to be early and by a person or persons having access to very early records and first-generation copies. This is what we today would call an "inside job." We should not be too surprised that this could happen, for in our own dispensation and with our own scripture, we have had a similar thing. We have suffered the loss of 116 pages of translation from the gold plates—what would have been the book of Lehi in the Book of Mormon. We also lost the earliest official history of the Church from 1830 to 1838 through the perfidy of the then Church historian, John Whitmer.

Having such a parallel in our own history, Latter-day Saints should be able to visualize the kinds of things that can happen to a sacred record, and that 1 Nephi 13 says *did* happen to the Bible centuries ago. The Book of Mormon was written for our day. It is written for our learning and understanding. Does it not seem apparent that Nephi's vision has been preserved by the Lord because he wants us to know these very things and have these views about the Bible? The vision was not for Nephi alone, but for us also.

Lack of an Adequate Manuscript

That the problem with the text of the Bible is much larger than translation of language or the misplacement of a few words was repeatedly taught by the Prophet Joseph Smith. We are dealing with a matter of transmission (which includes copying, translating, revising, editing, interpreting, adding to, and taking from) and not simply translation of language alone. Note several statements from the Prophet Joseph:

> From sundry revelations which had been received, it was apparent that many important points touching the salvation of men, had been *taken from* the Bible, or lost *before* it was compiled (1832).[1]
>
> I am now going to take exception to the present translation of the Bible in relation to these matters [the books of Daniel and Revelation]. Our latitude and longitude can be determined in the original Hebrew with far greater accuracy than in the English version. There is a grand distinction between the actual meaning of the prophets and the present translation (1843–44).[2]
>
> There are many things in the Bible which do not, as they now stand, accord with the revelations of the Holy Ghost to me (1843–44).[3]
>
> I believe the Bible as it read when it came from the pen of the original writers. Ignorant translators, careless transcribers, or designing and corrupt priests have committed many errors (1843–44).[4]

These and other statements by the Prophet show that he regarded problems in the present text of the Bible to be the result not only of translation of language, but also a loss of actual text, and a wilful changing and editing of the text in ancient times. As Moroni asked: "Why have ye transfigured the holy word of God . . . ?" (Mormon 8:33). These expressions give us a broader understanding of what is meant by the eighth article of faith: "We believe the Bible to be the word of God as far as it is translated correctly." Although he used the word *translated*, the Prophet obviously had in mind a wider meaning, such as the term *transmitted*; for as his own statements illustrate, there was more involved than mere translation of languages. From the words of Joseph Smith and also the vision of Nephi, we can see that the intended meaning of the eighth article is, "We believe the Bible to be the word of God, as far as it is *transmitted* correctly." Editing, adding to, taking from, as well as translating, have all contributed to the present condition of the Bible.

With this point firmly in place, we can see that the real condition of the Bible is not that we lack capable men or women who can read and translate from the ancient languages. The problem is the absence today of an adequate, complete, and accurate manuscript to translate.

Prophecies of the Restoration of Lost Material

I have noticed that whenever the Lord predicts a loss or a falling away, he also speaks of a restoration, a return of that which is lost. This is true not only of priesthood and of church organization, but also of scripture. As we see with the words of the angel to Nephi:

> Neither will the Lord God suffer that the Gentiles shall forever remain in that awful state of blindness, which thou beholdest they are in, because of the plain and most precious parts of the gospel of the Lamb which have been kept back by that abominable church, whose formation thou hast seen (1 Nephi 13:32).

The loss of so many plain and precious parts has rendered some doctrinal things in the Bible obscure and ambiguous. Also, the purposes of God are not so well discerned in the Bible as they were originally.

After explaining that the Gentiles in America will take the Bible to the Lamanites, the angel showed Nephi that the lost and missing parts will be restored:

> And after it [the Bible] had come forth unto them [the Lamanites] I beheld other books, which came forth by the power of the Lamb, from the Gentiles unto them, unto the convincing of the Gentiles and the remnant of the seed of my brethren, and also the Jews who were scattered upon all the face of the earth, that the

records of the prophets and of the twelve apostles of the Lamb are true.

And the angel spake unto me, saying: These last records, which thou hast seen among the Gentiles, shall establish the truth of the first, which are of the twelve apostles of the Lamb, and shall make known the plain and precious things which have been taken away from them; and shall make known to all kindreds, tongues, and people, that the Lamb of God is the Son of the Eternal Father, and the Savior of the world; and that all men must come unto him, or they cannot be saved. (1 Nephi 13:39—40.)

The "other books" and "last records" spoken of in these two verses no doubt include the Book of Mormon, Doctrine and Covenants, Pearl of Great Price, and the Joseph Smith Translation of the Bible. The "other books" could also include the record of the ten tribes that will yet come to us. These books, which are our standard works, do indeed make known many passages that are lost and also tell of whole books that are missing from the Bible. They also clarify many doctrinal concepts. Furthermore, they declare that the Bible is a divinely inspired record and that its fundamental message, though presently incomplete, is true. In spite of its loss, the Bible is still a testimony of the existence of God and of the mission of Jesus Christ as Redeemer of the world. It just does not testify as effectively as it would if it were precise and complete. A similar prophecy, telling of a loss and then a restoration of Moses' writings, is found in Moses 1:40—41.

The angel continues the theme of restoration by stating that the "words of the Lamb" of God, who is Jesus Christ, shall be established and "made known in the records of thy seed [the Book of Mormon], as well as in the records of the twelve apostles of the Lamb [New Testament]; wherefore they both shall be established in one; for there is one God and one Shepherd over all the earth" (1 Nephi 13:41). Every significant doctrinal question raised at the Nicene Council in A.D. 325, and in church councils and debates in the past sixteen hundred years of the apostasy, has been answered in the Book of Mormon and other latter-day revelation.

Additional Scripture Yet to Be Restored

The Book of Mormon not only confirms and certifies the truth of the biblical records, but by its very existence it shows that the Bible is not the complete source for the word of God. It makes clear that the Jewish record once had more books and that even the books we do have are reduced in size in some instances. We understand that these will eventually be restored to their original purity. We now have thirty-nine books in the Old Testament and twenty-seven in the New, making a total of sixty-six books in all. In our present Church Sunday School curriculum, we take one year to study the Old Testament and another to study the New Testament. At BYU we use two semesters on the undergraduate level to go through the Old Testament and two more semesters to study the New Testament. There are also graduate-level advanced courses with another seven hours for Old Testament and six hours for the New.

With the clearer insight concerning the Bible and the promise of eventual restoration, we will someday have to take a much longer time to study the Bible when we have it in its complete and restored form. I can mentally visualize that at some future semester at BYU, the Religion offering for the Bible will contain courses not only in the present two Old Testament courses, 301 and 302 (two hours each), but a semester in Brass Plates 303 (five hours), with an emphasis on the prophecies of Joseph in Egypt. We now have Old Testament 304 specializing in Isaiah. When the plates of brass are restored, we will need Old Testament 305, Zenock; 306, Zenos; and 307, the prophecies of Neum (each with three credit hours). At this rate, it could involve a student four years just to take the beginning courses in the Old Testament alone. Instead of the present thirteen hours in an Old Testament offering, there could be as many as forty credit hours with undergraduate and graduate offerings. An equal enlargement would be necessary with the New Testament. And we did not even mention courses in Lost Tribes 101, 102, and 103—three courses of two hours each, using as the text the record yet to come forth giving their history and an account of the Savior's visit to show his resurrected body to them (3 Nephi 17:4).

The Book of Mormon curriculum will likewise have to be enlarged. We will not only need the two beginning courses, 121 and 122, presently in the curriculum, but when the time of restitution really descends upon us, there probably will be courses in Book of Mormon 123, Readings from the 116 Lost Pages (two hours); Book of Mormon 124, The Twenty-four Gold Plates of Ether (four hours); 125, 126, and 127, The Sealed Plates containing a revelation "from the beginning of the world until the end thereof" (five hours each). Advanced courses might read as follows: 531, The Large Plates of Nephi, Mosiah; 532, Large Plates, Alma; 533, Large Plates, Helaman; and so on through the entire collection. This is in contrast to our offering today of a four-hour survey course on Book of Mormon, and a four-hour upper-division course, and eight hours of graduate course work in Book of Mormon, making sixteen in all. At some future day there will be so many records available on the Book of Mormon alone that we could sensibly have forty to fifty information-packed semester hours in the Book of Mormon and a like number of biblical course selections. And all this because of the restoration of records that are mentioned in the Book of Mormon that are yet to be made available to us.

All of these records, being sacred and being translated by the power of God, will contain the truth and will shed additional light on man's origin and man's history in the world and his early culture and high civilization. These new records will also confirm what we already know in the scripture we now have. Thus, there will be a need also on this campus for revised courses about the Ancient World and revised courses in American history before A.D. 1600. There will be a need also for revised courses in ancient civilization and in the origin of language, origin of writing, and the origin of man. Present courses on these subjects will no doubt be seen as inadequate and even erroneous in light of revealed knowledge.

The Law of Witnesses Is Operative with the Book of Mormon

It is not only *desirable* that the Book of Mormon should substantiate the Bible and supply certain missing parts, it is absolutely *necessary* for eternal justice. It appears that in the economy of God there must be more than one witness for the truths that are taught to mankind. Without a second or third witness, the law cannot be binding and valid in the day of judgment.

The law of witnesses is stated in Deuteronomy 19:15 as follows: "At the mouth of two witnesses, or at the mouth of three witnesses, shall the matter be established." This principle is referred to by Jesus in Matthew 18:16: "Take with thee one or two more, that in the mouth of two or three witnesses every word may be established." Paul likewise alludes to this law in 1 Timothy 5:19; 2 Corinthians 13:1; and Hebrews 10:28.

We have an interesting account of Jesus invoking the law of witnesses in John 5:31. The whole episode of John 5 is an encounter between Jesus and the Jewish rulers, with legal implications. Jesus says, "If I bear witness of myself, my witness is not true." In plainer terms, the meaning is this: "If I am the *only* witness, my witness is not legally valid and binding."

Jesus then established John the Baptist as a witness for him (verses 32–34). He further declares that he has more witness than the testimony of John. He identifies this further witness as the testimony of his divine works; the testimony that the Father has given of him (verse 37), and also the testimony of the scriptures (verse 39), especially those things written by Moses (verses 45–47). A short time later in John chapter 8, the Pharisees verbally attack Jesus and say: "Thou bearest record of thyself; thy record is not true [that is, not legally valid]" (John 8:13). Jesus replies:

> I am not alone, but I and the Father that sent me.
> It is also written in your law, that the testimony of two men is true.
> I am one that bear witness of myself, and the Father that sent me beareth witness of me. (John 8:16–18.)

An honest, candid reader with only a fourth-grade education can see that the Old and New Testaments teach that God himself establishes his truth in the earth by virtue of the law of witnesses and leaves men without excuse. The concept is clear and open and without argument or equivocation.

It must be equally clear to any reader that since Jesus invokes his Father as his second witness in John 8:18, the Father and the Son must be two separate men; otherwise, they are not two witnesses and could not fulfill the requirement wherein Jesus says, "I am one witness and the Father is the other witness."

We thus have this eternal and divine principle showing that God uses witnesses to establish his word. And so in like manner we have been given the Book of Mormon to establish the truth of the Bible—not just the truth of the Bible as history and as a cultural record, but to establish the greatest truth that the Bible was intended to declare, and that is to prove that the testimony of Jesus Christ contained in the scriptures is true and correct.

President Brigham Young gave this instruction:

> There is not that person on the face of the earth who has had the privilege of learning the Gospel of Jesus Christ from these two

books, that can say that one is true, and the other is false. No Latter-day Saint, no man or woman, can say the Book of Mormon is true, and at the same time say that the Bible is untrue. If one be true, both are; and if one be false, both are false.[5]

President Heber J. Grant adds this:

All my life I have been finding additional evidences that the . . . Book of Mormon is the greatest witness for the truth of the Bible that has ever been published.[6]

The Time Is Right for a Second Witness to the Bible to Appear

Most of the Christian world today professes to hold the Bible in high esteem as a religious record—both the Old Testament and the New Testament. Our Jewish brethren profess a belief in the Old Testament as a record of their fathers. Yet it seems evident that the Bible has suffered neglect at the hands of millions who, while having certain reverence for the Bible as a religious record, have multiple doubts about its inspiration and historical accuracy. We do not have to go very far to find biblical adherents who at the same time doubt the story of creation in Genesis (the Garden of Eden story), who hold the fall of man as a myth, who systematically reject the miracles of the Old and the New Testament, and who look upon Jesus Christ as a great teacher of ethics but hesitate to think of him as the divine and literal Son of God, and doubt that he rose from the grave with a tangible, physical, immortal body.

Millions professing faith in the Bible do not believe in the gift of prophecy, the ministry of angels, or the blessings of continued revelation. This is a great contradiction and inconsistency, but many seem to be in that situation. President Brigham Young had noticed this same tendency among the people and is reported to have said: "We take this book, the Bible, which I expect to see voted out of the so-called Christian world very soon, they are coming to it as fast as possible, I say we take this book for our guide."[7]

At another time President Young declared:

The Bible is true. It may not all have been translated aright, and many precious things may have been rejected in the compilation and translation of the Bible; but we understand, from the writings of one of the Apostles, that if all the sayings and doings

213

of the Savior had been written, the world could not contain them. *I will say that the world could not understand them.* They do not understand what we have on record, nor the character of the Savior, as delineated in the Scriptures.[8]

The way in which churches vote out the Bible is simply that they continue to use it for an ethical guide, but stop believing what it teaches historically and doctrinally.

We are in the habit of using the Bible to prove the Book of Mormon is true, but as we have seen in various passages used in this article, the opposite should be the case. We should gain a testimony of the Book of Mormon by the Spirit and use it to prove that the Bible is true. The Book of Mormon has come to us directly through the intervention of heavenly beings and revelation. One of its purposes, as declared by the Lord himself in D&C 20:11, is to prove to the world that the "holy scriptures [the Bible] are true."

Elder Bruce R. McConkie has written:

> There is, however, one great difference between the Bible and the Book of Mormon that shows why some people can disbelieve the Bible and let the matter drop, but disbelieving the Book of Mormon, they find themselves compelled to arise in wrath and defame the Nephite record. It is that people who believe the Bible, as they suppose, can also believe any creed of their choice and belong to any church that suits them. But belief in the Book of Mormon presupposes the acceptance of Joseph Smith as a prophet as well as membership in the church organized by him. . . .
>
> Further, the Bible is difficult to interpret and understand, and reasonable men, approaching it wholly from an intellectual standpoint, can reach divergent conclusions on almost all doctrines—hence, the many contending sects in Christendom. The Bible [because it has been flawed by man] is indeed the perfect tool to support every conceivable doctrinal view. But the Book of Mormon is otherwise; this American scripture sets forth the doctrines of salvation in simplicity and plainness so that reasonable men, even from an intellectual standpoint, can scarcely disagree. This leaves religionists in the position where they must freely accept or openly oppose the Nephite scripture. There is no middle ground, no readily available gray area, no room for compromise.[9]

It appears that the time is right in the history of mankind for the Book of Mormon to come forth from the Lord as another witness for the Lord Jesus Christ to sustain and support the truths already taught in the Bible. This has a double effect—first, it blesses the believer and guides him to the truth, and second, it leaves the unbeliever without excuse on the day of judgment.

We live in a materialistic and humanistic society in which it is popular to place one's trust in the learning of man, in worldly norms, and in physical comforts. Such a life-style does not require prayer, faith, sacrifice, or obedience to divine laws. It does not call for or expect, or even want, divine intervention. In such an environment, the things of God can be easily disregarded and neglected. In 2 Nephi 29:8–14, we read that the testimony of two nations is a witness for God. We are given to understand in that chapter that we will eventually have three major written sources of scripture: the record of the Jews—the Bible, which is a testament of Jesus Christ; the record of the Nephites—the Book of Mormon, which is another testament of Jesus Christ; and the record of the ten tribes—a third testament of Jesus Christ—three witnesses to the truth of the gospel of Jesus Christ: that he is the literal Son of God, that he shed his blood for atonement, died, and that he rose from the grave in splendor and physical perfection. And we are further invited to consider the fact that out of these records we shall be judged of God for our eternal salvation.

NOTES AND REFERENCES

1. *Teachings of the Prophet Joseph Smith*, comp. Joseph Fielding Smith (Salt Lake City: Deseret Book, 1976), pp. 9–10; italics added.

2. Ibid., pp. 290–91.

3. Ibid., p. 310.

4. Ibid., p. 327.

5. *JD* 1:38.

6. *Improvement Era*, November 1936, p. 660.

7. *JD* 13:236.

8. *JD* 14:135-36; italics added.

9. *A New Witness for the Articles of Faith* (Salt Lake City: Deseret Book Co., 1985), pp. 460–61.

14

A LAND OF PROMISE, CHOICE ABOVE ALL OTHER LANDS

Philip M. Flammer

It goes almost without saying that a wide disparity exists between the concept of a "promised land," as mentioned in the scriptures, and the exchanges of territory that went with such mighty endeavors as the growth of dynasties, the feudal system, and the promises of would-be conquerors. The latter were part of the enduring itch for aggrandizement, a condition aptly described by Machiavelli as "the disease of princes." On the other hand, the concept of a promised land, as defined in scripture, involved special lands offered to special peoples by God himself. Moreover, receiving and possessing the lands as an inheritance was confirmed by covenant, with God offering both temporal and spiritual blessings for high levels of righteous behavior. If the covenant was broken by man, the divine sanction and protection were forfeit and hence the loss of the land itself—at least for a season.

A "promised land," prepared and protected by the Lord and tied to the covenant that "inasmuch as ye keep my com-

---

Phillip M. Flammer is Professor of History at Brigham Young University.

mandments ye shall prosper in the land," is surely one of the more vivid and pervasive concepts of the Book of Mormon. Both the Jaredites and the Nephites occupied land on the Western Hemisphere under this condition and, failing to keep the covenant, lost it to their utter ruin.

It is uncertain when Lehi was first told of the promised land awaiting him and his posterity. It is Nephi who first mentions it in the Book of Mormon. The Lord personally told Nephi that he was blessed because of his faith,

> for thou hast sought me diligently, with lowliness of heart. And inasmuch as ye shall keep my commandments, ye shall prosper, and shall be led to a land of promise; yea, even a land which I have prepared for you; yea, a land which is choice above all other lands. (1 Nephi 2:19–20.)

Thus, the hasty departure from Jerusalem and the migration to the promised land was revealed as part of a great plan God had prepared and now set in motion.

As part of a great vision, Nephi and his father witnessed many wonderful things and were instructed as to their meaning. This included the "iron rod," the "tree of life," and the forthcoming birth and ministry of the Savior. An angel who acted as Nephi's guide, however, further spoke of the promised land. Again in vision, Nephi was allowed to see much that would befall his people, including a visit by the resurrected Savior and the ultimate disappearance of the Nephite civilization. He also saw that some descendants of Laman and Lemuel would survive, eventually dwindling in unbelief as a degenerate people "full of idleness and all manner of abominations" (1 Nephi 12:23).

The vision was further extended to include a number of events relative to the unveiling of the promised land and God's influence in bringing devout and freedom-loving people to its shores. In Nephi's words:

> And I looked and beheld a man among the Gentiles, who was separated from the seed of my brethren by the many waters; and I beheld the Spirit of God, that it came down and wrought upon the man; and he went forth upon the many waters even unto the seed of my brethren, who were in the promised land (1 Nephi 13:12).

Believers in the Book of Mormon recognize in this verse a clear reference to Christopher Columbus and his epic "discovery" of the "New World" in 1492. The traditional view, however, holds that Columbus's discovery was a lucky accident, a result of his belief that the world was round and his eagerness to discover a way to the eastern "Indies" by sailing west. Columbus himself would have found this explanation most unsatisfactory. A deeply spiritual man who concluded that the end of the world was not far distant, he believed himself predestined to assist in the fulfillment of certain biblical prophecies. Among other spiritual callings, he felt a special destiny in relation to Isaiah's "islands of the sea" prophecies and Christ's statement that "other sheep I have, which are not of this fold: them also I must bring, and they shall hear my voice; and there shall be one fold, and one shepherd" (John 10:16).[1]

"I come to your Majesty as an Emissary of the Holy Trinity," he wrote in asking King Ferdinand of Spain to support his venture. And, eight years after his discovery of the New World, he wrote, "God made me the messenger of the new heaven and the new earth . . . and he showed me the spot where to find it."[2] Indeed, his last will and testament included the statement that the "most holy Trinity . . . inspired me with the idea and afterwards made it perfectly clear to me that I could navigate and go to the Indies from Spain by traversing the ocean westward."[3]

Inspired latter-day prophets have underscored this important point. In a 1961 conference address, President Ezra Taft Benson, then of the Council of the Twelve, declared that as part of the "divine plan . . . to raise up the first free people in modern times . . . God inspired Columbus to overcome almost insurmountable odds to discover America and bring this rich new land to the attention of the gentiles in Europe."[4]

After the vision of Columbus in relation to the promised land, Nephi "beheld the Spirit of God, that it wrought upon other Gentiles; and they went forth out of captivity, upon the many waters" (1 Nephi 13:13). The fulfillment of this vision/ prophecy is also verified by history and by latter-day prophets.

The early Pilgrims and Puritans who left Europe for the New World did so because they sought the freedom to worship as they saw fit as well as freedom from the prevailing forms of economic bondage, important issues left largely unaffected by both the Renaissance and the Protestant Reformation. Indeed, even as these humble and devout people were preparing to leave Europe, the Thirty Years' War, renowned for its savagery as well as its durability, broke out between Protestants and Catholics. Aptly described as a war "in which fervent Christians were prepared to hang, burn, torture, shoot or poison other fervent Christians with whom they disagreed on the correct approach to eternal life,"[5] it decimated much of western Europe. Moreover, the seventeenth century, like the one preceding it, experienced the widespread and monstrous "witch craze" in which both the Protestant and Catholic elite joined in identifying "Satan's lieutenants"—usually by liberal use of judicial torture—and destroying them in the name of God. As one eminent historian put it:

> The more fiercely [witches] were persecuted, the more numerous they became. By the beginning of the seventeenth century the witch-doctors had become hysterical. Their manuals have become encyclopedic in bulk, lunatic in pedantry. They demand, and sometimes achieve wholesale purges. By 1630 the slaughter has broken all previous records. It has become a holocaust in which lawyers, judges, clergy themselves join old women at the stake.[6]

Even the better-known Reformers were personally intolerant. Luther's severity in the Peasants War, for example, is well known. Little known but worthy of mention is Luther's one-sided discussion with the Swiss reformer Ulrich Zwingli. The purpose of the conference was to promote much-needed Protestant unity, but Luther began by focusing on the eucharist. Holding close to the Catholic doctrine of transubstantiation, he precluded unity or compromise by writing *Hoc est Corpus Meum* (This is my body) on the table. "I take these words literally," he said; "if anyone does not, I shall not argue but contradict."[7] For his part, Zwingli, who had considerable control in Protestant Zurich, stood firm against the Anabaptists. These devout Christians emphasized spiritual matters over temporal ones and, among other things, insisted on baptism by immersion. Zwingli consented to having a number of them "truly immersed," that is, drowned in the Limat River.[8]

In Geneva, John Calvin clung to rigid precepts based on the doctrine of pedestination, declaring:

> Whoever shall now contend that it is unjust to put heretics and blasphemers to death will knowingly and willingly incur their very guilt. . . . It is not in vain that he [God] banishes all those human affections that soften our hearts, that he commands paternal love

and all the benevolent feelings between brother, relations, and friends to cease. . . . When his [God's] glory is to be asserted, humanity must be almost obliterated from our memories.[9]

True to his word, Calvin burned Michael Servetus for heresy and, among other things, ordered a child beheaded for striking its parents.[10]

Even after King Henry VIII's break with Rome, England was not tolerant of religious diversity. The Church of England proved dogmatic and intolerant and vigorously persecuted those who did not fall into line. Many dissenters were burned for heresy. Joseph Smith's fifth great-grandfather, the Reverend John Lathrop, initially a minister for the Church of England, was more fortunate. Finding much Church of England doctrine not in harmony with scriptures, he left the state church and became a minister of The First Independent Church of London. For this breach of policy, the Bishop of London had him arrested and cast into prison.

> While he was thus incarcerated, his wife died. He was not so much as allowed to attend her funeral, and his children were left with no one to care for them. He made repeated appeals for clemency, but the bishop refused even to listen to him. Finally the orphaned children went to the bishop as a group and personally pleaded for mercy. So pitiful were they . . . that the bishop was finally moved, and he released Lathrop on condition that he leave the country. This he did, and, with thirty-two members of his congregation, he went to America.[11]

In somewhat similar fashion, the Pilgrims that landed at Plymouth Rock in 1620 had first fled from England to Holland in search of greater religious and economic freedom. Finding neither to their satisfaction, they were among the first to come to America.

Nephi also beheld in vision that the Gentiles in the promised land grew to "many multitudes" and "the Spirit of the Lord . . . was upon the Gentiles, and they did prosper and obtain the land for their inheritance; and I beheld that they were white, and exceedingly fair and beautiful, like unto my people before they were slain" (1 Nephi 13:15).

Nephi also witnessed that the "wrath of God . . . was upon the seed of my brethren; and they were scattered before the Gentiles and were smitten" (1 Nephi 13:14), a consequence amply validated by the record of history. Much of this conflict stemmed from attraction of the western frontier, where good land, including tribal lands, was available by purchase or by conquest. While life was rarely easy for new immigrants to the promised land, opportunities were abundant and greatly enhanced by a level of freedom unknown in Europe. Indeed, the ever-increasing influx of immigrants bore ample witness that the New World was truly a land of promise, one where they could prosper to a degree not possible in Europe.

Nephi further saw that "the Gentiles who had gone forth out of captivity did humble themselves before the Lord; and the power of the Lord was with them" (1 Nephi 13:16). This pleasing combination explains much of their prosperity, which soon reached such proportions that alarmed British authorities decided to end what had been a "soft" policy of "benign neglect." Under the British policy of mercantilism, the colonies existed to be sources of raw materials and a controlled market for British manufactured goods. To establish firm control, the British imposed forms of economic sanctions. Besides increased taxes and import duties, the colonies were specifically forbidden to coin money or manufacture specific items such as iron and hats. Colonial reaction to such infringements on their freedoms and prosperity led to the Declaration of Independence and the American Revolution.

The American Revolution was a war the colonies won with divine assistance. In his vision, Nephi saw that

> the power of God was with them, and also that the wrath of God was upon all those that were gathered together against them to battle. And I . . . beheld that the Gentiles that had gone out of captivity were delivered by the power of God out of the hands of all other nations. (1 Nephi 13:18−19.)

It is an axiom of history that temporary, ill-equipped and poorly trained militia such as those available to the colonies cannot prevail over regular, well-equipped and well-trained forces backed by the resources of a wealthy nation, precisely the type of forces available to England. General George Washington often complained about the reliability of the militia, saying at one point:

> It takes you two to three months to bring new men in any tolerable degree acquainted with their duty. . . . Before this is accom-

plished, the time approaches for their dismissal, and you are beginning to make interest with them for their continuance on another limited period; in the doing of which you are obliged to relax in your discipline, in order as it were to curry favor with them, by which means the latter part of your time is employed in undoing what the first was accomplishing.[12]

The eventual victory of the Continental forces was indeed miraculous and was so recognized by many political and spiritual leaders of the time. And no man understood this better than George Washington, who spoke frequently of the influence of "Divine Providence." During the colonial siege of Boston, for example, Washington was gravely concerned that the British might learn his soldiers had fewer than nine rounds of ammunition per man. Well aware that they could not stop a British advance, he wrote, "If I shall be able to rise superior to these . . . difficulties . . . I shall most religiously believe, that the finger of Providence is in it, to blind the eyes of our enemies."[13]

The British missed a golden opportunity to end the revolution at Boston, at least for the time being. Other opportunities would be soon forthcoming, however. The British won at Long Island, Harlem Heights, Fort Washington, and Fort Lee while Washington was able to keep his demoralized troops intact only by retreating. The Continental Army won victories at Trenton and Princeton, but they were of little consequence other than to give the troops the will to endure Valley Forge. After the hard winter of Valley Forge, Washington wrote that

> Providence has a joint claim to my humble and grateful thanks, for its protection and direction of me, through the many difficult and intricate scenes, which this contest hath produced; and for the constant interposition in our behalf, when the clouds were heaviest and seemed ready to burst upon us.[14]

For all his tribulations, Washington was much heartened after Valley Forge. "The hand of Providence [he wrote] has been so conspicuous in all this, that he must be worse than an infidel that lacks faith, and more than wicked, that has not gratitude, enough to acknowledge his obligations. . . ."[15]

Washington firmly believed that without divine assistance, any one of several events could have brought the war to an unhappy conclusion. General Charles Lee's irresponsible if not cowardly retreat at Monmouth, for example, so disorganized colonial forces that, in Washington's words, it would have "proved fatal" to the cause except for "that bountiful Providence which has never failed us in the hour of distress." With that help, Washington was able to rally a "regiment or two" from the chaos and drive the enemy from the field.[16]

The fortuitous discovery of Benedict Arnold's attempt to betray the post and garrison at West Point into the hands of the British touched Washington deeply. "That overruling Providence which has so often, and so remarkably interposed in our favor, never manifested itself more conspicuously than in the timely discovery of [Arnold's] horrid design."[17]

While Washington personally experienced divine intervention again and again, many other Americans also saw and appreciated its results. According to historian James Hutchinson Smylie,

> The clergymen had compared America to Israel during the war. . . . Again and again they referred to the new nation as God's "American Israel," or as God's "New English Israel," or as "God's American Zion," and they were positive that God was involved inseparably in America's destiny as he had been involved in Israel's.[18]

Equally if not more dangerous to the growing tradition of freedom in America were the "mother Gentiles" in Europe who "gathered together upon the waters, and upon the land also, to battle" (1 Nephi 13:17) with the new inhabitants of the land of promise. Some, such as the French and the Spanish, incited the Indians to harass the settlers and discourage their westward expansion. Indeed, between 1688 and 1815, six general European wars spilled over into the New World. A number of colonial wars were fought between England and France in the New World and one—the French and Indian War (1754–1763)—spread to Europe where it became known as the Seven Years' War. When the English colonies broke from the parent government and the French government helped the Americans, it was not out of sympathy for the American effort but for revenge against England. Even so, France had no desire to see America become a great nation and at times conspired to limit its expansion.

During the Napoleonic Wars, which began in 1803, Napoleon sought to build a colonial empire in the New World. Its center would be in Haiti, but its breadbasket would be the vast Louisiana Territory, a sparsely inhabited wilderness west of the

Mississippi River, as large as the United States itself. France, however, did not own the territory, having ceded it to Spain in 1762 to compensate her for her losses to England in the Seven Years' War. Thus, Napoleon first had to extract it from Spain, a matter of grave concern to the Americans, for the territory included the mouth of the Mississippi River and the port of New Orleans. The Spanish had periodically closed the port to the Americans, disrupting American trade from as far away as the upper Ohio Valley. The idea of this port being in the hands of the French so alarmed President Thomas Jefferson that he seriously considered the possibility of a forced alliance with Great Britain. In a letter to Robert Livingston, the American minister in Paris, he wrote:

> There is on the globe one single spot, the possessor of which is our natural and habitual enemy. It is New Orleans. . . . The day that France takes possession of New Orleans, fixes the sentence which is to restrain her [the French Nation] forever within her low-water mark. . . . From that moment, we must marry ourselves to the British fleet and nation.[19]

In a series of events as remarkable as the evidence of divine intervention in the American Revolution, Napoleon abruptly decided to sell the Louisiana Territory to the United States for the astonishingly low sum of fifteen million dollars. (Jefferson's agents were authorized to offer ten million dollars for New Orleans alone.) Jefferson was not about to reject this golden opportunity, even though he had long insisted on strict adherence to the letter of the Constitution and knew he did not have authority to approve the sale. For his part, Napoleon deliberately left the western boundaries of the new territory uncertain, hoping to stir up trouble between the United States and Spain.

A few years later, the United States found herself in serious trouble with both England and France. Locked in the Napoleonic Wars, each antagonist forbade the United States to trade with the enemy. Both sides seized American merchant ships with abandon and, at one point, Britain and the United States went to war, partly because the British were stopping American ships on the high seas and forcibly impressing American sailors for near slave-like service on British vessels. It was during this War of 1812 that the British captured Washington, D.C., and burned government buildings, including the White House.

The "gentile nations" that harassed the budding United

States during these trying years had no intention of allowing the infant nation to become a powerful rival. Not until the United States gained international stature in its own right was it treated as an equal among the nations.

The birth and growth of the United States is easily one of the more astonishing events in human history, strong support indeed for the concept of divine assistance during that trying period. In particular, the nation evolved in a way counter to the usual patterns for developing nations. To suit the Lord's purposes, it was vital that freedom be an inherent part of that pattern in order to uphold the divine principle of free agency. Thus a democracy, the preferable form of political freedom, must not only cherish its freedom, it must remain anchored to a tradition of freedom so firmly rooted that it is very difficult to dislodge. This the United States achieved, largely because of divine assistance in its development as well as its founding (see 2 Nephi 1:8).

Since mankind has an affinity for mortgaging the future by exploiting resources rather than husbanding them, it is hardly surprising that the Spanish and Portuguese who followed Columbus directed their efforts to the lands of Central and South America. In their search for gold and other mineral wealth, they ravaged both lands and peoples. The Catholic Church was the only durable institution, and it too practiced economic exploitation.

How different this was from the temperate lands to the north which remained largely unexplored. These lands lacked the gold and silver which enriched Spain for a season and then left her sterile when the industrial revolution set a new standard for national wealth, power, and prestige. The lands that would form the United States possessed these resources in abundance. This provided, in time, for a new nation where people flocking to its shores could develop a firm tradition of freedom well able to withstand the powers that plotted against them. History offers no comparable development.

But perhaps most important of all, it was vital that the tradition of freedom be able to withstand internal pressures. A near universal truth of history is the seeming inevitability of a prosperous society to separate into classes and for the new "aristocracy" to seize power and use it to promote their own purposes. This was largely precluded in the United States by a divinely inspired Constitution married to a firm tradition of God-given liberty.

Still, even with freedom of worship guaranteed by the Constitution, the restored Church suffered intense persecution. And it is significant that enemies of the Church continually sought government assistance by claiming that the Church and its people were "in rebellion" against the nation and the states in which they settled. Not even the great exodus to Mexican territory in the West stilled those voices, a strong indication of what the Church could have expected in lands without a tradition of freedom guaranteed by a written constitution.

Having seen much of the future and having such a clear vision of the promised land and the role it would play in the divine plan, Nephi's account of the arrival of his group in the promised land underscores the validity the angel's statement to Nephi that their destination was indeed a covenant land "choice above all other lands" (1 Nephi 13:30).

> We did arrive at the promised land; and we went forth upon the land, and did pitch our tents; and we did call it the promised land.
>
> And it came to pass that we did begin to till the earth, and we began to plant seeds. . . . And it came to pass that they did grow exceedingly; wherefore, we were blessed in abundance.
>
> And it came to pass that we did find upon the land of promise, as we journeyed in the wilderness, that there were beasts in the forests of every kind, both the cow and the ox, and the ass and the horse, and the goat and the wild goat, and all manner of wild animals, which were for the use of men. And we did find all manner of ore, both of gold, and of silver, and of copper. (1 Nephi 18:23–25.)

The great vision of the promised land given Lehi and Nephi surely sustained them during those difficult years en route to the promised land. Their long and difficult journey was one with divine purpose and hence profound meaning. By the same token, Laman and Lemuel's festering resentment and animosity towards those with that vision is partly attributable to their total lack of understanding as to its meaning. For them, the exodus was nothing more than a foolish and unnecessary flight from Jerusalem. Thus, the hardships they faced were also unnecessary, their father Lehi a foolish visionary, and Nephi a sanctimonious and domineering younger brother. All that might have changed had they understood the concept of the promised land which they would share, and which was explained with utmost clarity.

Some time after their safe arrival, Nephi was approached by his rebellious brothers as he was studying the brass plates taken from Laban. Asked whether certain things mentioned on the plates were to be understood temporally or spiritually, Nephi spoke prophetically about the promised land on which they now stood. He spoke of its relationship to the restoration of the gospel in the latter days, together with the bringing of that gospel to the scattered remnants of their own seed.

> And . . . the time cometh that after all the house of Israel have been scattered and confounded, that the Lord God will raise up a mighty nation among the Gentiles, yea, even upon the face of this land; and by them shall our seed be scattered.
>
> And after our seed is scattered the Lord God will proceed to do a marvelous work among the Gentiles, which shall be of great worth unto our seed; wherefore, it is likened unto their being nourished by the Gentiles and being carried in their arms and upon their shoulders.
>
> And it shall also be of worth unto the Gentiles; and not only unto the Gentiles but unto all the house of Israel, unto the making known of the covenants of the Father of heaven unto Abraham, saying: In thy seed shall all the kindreds of the earth be blessed. (1 Nephi 22:7–9.)

How that understanding of God's plan must have thrilled Nephi! To the blessings inherent in possessing the promised land and keeping the covenants, there was the added knowledge that this land would one day be the citadel of freedom essential to the restoration of the gospel. It would be God's "base of operations" for sending the gospel to the nations of the world prior to the second coming of Jesus Christ.

NOTES AND REFERENCES

1. See Pauline Watts, "Prophecy and Discovery: On the Spiritual Origins of Christopher Columbus's 'Enterprise of the Indies,' " *American Historical Review*, Feb. 1985, pp. 73–102. See also Hugh Nibley, "Columbus and Revelation," *Instructor*, Vol. 88 (October 1953), pp. 319–20.

2. Watts, p. 73.

3. Cited in Mark E. Petersen, *The Great Prologue* (Salt Lake City: Deseret Book Co., 1975), p. 29.

4. Ezra Taft Benson, Conference Report, October 1961, p. 69.

5. General Sir John Hackett, *The Profession of Arms* (New York: Macmillan Publishing Co., 1983), p. 75.

6. H. R. Trevor-Roper, *The European Witch-Craze of the Sixteenth and Seventeenth Centuries* (New York: Harper and Row), p. 97.

7. James E. Barker, *Apostasy from the Divine Church* (Salt Lake City: Bookcraft, 1984), p. 716.

8. Ibid., p. 740.

9. Ibid., p. 750.

10. Ibid., pp. 749–50.

11. Petersen, pp. 34–35.

12. Lynn Montross, *War Through the Ages* (New York: Harper and Brothers, 1960), p. 419.

13. John C. Fitzpatrick, *The Writings of George Washington.* 31 vols. (Washington: GPO, 1932–1944), 11:243.

14. Ibid., 11:492.

15. Ibid., 12:343.

16. Ibid., pp. 156–57.

17. Ibid., 20:213.

18. James Smylie, unpublished Ph.D. dissertation (Princeton Theological Seminary, 1946), cited in pamphlet by Michael L. Chadwick, *God's Hand in the Founding of America as Acknowledged by the Early Clergymen of the United States* (Salt Lake City: The Center for Constitutional Studies, 1980), p. 3.

19. Thomas A. Bailey, *A Diplomatic History of the American People* (New York: Appleton-Century-Crofts, 1974), p. 105.

15

FROM SMALL MEANS THE LORD BRINGS ABOUT GREAT THINGS

Clark V. Johnson

The experiences of Lehi's family in the wilderness illustrate how God works with his children to bring them closer to him. They describe their experience as one of trials, discomfort, near starvation, rebellion, and death that occurred while they traveled from near the borders of the Red Sea to a place called Bountiful (1 Nephi 16:14). Daily crises were not reserved for Lehi's family but are common to us all. The experiences of Lehi's family illustrate that it is not position in life but reaction to daily adversity and prosperity that determines our eternal destiny. Through "small means" provided by God to meet our daily circumstances he brings about "great things"—our salvation as his children. Chapters 16 to 18 of 1 Nephi contain at least four keys that serve as guideposts to us as we try to build a successful relationship with our Father in Heaven and obtain salvation.

Clark V. Johnson is Associate Professor of Church History and Doctrine at Brigham Young University.

Obedience

Traveling in the desert for eight years, Lehi's group arrived at a place on the Indian Ocean which they named Bountiful (1 Nephi 16:13; 17:1, 5).[1] Even though their trials were great and should not be minimized, Nephi knew that the Lord had provided for them because they had kept the commandments (1 Nephi 17:3). He knew that "the commandments of God must be fulfilled," and that if "men keep the commandments of God he doth nourish them, and strengthen them" (1 Nephi 17:3). Nephi understood that he could accomplish all things, even to the point of changing the elements if the Lord required him to do so (1 Nephi 17:50). This is one of the keys: if the Lord requires it of you, you can do it!

Throughout 1 Nephi one cannot help but be impressed with Nephi's personal righteousness. After counseling with his brothers and giving them the interpretation of their father's dream of the tree of life, Nephi admonished his brothers to change their lives. He reasoned that "the kingdom of God is not filthy, and there cannot any unclean thing enter into the kingdom of God" (1 Nephi 15:34). When he had finished speaking to them, his brothers replied: "Thou hast declared unto us hard things, more than we are able to bear" (1 Nephi 16:1). Nephi agreed that he had spoken hard things against the wicked, but held out great hope for the righteous (1 Nephi 16:2–4). Laman and Lemuel, like many of us at times, had forgotten that the Lord gives us commandments to inspire us to righteousness, not to restrict us (D&C 20:7). It seems that before God helps his children they must approach him by striving to live in harmony with his commandments. Hence, Abinadi taught the rebellious Noah and his priests the Ten Commandments, which are the basis for establishing a relationship with God (Mosiah 12:31–37; 13:11–25). He further taught them of Noah that the wicked become angry when they hear the "truth," and that the word of God "cuts [the wicked] to [their] hearts" because of their sins (Mosiah 13:4, 7).

During the years prior to their arrival at the promised land, Laman and Lemuel and others in the group complained repeatedly about almost everything—departing into the wilderness, returning to Jerusalem after the brass plates, the broken bow, the death of Ishmael—and thought it ridiculous that the Lord would require them to help Nephi build a ship (1 Nephi 3:2–6; 4;

16:17—23, 31—32, 34—35; 17:17—22). It must also be remembered that during these trials they had had several faith-building experiences. Even though an angel had appeared to them, they had had revelatory help in finding food, and they were shocked by the power of God (which convinced them to help Nephi build the ship), they never experienced the growth that comes from obedience to principles (1 Nephi 7:16—20; 16:37—39; 17:45—55; 18:8—22).[2] The Lord demonstrated his power again and again, but they would not respond. They never acquired faith in the mission of their father (1 Nephi 17:20). They never learned that obedience is the key to obtaining salvation as taught in these chapters and revealed again through Joseph Smith. The prophet taught that,

> There is a law, irrevocably decreed in heaven . . . upon which all blessings [or cursings] are predicated—and when we obtain any blessing [or cursing] from God, it is by obedience [or disobedience] to that law upon which it is predicated (D&C 130:20—21).

Nephi repeatedly tried both to warn and to teach his brothers and their families, and just when he felt that he might be successful, they always reverted to their old ways—complaining and plotting against him and their father until they had arrived at the point where they were "past feeling" (1 Nephi 17:45).

The Use of the Scriptures

Sometime after the Lehi colony had arrived at the land Bountiful, Nephi was commanded to build a ship to make possible their journey to the promised land. His brothers laughed at and ridiculed him. They also began once again to plot against Nephi, threatening to take his life (1 Nephi 17:48).[3] They lamented that they were not still enjoying the comforts of Jerusalem (1 Nephi 17:21). Nephi spoke to them at great length trying again to persuade them to follow Lehi.

When Laman and Lemuel insisted that the people at Jerusalem were righteous and inferred that their father had deceived them, Nephi taught them out of the brass plates concerning the obedience of Abraham, Isaac, and Jacob (1 Nephi 17:40). He reminded them that even after God had delivered the children of Israel from Egyptian bondage, had destroyed the armies of Pharaoh by drowning them in the Red Sea, and had helped Israel conquer the land of Canaan, they still turned against the Lord and rejected his prophets. He explained that when in the wilderness the children of Israel were bitten by fiery flying serpents and many people died, God prepared a way for them to be healed. All they had to do was to "look; and because of the simpleness of the way . . . there were many who perished" (1 Nephi 17:23–29, 41–42). Showing from scripture the history of the destruction of those who lacked the faith to believe, Nephi spoke prophetically of the coming destruction of the Southern Kingdom [Judah] by the Babylonians saying that "they are at this day about to be destroyed . . . and led away into captivity" (1 Nephi 17:43).[4] Nephi explained to them that God had led the righteous away from the wicked and testified that they would have been destroyed had they not followed their father (1 Nephi 17:38).[5] He taught them that God created the earth and man for a purpose, and that he blesses those who will have him to be their God (1 Nephi 17:36, 39–40, 45). He warned his brothers that the "righteous" are "favored of God" and that the reason Israel was led to Canaan anciently was the inhabitants of that land had become "ripe in iniquity" and God "did curse the land against them," but he blessed the land for ancient Israel (1 Nephi 17:35).

Nephi instructed his brothers concerning the miraculous preservation of ancient Israel by the hand of the Lord, but they resented his teachings from the brass plates. It was only after a convincing demonstration of the power of God that they acknowledged his power and the righteousness of Nephi's position (1 Nephi 17:48, 53–55). Nephi's reference to God's preservation of ancient Israel was analogous to God's preservation of his father's family (1 Nephi 17:23–24, 41–46).

While the teachings from the brass plates had a negative effect upon Laman and Lemuel, they had a positive effect upon other members of Lehi's family. Lehi used the scriptures (brass plates) in a positive way to teach his son Joseph about his namesake, Joseph of Egypt. He spoke of the good qualities of Joseph who was sold into Egypt, and also related some of the prophecies of the ancient Joseph to his own son, noting that because he was a descendant of Joseph he would be blessed (2 Nephi 3).[6] It is clear that Nephi also believed that the teachings from the brass plates were applicable to them, for he wrote: "I did liken all scriptures unto us, that it might be for our profit and learning" (1 Nephi 19:23). Perhaps this is one of the reasons that President

Spencer W. Kimball continually pled with us to study the scriptures. He wrote on one occasion:

> Let us this year seek to read and understand and apply the principles and inspired counsel found within the [scriptures]. If we do so, we shall discover that our personal *acts* of righteousness will also bring *personal revelation* or *inspiration* when needed into our own lives.[7]

Thus the third key to obtaining salvation as illustrated by Nephi and Lehi is to study the scriptures.

Within the scriptures are lesson-filled stories about the ancients illustrating the principles that we need to acquire in order to come to know God and to receive personal revelation from him. A primary scripture for us today is the Book of Mormon. President Ezra Taft Benson has said:

> The Book of Mormon was written for us today. . . . It is a record of a fallen people, compiled by inspired men for our blessing today. Those people never had the book—it was meant for us. Mormon, the ancient prophet after whom the book is named, abridged centuries of records. God, who knows the end from the beginning, told him what to include in his abridgment that we would need for our day.[8]

Prophets and Prophet-Fathers

One of the great lessons in revelation and obedience is contained within the experience of Nephi's broken bow. When the small colony was unable to obtain food, many accused Nephi of being careless and they rebelled against God for getting them into such a predicament. Even father Lehi's faith faltered and he murmured against God (1 Nephi 16:18, 20).

Rather than murmur, Nephi made a wooden bow and some arrows, and then asked his father to inquire of the Lord where he should go to find meat (1 Nephi 16:23). Elder Marion D. Hanks said of this event:

> "Whither shall I go to obtain food?" It is a simple thing, isn't it? . . . This means that Nephi went to his father and said, "Dad, the Lord has blessed you. You are his servant. I need to know where to go to get food. Dad, you ask him, will you?" Oh, he could have gone to his own knees. He could have taken over. I

count this one of the really significant lessons of life in the book. . . . A son who had strength enough, and humility enough, and manliness enough to go to his wavering superior and say, "You ask God, will you?" because somehow he knew this is how you make men strong, that wise confidence in men builds them. Lehi asked God and God told him, and Lehi's leadership was restored.[9]

Sometimes one fails to realize that Nephi was just as hungry as the rest, and in addition had been the object of their scorn. It would have been easy for him to have gone to the Lord himself, but he recognized the position of leadership held by his father, Lehi, and sought counsel from his prophet-father. What most of us fail to realize is that it is our reaction to daily crises which produce rebellion or righteousness.

When Lehi sought counsel from the Lord he not only learned where to send his son for meat but was also chastised by the Lord, which caused him to "fear and tremble exceedingly" (1 Nephi 16:27). None is exempt from the growing experience of being tried and chastened by the Lord. Father Lehi needed to be reprimanded by the Lord for his lack of faith. Unlike Laman and Lemuel, however, he repented. Joseph Smith attributed his own lack of revelation early in the Restoration to his foolishness and vain ambitions and was chastened by the Lord (Joseph Smith—History 1:28). Later in his life, the Lord chastised the Prophet for not teaching his family the commandments and included other members of the First Presidency as well (D&C 93:41–50). In a revelation to Brigham Young, the Lord taught that a person that will "not bear chastisement" is not worthy of his kingdom (D&C 136:31). Blessings received from a father or Church leader may include chastening from the Lord. The Lord gives instructions concerning what one must do on his own to help himself before he can expect help from the Lord. In evaluating their experience one notes that the Lord tells them exactly what to do to become worthy of further revelation. Many men and women when they receive chastenings in their blessings turn away, convinced that the Lord does not love them and will not help them. Thus they fall into the Laman and Lemuel trap and are not like Lehi, who accepted the rebuke and repented and continued to receive revelation from God.

From the life of Lehi we learn that revelation is a continuing process. Many assume that once they have received an answer to prayer that is sufficient and all that God requires of them. Nephi pointed out that after the people at Jerusalem had refused to receive Lehi's words, after Lehi had obeyed the Lord's commandment to take his family and leave Jerusalem, after he had sent his sons back to Jerusalem to acquire the brass plates, after they had brought Ishmael's family into the wilderness, and after the children from the two families had intermarried, Lehi had fulfilled all the commandments the Lord had given him (1 Nephi 16:8).

But the Lord was not through with this father-prophet. After keeping all the commandments he had been given, Lehi received further revelation which commanded him to continue traveling in the wilderness. Thus we see that revelation is a steady, repeated process as God seeks to guide and direct our lives. This concept of continuous revelation was taught by the Prophet Joseph Smith.

> Happiness is the object and design of our existence; and will be the end thereof, if we pursue the path that leads to it; and this path is virtue, uprightness, faithfulness, holiness, and keeping all the commandments of God. But we cannot keep all the commandments without first knowing them, and we cannot expect to know all, . . . unless we comply with . . . those we have already received.[10]

As Lehi's family made preparations to continue their journey, the Lord provided a new source of revelation, the Liahona (1 Nephi 16:10).[11] This remarkable instrument not only acted as a compass (1 Nephi 16:16), but also writing appeared upon it giving the group instructions. Nephi noted that the instrument worked only according to the obedience and faith of the group.

When Nephi sought directions from his father as to where he could find meat during a time of privation and starvation, Lehi consulted the Liahona. This instrument which Nephi calls a small means for the Lord to bring about great things, not only gave directions to Nephi, but also gave Lehi and other members of his family information that caused them to fear and tremble (1 Nephi 16:27–30). In the revelatory sense it was not unlike the seer stones possessed by a later Nephite prophet-king, Mosiah (Mosiah 8:13–18).[12] Receiving revelation is the duty of those who preside in the priesthood of the Church. For example, the prophet is to receive revelation for the whole Church, a stake president for the members within his stake, a bishop for the members of his ward and a father for the members of his family.

Near the end of his life Lehi responded to his revelatory responsibility to his children and gave each of his sons (and through them their families) a patriarchal (father's) blessing (2 Nephi 1-4). Thus, Lehi was a father-prophet who understood revelation and kept the commandments of God (1 Nephi 16:8). This is the fourth key for our obtaining revelation: follow the prophet, Church leaders, and honor our fathers.

Conclusions

From the events in the lives of Lehi and his family come more than just experiences and difficulties in desert travel. Each crisis caused them to react. For the most part Lehi, Nephi, and others were faithful and grew from their experiences. They grew stronger physically, and they grew more sensitive spiritually. Their sensitivity caused them to appreciate the blessings that God had given them. Through personal obedience Nephi became a prophet. He sought the Lord in the temporal as well as the spiritual aspects of his life. The Lord responded to Nephi and directed him through continuous revelation so that he prospered in both areas.

Unlike their brother Nephi, Laman and Lemuel were too busy complaining to recognize the blessings of the Lord. Through disobedience they became "past feeling."

Nephi tried to teach his brothers from the scriptures. He used the stories of the ancient patriarchs and Moses to teach the principles of righteousness to his people. He taught them that even though the Lord had blessed Israel during the days of Moses, the Israelites rejected revelation and living prophets.

These chapters in the Book of Mormon illustrate for us the principles by which we must live if we are to live successfully in the Lord. Keeping the commandments, receiving personal revelation, and following living prophets give men and women happiness in this life and lead them to God, who rewards them with eternal life.

NOTES AND REFERENCES

1. *Bountiful* means plentiful. They named the place Bountiful "because of its much fruit" (1 Nephi 17:6).

2. See also 1 Nephi 3:29; 4:3.

3. Previously they had sought to kill their father Lehi as well (1 Nephi 17:44). Laman and Lemuel had developed the disposition to commit murder (1 Nephi 16:37–38).

4. In about 721 B.C. Assyria conquered the Northern Kingdom, and Jerusalem fell to the Babylonians about 587 B.C. (LDS Bible Dictionary, pp. 638–39). The Lehi colony camped at Bountiful and built a ship about 591 B.C. (Book of Mormon, footnote p. 40.) After their arrival in the promised land Nephi declared to his people that Jerusalem had been destroyed. He had seen it in a vision. (2 Nephi 1:4.)

5. He pointed out that the people at Jerusalem had sought their father's life (1 Nephi 17:44).

6. See 2 Nephi 3:23, which points out that Joseph, Lehi's son, will be blessed because of the covenants Joseph of Egypt made with the Lord.

7. Spencer W. Kimball, "Always a Convert Church," *Ensign*, September 1975, p. 4.

8. Ezra Taft Benson, Conference Report, April 1975, p. 94. See also *Ensign*, May 1975, p. 63.

9. Marion D. Hanks, "Steps in Learning," Brigham Young University *Speeches of the Year*, 4 May 1960, p. 7.

10. *Teachings of the Prophet Joseph Smith*, comp. Joseph Fielding Smith (Salt Lake City: Deseret Book, 1976), pp. 255–56.

11. 1 Nephi 16:16, 27–30; see also Mosiah 1:16; Alma 37:38–40; D&C 17:1.

12. Mosiah II in addition to being a king of the people in Zarahemla was also a seer. He had the "interpreters" which allowed him to translate and see, giving him knowledge of the past, present, and future. (Mosiah 8:13, 17.)

16

LEHI'S JOURNEYS

Paul R. Cheesman

The story of the Book of Mormon and Lehi's exodus from the Old World begins in Jerusalem, the capital of the kingdom of Judah and the most prominent city in all Israel. Latter-day Saint visitors to Jerusalem, who are inspired by these surroundings as they relate to the life of Christ, should also remind themselves that this is where the prophet Lehi lived. In Lehi's time, priests and Levites who officiated in the ordinances of the law of Moses, worshippers from the other tribes of Jacob, merchants from Egypt and neighboring countries, and artisans in various trades—all considered Jerusalem a center of civilization in the Near East.

The country was divided into two parties—pro-Egyptian and pro-Babylonian. Most of the people favored the Egyptian influence. Hugh Nibley has suggested that Lehi had been closely associated with Egypt as a merchant and thus had traveled between the two countries.[1] This experience would have been a

Paul R. Cheesman is Professor Emeritus of Ancient Scripture at Brigham Young University.

great advantage to Lehi for the journey that he was eventually commanded to undertake. Lehi probably spoke and wrote Egyptian, which he taught his sons.[2]

The story of Lehi's leading the company of Israelites from Jerusalem to America is told in 1 Nephi 2–18. Many of these chapters, however, deal with Nephi's visions (1 Nephi 11–15) and his comments on the records he is keeping (1 Nephi 6, 9). That leaves about twenty-five pages wherein the group's travels are recorded, and most of these pages record opposition of the elder sons Laman and Lemuel to their father and younger brother Nephi. The result is that we have only a sketchy account of Lehi's travels given us in the Book of Mormon. We are therefore left to surmise several related things based upon consideration of other evidences.

That Lehi lived in Jerusalem did not necessarily mean that he dwelt in the *city* of Jerusalem. The *land* of Jerusalem encompasses much more of the immediate area surrounding the city. We are of the opinion that Lehi's property lay somewhere in the land of Jerusalem and not within the walls of the city.

Lehi was of the tribe of Manasseh and was obviously a man of considerable wealth (Alma 10:3–4). He and his wife, Sariah, had four sons and some daughters. He received many dreams and visions in which the Lord instructed him to warn the people of Jerusalem to repent. Rather than listen and repent, the people were angry with Lehi and sought his life. As a result, he was commanded to leave Jerusalem. He went into the wilderness and left behind great treasures of gold, silver, and other precious items, carrying with him only the necessities for traveling and existing in the wilderness (1 Nephi 2:4).

Lehi's wealth seemed to reflect the possibility of his being a trader, acquiring all manner of "precious things" (1 Nephi 2:4, 11). We can assume that he was an experienced traveler because his preparation for the trip into the wilderness was so complete that he did not have to send back for any provisions. Nibley reminds us that Manasseh was the tribe living in the most remote part of the desert.[3]

From Jerusalem to the Valley of Lemuel

There are three possible routes from Jerusalem to the Red Sea: (1) from Jerusalem northeast to Jericho, east across the Jordan River, and then south on the east side of the Dead Sea; (2)

from Jerusalem to Jericho and down the west side of the Dead
Sea; and (3) from Jerusalem southwest through Hebron, then
east or southeast to a point below the Dead Sea. All three routes
converge south of the Dead Sea and lead to Aqaba.

Lynn M. and Hope Hilton have suggested that Nephi could
have seen metal smelting and shipbuilding at Aqaba that would
have benefited him later.[4] From Aqaba Lehi's group journeyed
"three days in the wilderness" and camped in the "valley of
Lemuel" (1 Nephi 2:10, 14). After traveling in this area, the
Hiltons conclude that the valley of Lemuel is most probably the
place now known as Al Beda in the Wadi El Afal, in Saudi
Arabia. Al Beda contains the ruins of what has been considered
the traditional home of Moses' father-in-law Jethro. The ruins
are still called by his name. Lehi's colony could have stayed at Al
Beda several seasons.[5]

In this valley Lehi built an altar and offered a sacrifice to the
Lord, giving thanks for their journey. His description of the
valley's being firm and steadfast and immovable is in contrast to
the modern vernacular of Joseph Smith, who probably would
have referred to the mountains and hills as the everlasting and
stronghold areas. To the Arabs, the *valleys*, not the mountains,
are the source of their strength and permanence.[6]

It seems to be a tradition among Semitic people to name
even already-known places after their current personal experiences, perhaps to give greater meaning to the areas.[7]

It was in the valley of Lemuel that Lehi had a dream com-
manding him to send his sons back to Jerusalem to obtain the
brass plates. After a successful mission, the sons returned with
the brass plates and also with Zoram, the servant of Laban, who
was the keeper of the plates.[8]

Nephi had made Zoram take an oath that he would not
return to Jerusalem. One might consider this a strange custom,
but to the people of that day there was "nothing more sacred
than the oath among the nomads."[9] Such action supports the
Book of Mormon as an ancient Israel document.

The Lord also counseled Lehi to have his sons return to
Jerusalem a second time to bring the family of Ishmael, who was
of the tribe of Ephraim, to join them on their journey. Again the
mission was successful and the family of Ishmael, including his
sons and their wives and children, plus Ishmael's single daughters, left Jerusalem and joined the family of Lehi in the wilderness. This allowed the sons of Lehi the opportunity for marriage
and family.

According to Erastus Snow, Joseph Smith said that Ishmael's "sons [had] married into Lehi's family."[10] This combination of families would increase the number who continued the journey to approximately twenty to thirty people, depending on the number of children among them. This number increased during this eight-year wilderness journey as two sons, Jacob and Joseph, were born to Sariah and Lehi (1 Nephi 18:7), and other families also bore children (1 Nephi 17:1, 20).

From the Valley of Lemuel to Bountiful

The Book of Mormon indicates that after the group left the valley of Lemuel, they traveled for the space of four days in a "south-southeast direction" (1 Nephi 16:13). Most researchers believe that the trail Lehi took was near or on the passage most commonly taken by travelers, and known as the Frankincense Trail. It is reported that Joseph Smith was of the opinion that Lehi's party "traveled nearly a south-southeast direction until they came to the nineteenth degree of north latitude; and then nearly east to the sea of Arabia."[11] The exact route is not known. It was revealed to Lehi where he was to go, and so it is not possible or necessary to establish the exact route.

Reynolds suggests that the ancient Aztec map known as the Boturini Codex bears certain figures in hieroglyphic drawing which might depict Lehi's travels.[12]

The Lord gave directions through "a ball of curious workmanship" (1 Nephi 16:10), which Nephi refers to as a compass (1 Nephi 18:12). Alma records the name of the instrument as the Liahona (Alma 37:38). But the Liahona should not be compared to a mariner's compass. Lehi's "compass" indicated the directions in which Lehi *should* go; the mariner's compass only tells the traveler *which way* is magnetic north. The Liahona worked on the principle of faith and according to the diligent attention given to it (Alma 37:40). Mosiah refers to it as a director (Mosiah 1:16). It not only gave directions to the travelers, but writing also appeared on the ball (1 Nephi 16:26).

It is believed by some that the word *Liahona* means "To God Is Light"; that is to say, God gives light as does the sun.[13] The unique quality of the Liahona was in providing spiritual guidance as well as travel direction.

It was approximately eight years from the time the Lehi colony left the valley of Lemuel until they reached a place they called Bountiful. Since they carried seeds of every kind, we can suppose they took time to plant along the way and also wait for the harvest before proceeding. This would mean that their travels may have been seasonal. Perhaps they traveled in the cooler months of the year. It is estimated that their trip to the Arabian Sea was somewhere near twenty-five hundred miles in length.

The company would probably travel for a few days, rest, hunt, and then take up their journey as the Liahona directed. Perhaps when they found good soil and water they would plant seeds and harvest the crops.

The food eaten on this trip probably consisted of their own crops and probably grapes, olives, and figs, which grow in the area, and also meat (1 Nephi 16:31; 17:1–2). Other fruits which are grown in the Middle East and could have been used include dates, coconuts, and pomegranates.

An average encampment was calculated to be about twelve days long, but some crop-growing ones were perhaps as long as six months.[14] How fast did the Lehi company travel? Major R. E. Cheesman, an experienced traveler in that area in the 1920s, has estimated that the average caravan could travel thirty miles a day.[15]

During this journey, the group also may have fished along the coasts of the Red Sea, as this body of water contains mackerel, tuna, sardines, and horgie.[16]

On the probable trail which Lehi traveled there are today 118 waterholes, spaced (on the average) eighteen miles apart.[17] It was the custom of experienced travelers in Arabia that they never built a fire, as it could attract the attention of a prowling, raiding party.[18] As a result, they ate much of their food raw, as recorded in the Book of Mormon (1 Nephi 17:2). Attacking and plundering camps still seems to be the chief object of some Arab tribes.

Lehi's journey, besides being difficult because of the terrain, also became troublesome because of the constant rebellion of Laman and Lemuel and some of Ishmael's children.

It seems that the keynote of life in Arabia is and was hardship. Albright notes concerning the general area where we know Lehi had traveled that it is a land of "disoriented groups and of individual fugitives, where organized semi-nomadic Arab tribes alternate with . . . sedentary society, with runaway slaves, bandits, and their descendants."[19]

How did they travel through this difficult terrain and environment? From all observations, camels seem to be the mode of travel. No matter which route Lehi took to the Red Sea, he would have encountered camel markets which would have allowed him to use this animal even if he started only with donkeys. Camels can take two 150- to 180-pound packs on their backs, and Lehi brought his tents, provisions, and seed with him to plant and harvest en route and to use in his promised land. Although the Book of Mormon does not mention camels, it may be that they were not mentioned because they were taken for granted.

After traveling four days from the valley of Lemuel, the company camped in a place they called Shazer (1 Nephi 16:13). Calculating their average traveling distance, this place could be the modern oasis of Azlan in the Wadi Azlan. Even another harvest season could have elapsed in this area. Because of the spelling and pronunciation of similar place names in Palestine, Nibley proposes that this could have been a name given to a place where trees grew.[20]

After leaving Shazer, the narrative indicates that Nephi broke his bow and the colony was desperate for food (1 Nephi 16:18ff). Nephi found wood to build a new bow (1 Nephi 16:23). Archaeologist Salim Saad calls our attention to the fact that wood from the pomegranate tree which grows around a place called Jiddah would make a good bow. These particular trees, with especially hard wood, were an absolute necessity for bow-making purposes. Evidently the areas where Nephi could have found wood suitable for a bow were not plentiful, hence the need for divine guidance at this point in the journey. It was also providential at this point that this area contained many animals suited for food.[21]

Nibley cites another witness to the building of a new bow. According to Arab writers, the only bow wood available grew near the mountains of Jasum and Azd.[22] As nearly as we can surmise, this is where the Lehi group was encamped when Nephi broke his bow and sought to make another (1 Nephi 16:23). Jiddah is also a shipbuilding city and perhaps Nephi could have observed craftsmen in this area which would have benefited him later.

Moving on in the same easterly direction, they came to a place that was called Nahom. It was not named by Lehi but was apparently a desert burial ground. It was here that Ishmael died and was buried (1 Nephi 16:34). Nibley explains the possibility that the name *Nahom* is related to an Arabic root word meaning "to moan." When Ishmael died, the "daughters of Ishmael did mourn exceedingly'' (1 Nephi 16:35). It seems that among the desert Arabs, mourning rites are monopolized by the women.[23] A possible site of Nahom where Ishmael was buried is thought by the Hiltons to be al Kunfidah in Arabia. Rows of graves found in Al Kunfidah sustain the possibility that it was an ancient burial ground.[24]

Bountiful by the Sea

After traveling in an easterly direction, as the Book of Mormon indicates (1 Nephi 17:1), the party went through an area where they "did wade through much affliction." This arid wasteland was perhaps the worst desert of all. It did merge, however, into a paradise by the sea which they named Bountiful. There is just such an area in the Qara Mountains on the southeasterly coast of Arabia. There is one place in the entire fourteen-hundred-mile southern Arabian peninsula that meets the description of Bountiful in the direction from Nahom suggested in the Book of Mormon and by the Prophet Joseph Smith as noted earlier (note 12). This is modern Salalah. They called the new land "Bountiful, because of its much fruit and also wild honey" (1 Nephi 17:5). Hilton reports that today in Salalah a person finds many fruits growing—citrons, limes, oranges, dates, bananas, grapes, apricots, coconuts, figs, and melons.[25]

It was at Bountiful where Nephi was commanded to build a ship (1 Nephi 17:7–8). The Lord himself instructed Nephi on the details of building the ship that carried the Lehi colony to the promised land. It must have been a unique structure, since we are told that it was not built after the manner of men (1 Nephi 18:1–2). Consequently, we cannot compare it to the traditional ships built in that time period. Even Nephi's brethren remarked on the workmanship as being unusually good (1 Nephi 18:4). Even though building a ship was a new experience for Nephi, he surely would have observed native shipbuilders in the many villages he passed as he traveled along the coast of the Red Sea.

The sycamore-fig shade tree that grows in the desert produces a very hard wood, is strong, resistant to water, and almost free from knots. These trees still grow in the area of Salalah, where Nephi might have been when he was instructed to build his ship. Surely the wisdom of the Lord was involved in the selection of areas where the Nephites lived in the wilderness as he directed their journey via the Liahona.

Because of the length of time involved in this exodus—eight years to make the journey from the valley of Lemuel in addition to the years required for building the ship—the number in Lehi's extended family could have enlarged to as many as forty or fifty people. If the numbers were that high, the ship would have had to be at least sixty feet long to accommodate such a large group, especially if there was enough space for dancing, which the record states that they did (1 Nephi 18:9). The ship was built and the people sailed for the promised land.

Conclusion

The weather and geography of Arabia have changed little, if any, since Lehi's day.[26] Most LDS scholars are of the opinion that current studies of Arabic geography and history are in complete harmony with Lehi's story.[27] It is also the opinion of those who have traveled and studied the area involved in Lehi's exodus that everything recorded in 1 Nephi concerning the travels of Lehi actually could have happened.[28]

With the passing of time and with continued study, the case for the Book of Mormon record will increase in strength. I can foresee the day when the world of scholarship and archaeology in academic circles outside the Church will continue to uncover and unearth such thrilling evidences that the world will be left without excuse. It is my hope that all of our endeavors will be in studies that will sustain and support the truth in this marvelous record of Lehi's extended family. It is my desire to eliminate obstacles so that the student and scholar will become so impressed and fascinated with this sacred record that they will eventually *open* the Book of Mormon, *read it*, and gain a testimony of its eternal truths.

NOTES AND REFERENCES

1. Hugh W. Nibley, *Lehi in the Desert and the World of the Jaredites* (Salt Lake City: Bookcraft, 1952), pp. 8, 12–13, 36–38.

2. Although Lehi wrote Egyptian as well as Hebrew, the language of the Book of Mormon was Reformed Egyptian, a combination of Hebrew and Egyptian that was known only to the Nephites; see 1 Nephi 1:2; Mosiah 1:4; Mormon 9:32–33.

3. Nibley, *Lehi in the Desert*, p. 41.

4. Lynn M. Hilton and Hope Hilton, *In Search of Lehi's Trail* (Salt Lake City: Deseret Book Co., 1976), p. 39.

5. Ibid., p. 74.

6. Nibley, *Lehi in the Desert*, p. 105.

7. Hilton and Hilton, p. 27.

8. This record contained the first five books of the Bible and other biblical books to the time of Jeremiah (1 Nephi 5:1–14). It documented God's dealings with his covenant people. When these young men were asked to return to Jerusalem to obtain the brass plates, the idea of records being kept on metal plates certainly was not new or strange to any of them. For a treatise of evidence that ancient records were kept on metal plates, see Paul R. Cheesman, *Ancient Writing on Metal Plates* (Bountiful, Utah: Horizon Publishers, 1985), p. 85.

9. A. Janssen, "Judgements," *Revue Biblique XII* (1903), 259 CF Surv. Wstn. Palest., p. 327, as quoted in Nibley, *Lehi in the Desert*, p. 118.

10. Erastus Snow, *Journal of Discourses*, 23:184.

11. B. H. Roberts, *New Witnesses for God*, 3 vols. (Salt Lake City: Deseret News Press, 1951), 3:501–3. "In a compendium of doctrinal subjects published by the late Elders Franklin D. Richards and James A. Little, the following item appears: 'Lehi's travels.—Revelation to Joseph the seer: The course that Lehi and his company traveled from Jerusalem to the place of their destination: They traveled nearly a south, southeast direction until they came to the nineteenth degree of north latitude; then, nearly east of the Sea of Arabia, then sailed in a southeast direction, and landed on the continent of South America, in Chili, thirty degrees south latitude.'

The only reason so far discovered for regarding the above as a revelation is that it is found written on a loose sheet of paper in the handwriting of Frederick G. Williams, for some years second counselor in the First Presidency of the Church in the Kirtland period of its history, and it follows the body of the revelation contained in Doctrine and Covenants, section vii., relating to John the beloved disciple, remaining on earth, until the glorious coming of Jesus to reign with his Saints. The handwriting is certified to be that of Frederick G. Williams, by his son Ezra G. Williams, of Ogden; and endorsed on the back of the sheet of paper containing the above passage and the revelation pertaining to John. The indorsement [sic] is dated April, the 11th, 1864. The revelation pertaining to John has this introductory line: "A Revelation Concerning John, the Beloved Disciple." But there is no heading to the passage relating to the passage about Lehi's travels. The words "Lehi's Travels," and the words "Revelation to Joseph the Seer," are added by the publishers, justified as they supposed, doubtless, by the fact that the paragraph is in the handwriting of Frederick G. Williams, Counselor to the Prophet, and on the same page with the body of an undoubted revelation, which was published repeatedly as such in the life time of the Prophet, first in 1833, at Independence, Missouri, in the "Book of Commandments," and subsequently in every edition of the Doctrine and Covenants until now. But the one relating to Lehi's travels was never published in the lifetime of the Prophet, and was published nowhere else until published in the Richards-Little's Compendium.

12. George Reynolds and Janne M. Sjodahl, *The Story of the Book of Mormon* (Salt Lake City: Deseret News Press, 1955), pp. 10–11.

13. Daniel H. Ludlow, *A Companion to Your Study of the Book of Mormon* (Salt Lake City: Deseret Book Co., 1976), p. 113.

14. W. E. Jennings-Bradley, *The Bedouin of the Sinaitic Peninsula,* PEFQ, 1907, p. 284.

15. Cheesman, *In Unknown Arabia*, pp. 27, 52.

16. Hilton and Hilton, p. 90.

17. Ibid., p. 33.

18. Cheesman, *In Unknown Arabia*, pp. 228, 234, 240, 280.

19. W. F. Albright, *Archaeology and the Religion of Israel* (Baltimore: Johns Hopkins Press, 1942), p. 101.

20. Nibley, *Lehi in the Desert,* p. 90.

21. Hilton and Hilton, pp. 81–83.

22. Nibley, *Lehi in the Desert*, p. 68.

23. Ibid., pp. 90–91.

24. Hilton and Hilton, p. 95.

25. Ibid., p. 105.

26. Ibid., p. 116.

27. In addition to Hugh Nibley and the Hiltons, see Eugene England, "Through the Arabian Desert to a Bountiful Land: Could Joseph Smith Have Known the Way:" in *Book of Mormon Authorship: New Light on Ancient Origins* (Provo, Utah: Brigham Young University Religious Studies Center, 1982), pp. 143–56.

28. Nibley, *Lehi in the Desert*, p. 129.

17

TRANSOCEANIC CROSSINGS

John L. Sorenson

The three crossings of the ocean to the New World reported in the Book of Mormon are treated in differing degrees of detail. Events of the earliest, by Jared's group, are recounted at considerable length but with little nautical information in Ether 2:13–25; 3:1–3, and 6:2–12. The voyage by Lehi's party is treated in 1 Nephi 17:5–18, 49–51, and in chapter 18. Concerning the voyage that brought Mulek, we have only two brief statements, Omni 1:15–16 and Helaman 8:21.

The fragmentary information in the text has led Latter-day Saints to pay but cursory attention to the voyages and their significance for the history and culture of Book of Mormon peoples. This paper analyzes the Lehi trip, for which we have the most textual and external comparative information, and demonstrates how we can expand our understanding of such events.

John L. Sorenson is Professor Emeritus of Anthropology at Brigham Young University.

A Paradigm for Voyages

The intent of this paper is to help us understand this voyage better. I consider that we understand an event when we have gained the widest feasible perspective on why and how it took place. This is akin to the aim regarding scripture in general urged upon us by Brigham Young.

> Do you read the Scriptures, my brethren and sisters, as though you were writing them, a thousand, two thousand, or five thousand years ago? Do you read them as though you stood in the place of the men who wrote them? If you do not feel this, it is your privilege to do so.[1]

To understand in this sense, we need to accumulate the largest possible body of information on the voyage described in 1 Nephi. An exhaustive set of questions will serve to alert us to new facts about the event, jarring us out of the mental rut induced by simply reading the text again and again. Once we have obtained reasonable answers to our questions, we should then know enough either to compose a monograph-sized history of the voyage and its setting close enough to the way things really were to be free from anomalies, or to produce a plausible historical novel, a dramatic production, or a series of artistic representations. Even if certain questions remained unanswered, they would provide a guide to further research.

The brevity of the Book of Mormon prevents our getting all the data we would like firsthand, but we can still consult other sources about voyages comparable to Lehi's. Thus we need to phrase our questions in two forms: those addressed directly to the scriptural voyage, and those intended to elicit complementary data from parallel cases. In the following list, questions of the second type are in parentheses:

I. Questions About the Origin of the Voyage

    1. (What voyages can be usefully compared with this particular case?)

    2. What historical and cultural factors led to this voyage? (What historical and cultural factors led to voyages in comarable cases?)

3. What did members of this party know about destinations, routes, and nautical technology? (What did comparable voyagers know of these matters?)

4. Was this voyage referred to in later history in the area of origin? (Were comparable voyages known to later history in their areas or origin?)

II. Questions About Preparations

5. What vessel technology was available to the voyagers in this case? (What vessel technology was available in comparable cases?)

6. Was a suitable vessel procured or procurable without new construction of one? (In comparable cases was a suitable vessel procured or procurable without new construction?)

7. What materials, tools, and knowledge were obtained in order to construct the vessel, and from where and how were they procured? (From this point on, the questions for comparable cases will be assumed.)

8. What was the design of the vessel, and how was it constructed?

9. How long did construction take?

10. What supplies and other materials were taken aboard in preparation for the voyage?

11. What training was necessary to prepare the crew for the voyage?

12. What port facilities were used for all the above actions?

13. What was the ethnic, social, and cultural composition of the group making this voyage?

14. What ritual, spiritual, psychological, ideological, etc., preparation of voyagers was carried out?

15. What seasonal timing was involved in preparation and departure?

16. How was the vessel launched?

III. Questions About the Voyage

17. How was a course laid and maintained, and how was the vessel operated?

18. What route was followed? Were other routes to the same destination feasible? What natural conditions were met and would likely have been met on alternate routes?

19. What were living conditions and routine aboard ship? Did these change during the voyage?

20. What emergencies occurred, and how were they met?

21. What stops were made, why, and for how long?

22. How long did the voyage take? Was this normal?

23. How were the personnel on board organized?

24. What effects on mortality, health, and psychological/spiritual outlook did life on board have?

25. Where did the vessel land, and what environment did the voyagers encounter at the landing place?

IV. Questions About Consequences of the Voyage

26. What happened to the vessel after the landing?

27. What modifications in their social organization resulted from the party's moving from ship to land?

28. How did the situation ashore change the party's activity patterns?

29. What elements of the culture of the group's area of origin were filtered out, newly emphasized, or otherwise modified by the voyage and new settlement?

30. What, if any, other people interacted with the immigrants soon after the landing, and what was the nature of the interaction?

31. Did the newcomers move from the landing site? If so, when, why, and to where?

32. What biological effects did the setting(s) in the new land produce in the newcomers, and they in their neighbors?

33. What spiritual and psychological effects did the new scene(s) produce in the newcomers?

34. What traditions about the voyage did descendants or neighbors maintain or construct in later generations? Was the landing area later perceived in any special manner?

35. How was voyaging as an activity viewed once the incoming group was settled in the land?

36. How did remembrance of the voyage enter into subsequent social, cultural, and political life (for example, as validation of leadership or rivalry)?

My queries lack the advantage of direct shipbuilding and sailing experience. Surely blue-water sailors would revise and rephrase my list to advantage and would produce better answers.

Answering the Questions

Several types of sources in addition to the scriptures deserve consideration as we search for answers. In descending order or value, the types are:

1. The scriptural text itself
   a. relatively unequivocal statements
   b. straightforward inferences from scriptural statements

2. Reports of premodern voyages that are
   a. comparable in time and location to Lehi's trip
   b. indirectly comparable, that is, at another time but over the same route and under like conditions
   c. not comparable in time or space but comparable in some ways in technology, sociology, meteorology, oceanography, etc.

3. Reports of voyages in recent centuries
   a. routine voyages under conditions similar to those of ancient times
   b. experimental voyages using replicas of early vessels

4. Inference from indirect evidence of voyaging established by archaeological, ethnological, or linguistic parallels

5. Modern calculations and reasoning (for example, what volume of supplies can be accommodated on a vessel of such and such size?)

Space limitations permit me to treat only type 1 information here. However, a large bibliography is available (see note 26) of references to the most important literature in which information from source types 2 through 5 can be pursued.

The Paradigm Applied to the Lehi Group's Case

Here I address as many of the thirty-six questions concerning this voyage as the Book of Mormon deals with directly or by inference. The numbers introduce discussions of the corresponding questions in the list above.

2. According to the Book of Mormon, the historical and cultural factors involved in the departure of the Lehi group from the land of Jerusalem center in the fact that the sociopolitical establishment there had rejected Lehi's warning message and standing as a legitimate prophet. The reasons for his rejection are not expounded in the text, but 1 Nephi 7:14 implies that they were generally the same as for his contemporaries in the Old Testament—Nahum, Habakkuk, Zephaniah, and Jeremiah (compare 2 Chronicles 36:11–16). The Bible indicates that it was their political impact that was most unwelcome, but spiritual, ritual, cultural, and social implications of their criticism of rulers

and people were, of course, also involved.[2] Beyond the pressures to flee, however, Lehi had a positive reason for departing—the Lord had given him a "land of promise" as a refuge and a reward (1 Nephi 5:5; compare 2:2. Hereafter, when only chapter and verse are cited, reference to 1 Nephi is to be understood).

This same question may also be asked in reference to the land of Bountiful as an origin area: What factors led to Lehi's departure from there? The record of Nephi before the eighteenth chapter does not make explicit but does imply that the Lord intended Bountiful to be only a stopover on a longer journey. Lehi and Nephi understood that (10:13), but it appears that Laman and Lemuel and perhaps others in the party did not see it that way (17:5–18, especially verse 17). They seem to have expected to stay in Bountiful. Nothing is even hinted about conditions in that area that pushed them to emigrate; only the command of the Lord to Nephi is indicated as impelling their departure. It could be, however, that Laman's and Lemuel's perception that Bountiful offered only limited prospects for the prosperity and ease they hoped to attain could have persuaded the brothers that moving on might be better than staying where they were.

3. No hint can be found in the text that anyone in Lehi's party had any knowledge whatever of nautical matters, nor is it likely that any had even been on a vessel before. Upon arrival in Bountiful they were impressed by the green land, as most desert travelers would have been (17:5–6), but they may also have been in awe of the sea. The waters off Arabia had high symbolic value. Note the brothers' unbelief that they could cross "these great waters." Nor did they manifest any belief or interest in the possibility of constructing a ship, even though the mercantile connections their father apparently enjoyed at Jerusalem probably had acquainted them with the existence of commercial destinations around the Indian Ocean.[3]

4. Regarding the secrecy attending the group's flight from the land of Jerusalem, we are specifically told (4:36) that they did not want "the Jews" to know of their flight, for they might "pursue . . . and . . .destroy" the small party. But once they were at a substantial distance from Jerusalem, they were no longer likely to be concerned about what the Jews could do to hinder them. In the wilderness, the instruction of the Lord that they not use "much fire" (17:12) suggests a defensive tactic against desert raiders rather than against Jewish pursuers.[4] Their

policy of secrecy probably ensured that no public record of their departure from the homeland was kept, although Lehi's or Ishmael's kin might have held a tradition of the event, and remaining prophets could have known of it by revelation.[5]

As to a tradition or record of their leaving the land of Bountiful, there is no apparent reason why local inhabitants of that area (who are not noted in Nephi's record but unquestionably were present, as archaeology and linguistics show[6]) would have known of their departure or would have paid particular attention to it. On the south coast of the Arabian peninsula where their vessel was built, the possibility is tiny that this one among a number of vessels constructed in that day would be specifically noted in local tradition or records. Nephi's record gives us no reason to suppose that the departure was noted by others.

5. At least some of the technology Nephi used on his ship differed from that used by contemporary shipbuilders (18:2). His statement to this effect implies that he was sufficiently familiar with what those others did that he could clearly distinguish his techniques from theirs. Nevertheless, he used only tools he himself was capable of manufacturing and materials that his party could obtain by their own efforts. We have no reason to suppose that the repertoire of skills he and his family possessed were superior to or even different from those common among nonspecialists in the Jerusalem area in his day. So even though the Lord showed him the "manner" after which he was to build the ship, he and his brothers still "work[ed] the timbers" with those simple tools; their technique would have to be broadly similar to that of other shipwrights of his era. The implication is that the chief differences were in quality of workmanship and some aspects of design. (Compare 2 Nephi 5:16 for a parallel situation in the case of the temple Nephi built. Although he constructed it "after the manner of the temple of Solomon," still "it could not be built like unto Solomon's temple" in certain aspects. Consider too the case of the Salt Lake Temple, for which Brigham Young reported visionary guidance as to its plan,[7] although the techniques, materials, and architecture employed remained within a range not surprising to nineteenth-century American craftsmen.)

6. The text implies that no existing vessel was available, or suitable, for the party's use in or near the Bountiful area. The family had been wealthy (2:4); had the Lord desired that they purchase a ship, presumably they could have brought sufficient

portable wealth through the desert to buy one. Moreover, they could have been led this way or that a few hundred miles from where they were to some other destination on the Indian Ocean coast that could have provided such a ready-made vessel, had there been a superior one about. Much time and labor would have been saved had they not had to build one, but perhaps they needed the experience to toughen them physically and spiritually for the arduous voyage and to enhance group cohesion.

Other vessels might indeed have existed, but the emphasis in 18:1–4 on the unusual and superior workmanship suggests that a vessel of more conventional design and technique might not have held up on such a singular trip as the one intended. (Compare 18:13–15 about storm stress on the vessel; and note that the answer to this question in the case of Mulek's party, which likely departed from Egypt via the Mediterranean Sea, could be quite different.)

7. We learn from 17:9–11 and 16 that Nephi began from scratch, personally locating and surface mining ore, constructing bellows and starting fire in order to manufacture woodworking tools. The ore seems to have been obtained and refined and the tools prepared while he was on "the mountain" (17:7) where he had gone for divine instruction. He showed his brothers the tools only after those were finished. And note that specification of "the" mountain intimates that only one rather obvious one was near or perhaps visible from their camp.

Copper hardened with arsenic or tin or simply by heating and hammering was the likely metal a lone worker could deal with successfully; its cutting edge would be suitable for the intended purpose. Iron is a less likely possibility. At least earlier on their journey Nephi was unable to repair his "steel"-backed bow and had to use an all-wood substitute (16:18–23). Samuel Shepley and John Tvedtnes have each proposed that Lehi was a smith, not a merchant as proposed by Hugh Nibley; or perhaps he was both.[8] The evidence is not decisive either way. If Lehi possessed metallurgical skills, it seems odd that a much less experienced Nephi would go off alone to do a task with divine help that his father could have carried out routinely. But Nephi must have been acquainted with the basic skills of the craft, as evidenced by the fact that he did not have to ask the Lord what tools to make nor how to make a workable bellows (17:9–11). In the New World, moreover, he immediately sought out and recognized various ores and confidently made plates for record keeping (19:1). In favor of the notion that the whole family was familiar with metal work is the fact that even his brothers showed no surprise at his ability to make tools, although they did scoff at his ability to build a ship.

Adequate timbers likely would not have been available to them on the immediate coast, only back in the hills a certain distance.[9] Probably not more than five or six men in such a small group would be available to "go forth" (18:1) to the hills for timber. Hauling it would have been arduous and time-consuming, as would sawing planks. (Given the relatively short trees available in that part of Arabia, a boat of suitable size for their purpose probably had to be made of planks.) Saws, mauls or hammers, axes, chisels or adzes, and awls would also have been required. What the sails (implied by 18:8–9) and cordage were made of we cannot guess from the text. Nothing hints other than that the party made all their tools and did all the construction by themselves, perhaps because their poverty did not allow paying local craftsmen.

8. Questions of the ship's design cannot even be approached from the text aside from a few generalities. First, because the vessel was sail powered, it had to have at least one mast, sail(s) and rigging, and it probably was keeled and had some type of rudder (18:13). Second, given the amount of stores implied (18:6), it is likely to have been decked, with supplies secured below from storm (18:15; compare verse 6: "we did go *down into* the ship, with all our loading"; italics added). Third, we can suppose, given the effective limits on the number of workers available to them, that no larger ship would be built and thus no more time wasted than would be just adequate for the small group. The Hiltons estimate that the party by this time consisted of around seventeen adults and thirty-two children, requiring a sixty-foot ship.[10] Perhaps, but it could have been smaller. Note that Columbus's *Nina* may have been only sixty feet long.[11]

9. The length of time it took to build the vessel can only be surmised. The Hiltons[12] suggest under two years. Given the builders' inexperience and small number and the necessity of carrying out other routine tasks simultaneously, it could well have taken more.

Another chronological consideration is also involved. In 2 Nephi 1:4 we are told that Lehi, recently arrived in the American promised land, reported having seen a vision that Jerusalem had been destroyed (compare 17:14). We do not know how long after the event the vision came to him. Had the party stayed in south Arabia, normal communication from Jerusalem down the frankincense caravan route might have informed them of the fall of their homeland to the Babylonians within a few months without the need for a vision. Lehi probably left Jerusalem in the first year of the reign of Zedekiah. The fall of Jerusalem occurred something more than ten years into that reign (2 Kings 24:18–25:3). With eight years in the wilderness Lehi's group would have at most three years (reduced by the "many days" mentioned in 17:7 before they got to work) to prepare the ship before word of Jerusalem's fall would be likely to reach them. But they probably left in the prime sailing season on that coast (mid-March to early May; a brief second possibility for leaving occurs in late August), so they may actually have had no more than two years to build the boat. However, a number of assumptions lie behind these calculations and make them uncertain. For example, the arrival of caravans from Israel might have been taking longer than two months, for the frankincense harvest was seasonal, taking place mainly in winter but perhaps also in spring,[13] and presumably the caravan season coincided. Thus Lehi's group might have had until the opening of the sailing season the following March to get under way before news from the north about Judea's fall would arrive. That might have allowed three years for their shipbuilding.

10. At first glance, the phrasing of 18:6 seems to indicate almost overnight preparation of stores for the voyage, but that would be impossible. The expression "after we had prepared all things" must point to a period of at least weeks during which hunting and collecting were pursued intensively. (No indication is given that the party cultivated crops while in Bountiful, although a point is made of such activity immediately upon their arrival in America—see 18:24. The silence is significant.) "Fruits and meat from the wilderness" could not have been obtained without a good deal of time, effort, and movement within the region. Given their Arabian coastal location, dates were probably an important item in the category *fruit*. Honey is specifically mentioned; presumably they could only have obtained their large supply of it at a certain season.

Finally, it is likely that the catch-all term *provisions* referred to grains, for fruit, meat, and honey would not constitute an adequate diet. Olive or another oil would also be probable. Very likely these "provisions" would have been obtained by trading surplus wilderness products such as skins to local inhabitants. If the group had succeeded in bringing camels or asses with them all the way from Jerusalem, those might have been traded, but it seems unlikely that they had survived beyond the time of extreme hunger described in 16:18–20. Of course they had taken "provisions" with them upon leaving their first major camp at the river Laman (16:10), but these were apparently being consumed continuously from Jerusalem on, for verse 11 speaks of "the remainder" of the provisions left to them at that juncture. They likely arrived at Bountiful with little stock of food.

They still did have "seeds" intentionally saved to carry to the New World (16:11). In addition to the seeds brought from the Jerusalem area, probably more were added from Bountiful. (Smith discusses crops probably present in that area.[14])

A final item of provisioning would obviously be a supply of fresh water and perhaps wine (compare 18:9) in either pottery vessels or skin bags.

11. People of the desert would certainly require training in even the most rudimentary management of a vessel before they set sail. The most plausible way to get that knowledge would be instruction by sailors on boats already in that vicinity. One can imagine also a combination of inspiration and trial and error as a means, particularly if Nephi's ship was of novel design.

13. The text is clear enough that apart from Zoram, only Lehi's and Ishmael's family members were in the voyaging party. All were Hebrew-speakers and at home with cultural ways of the Jerusalem area and not ethnically or socially varied among themselves, however cosmopolitan some of them might have been due to travel or learning.

14. They adhered to a version of Mosaic ritual (for example, 1 Nephi 2:7; 4:16; 2 Nephi 25:24), although their practices probably were different from the semi-pagan ways then prevalent in Jerusalem (compare 2 Chronicles 36:14). At least they likely carried out sacrifice and prayer before embarkation. The voice of the Lord to Lehi (18:5) was itself also preparatory in the sense of this question. Moreover, the language in 18:6 about entry into the vessel—"every one according to his age"—implies a special ritual. Further, the whole set of experiences, practical and spiritual, of the ten years since they had left Jerusalem, constituted a preparation for the voyage in the same sense that Zion's Camp proved a preparation of early Latter-day Saints for their trek to the Great Basin.

15. Being "driven forth before the wind" (18:8) implies dependence on the monsoon winds from the west to bear the vessel across the Indian Ocean (see the answer to question 9 above).[15] Typically, ships left the Arabian coast on that wind between mid-March and early May, although a date a bit later or in late August–early September cannot be ruled out.

16. All that is said about launching is that "we did put forth into the [out to?] sea" (18:8). I suppose that the sizable vessel had already been put into the water from the beach (on rollers?) and had undergone shakedown sailing off the coast even before provisioning, let alone departure.

17. A course was laid by observing one of the spindles inside the Liahona or "compass," which "pointed the way whither we should go" (16:10; 18:12, 21). I see no reason at all to suppose this device was magnetic, despite the term *compass*. Rather it was faith operated; when Nephi was tied up by his brothers, the pointer would not function, but when he was unloosed, he "took" the compass and "it did work whither I desired it," so that he could know in what direction to "guide the ship" (18:21–22). This language about how the device served to point out the course is operationally enigmatic, but that the vessel was actually kept on course by a combination of adjustments to rudder and sails is obvious.

18. The most economical explanation of the course followed supposes that the Lord typically uses natural forces familiar to us to accomplish his ends. In this case, he would have directed the party over a course where winds and currents would carry any vessel toward the intended spot in America with a minimum of miraculous intervention. No doubt other seafarers would already have passed over certain legs of the same route, though probably not the whole of it. (Compare the LDS pioneers of 1847 crossing the plains to the Great Salt Lake via the sensible North Platte River valley, and so on, rather than through mountain-cluttered New Mexico, Colorado, or Montana.)

Across the Indian Ocean the routine course taken by sailing ships in premodern times followed near 15 degrees north latitude, which carried them straight east to the Malabar coast of India. From there they would round Sri Lanka (Ceylon) and sail east near 10 degrees north latitude to the Straits of Malacca and past the site of modern Singapore.[16] One feasible course thereafter would wend between major islands of today's Indonesia to the Admiralty group north of New Guinea, thence past Tonga and through Polynesia near the Marquesas. Recently scientists have discovered that every dozen years or so what is known in the meteorology of the eastern Pacific as the "El Niño condition" develops in which unusual winds from the west replace the typical trade winds. At such time sailing eastward across the mid-Pacific and even on to America is feasible.[17] However, this was not the only possible route, for the sea off China and across the north Pacific between 25 and 40 degrees north could also have served.[18]

The Book of Mormon is silent about conditions encountered after the ship met with the tropical storm (18:9–21), which was probably in the Indian Ocean or the Bay of Bengal. Failure of the record to mention other difficulties on the voyage may imply that no life-threatening situations were encountered after the one great storm, or at least none significant enough for Nephi to describe on the small plates. Either route suggested would offer, but not guarantee, the possibility of a safe trip across the ocean. (Contrast the vivid language about the continuously stressful Jaredite journey in Ether 6:5–11, which fits conditions only on a north Pacific route around 45 degrees north.) Nephi simply said that "after we had sailed for the space of many days we did arrive at the promised land" (18:23).

21. Arab ships on the Indian Ocean route typically stopped ashore to repair storm damage, such as obtaining a new mast, as well as to scrape speed-impeding barnacles off the hull.[19] Especially after the one almost disastrous storm, the need to stop for repairs seems likely, perhaps in Sri Lanka or Sumatra. Another reason for stops would be to take on a new supply of water and fresh, anti-scurvy foods. Also, they may have spent periods in port, waiting for seasonal winds to turn the right direction or avoiding a storm. Some of the waits could have been fairly long. After all, if the journey through Arabia consumed eight years, we need not suppose the Lord would hasten the party across the ocean, more than ten times as far, in hasty, uninterrupted fashion. Stops would also have broken the tedium of the long voyage for those aboard the ship and given them—especially the children!—a welcome opportunity to escape the psychological and physical confines of their small vessel. In addition, being on land could give them a chance to conduct Mosaic sacrificial ceremonies impossible on the vessel because of lack of animals.

22. No information is given about duration, but the distance alone allows us to estimate time. This distance traveled would have been on the order of seventeen thousand miles. We

get valuable comparative data about rates of travel in the mid-Pacific by examining a recent voyage under pre-European conditions by the reconstructed Polynesian double-hulled canoe named *Hokule 'a*. The vessel traveled eight thousand miles in six legs, ranging from three hundred to three thousand miles: Hawaii to Tahiti, Tahiti to the Cook Islands, on to New Zealand, then Tonga, Samoa, and back to Tahiti and Hawaii. Total sailing time was nearly eighty-two days, for an average of ninety-eight miles per day. Surprisingly, the speed sailing east "against the trade winds" was twice what it had been going west.[20] This practical experience confirms warnings by nautical experts that maps that show "average" wind velocities and directions are meaningless as predictors of what may happen on any particular voyage.[21] Had Lehi's ships been able to travel continuously at the same rate as *Hokule 'a*, the entire voyage would have taken only about half a year. But we cannot assume such a thing. The storm mentioned in 1 Nephi 18 drove them "back" for four days, meaning an overall loss of at least eight days; that did not happen to *Hokule 'a*. Thereafter surely the winds were not always with Lehi's group, so delays due to weather alone must have caused significant waits; we know that for the Indian Ocean portion of the route, Arab, Chinese, and Portuguese ships sometimes waited for months for desired winds. Also, as mentioned in the answer to question 21, stops to maintain the vessel and restock food and water could well have consumed considerable time. *Hokule 'a*'s eighty-two days at sea actually stretched over more than a year, as crew members flew home to Hawaii for rest after each leg of the trip! Moreover, the Polynesian crew already had accumulated a large body of lore and expertise about sailing in that particular part of the Pacific, while Nephi was always traveling under unfamiliar conditions. And his vessel almost certainly would not have been designed like the Polynesian vessel, likely being slower.[22] Given these conditions, a full year seems a minimum period to accomplish the long voyage from Arabia to (Central) America. Two years are not unlikely.

23. What was the social organization aboard the ship? All we know is that Nephi, the nominal captain, proved to have limited power (18:10ff) during his brothers' mutiny. But a ship simply could not be operated without regular tasks such as helmsman and watch being performed. The overall success of the voyage assures us that the men aboard did carry out at least minimal routine tasks. Studies of parallel situations could no

doubt tell us more about this subject as well as about shipboard routine of concern in question 19.

The reference in Mosiah 10:12 to a tradition among the Lamanites that their ancestors "were also wronged while crossing the sea" may have reference to the occasion when Nephi retook control of the ship (18:20–22) during the great storm, or it might refer to another incident, but likely the issue was one of power and control, whenever the event. (Note 2 Nephi 1:2 which refers to "their rebellions [plural] upon the waters.")

25. Nephi does not give us useful information about where the ship landed, but two later statements in the scripture do. Mosiah 10:13 mentions "the land of their [the Lamanites] first inheritance, after they had crossed the sea." Then Alma 22:28, as part of a comprehensive description of geography in the land of promise, speaks of Lamanites spread in the wilderness "on the west in the land of Nephi, in the place of their fathers' first inheritance, and thus bordering along by the seashore." When this information is put together with other geographical statements, it becomes clear that the land referred to was on the "west sea" coast at the southern extreme of the territory spoken of in the Nephite record. In the first century B.C. it was considered part of ("in") the land of Nephi (whose primary area was in the highlands), hence the coastal zone must have been thought of as a mere wilderness adjunct to Nephi, a hint that the land of first inheritance was not a very large or important region in its own terms. We learn from 18:25 that the area was dominated by forests.

The most plausible correlation of Book of Mormon geography with today's map identifies the land of first inheritance or initial landing zone with a stretch of the Pacific coast a few score miles on either side of the Guatemala-El Salvador border.[23] That zone features swamps and lagoons just inside a beach, mixed with areas of seasonal forest. Within a couple of miles of the beach, taller forest is found, interspersed with grassland (conditions anciently could certainly have been somewhat different). Rainfall is light to moderate (increasing markedly inland as the land rises), but temperature and humidity are quite high year round. The zone is uncomfortable for human habitation but at times has been productively farmed. Except for a few periods of fairly heavy inhabitation, the area can truly be called jungly wilderness.

26. After leaving the ship (18:23), the group paid no attention to it again, it appears. Likely this was in part because

they were delighted to be free from its confines. Nothing is said later to suggest that seafaring was attractive to them, for over five hundred years at least, although, of course, a fuller record might give a different picture. One supposes that the vessel was in pretty poor condition by the moment of landing, and with all attention necessarily given to pioneering agriculture and exploration (18:24–25), it is no wonder that nobody looked to the sea again.

27. The routine tasks upon which members of the party had settled during the voyage were now a thing of the past. New problems and a new division of labor were suddenly thrust upon them. The pattern of organization among them must have changed; however, the nominal pattern still held Lehi to be dominant (for example, see 2 Nephi 4:10). The relationship between the challenges of the new environment and the issue of rulership precipitated by Lehi's death is not clear. It is implied in 18:24–25 that at least one crop was harvested and considerable exploration done even before Nephi made his plates, and by then he had a good deal to record (19:1). Lehi might have lived ashore for several years, thus the events of 2 Nephi 4:13 and 5:1–5 could have been so far removed from the time of landing as not to deserve consideration in this analysis.

28. At the least, the daily routine of all the party would have been totally restructured on land. Preparation of fields, the planting, care and harvesting of crops, and exploration tasks are mentioned or implied. Even before crops were harvestable, however, the settlers had to feed themselves currently. Hunting is indicated (18:25) and various foods such as shellfish could have been gathered in these tropical lowlands; processing would require new skills and perhaps new equipment on the part of both men and women. Also implied is the need for different forms of shelter constructed from the newly available materials, as well as a fresh supply of clothing and household goods.

29. Despite silence in the record about explicitly cultural changes, it is apparent that the conditions the group had endured during eleven or more years since they had lived in the Jerusalem area would have changed some of their ways drastically. This is confirmed in 2 Nephi 25:2 and 6 where Nephi says that he had allowed his people's poor recollection of the Old World ways to wipe part of the slate clean, permitting him to create a new, modified form of Israelite culture (compare 2 Nephi 5:14–19). Recall that among his group, only he, his brother Sam, Zoram, and perhaps their wives, had experienced the Old World culture

as adults. The same situation must have prevailed among the Lamanite faction.

30. Nothing is said in the record about interaction between the immigrants and possible inhabitants of the land found by them on arrival, just as it is silent about relations with inhabitants in the south Arabian Bountiful. That such people were present in both areas is beyond question.[24] A sure evidence of that fact for the Nephites is the later reliance on "corn" (maize) documented for the land of Nephi in Mosiah 7:22; 9:9. Maize is a native American plant "so completely dependent on man that it does not grow in the wild."[25] Hence the immigrants had to have received the seed and instruction about how to cultivate it from people already on the scene.

31. Since we do not know how long it was before they moved from the landing area, we cannot be sure of impelling factors, but discomfort due to the climate could easily have been one.

32. That biological changes would have been entailed in Lehi's descendants on the new scene is obvious from the point of view of biological anthropology. Exposure to new diseases, foods, climate, pests, etc., would have had immediate effects, although generations would probably have had to pass for the full range of consequences to become apparent. Also, we can reasonably suppose that they themselves imported Old World diseases to which they had developed immunity but which could have had serious consequences for peoples whom they contacted. Their imported plants could also have brought along damaging diseases.

33. Two documented results on spirit or psychology are noted. According to Nephi's perception, the Lamanites "did become an idle people, full of mischief and subtlety" (2 Nephi 5:24). We cannot tell what if any connection there might have been between the curse put upon them and the conditions of their life in the new natural setting. As for the Nephites, a long generation later they were characterized thus: "Our lives passed away like as it were unto us a dream, we being a lonesome and a solemn people, wanderers, cast out from Jerusalem, born in tribulation, in a wilderness, and hated of our brethren . . . wherefore, we did mourn out our days" (Jacob 7:26). But we remain uncertain how these characteristics might relate to question 33.

If we consider the Book of Mormon a real book about real people, the kind of exercise this paper constitutes should be repeated a hundred times.[26]

NOTES AND REFERENCES

1. John A. Widtsoe, ed., *Discourses of Brigham Young* (Salt Lake City: Deseret Book Co., 1941), p. 128.

2. Hugh Nibley, "Two Shots in the Dark," in *Book of Mormon Authorship: New Light on Ancient Origins*, ed. Noel B. Reynolds (Provo, Utah: Brigham Young University, 1982), pp. 110–11.

3. The symbolism associated with "Irreantum" or "many waters" can be glimpsed in citations in *Book of Mormon Critical Text, Vol. 1. 1 Nephi–Words of Mormon*. Second Edition (Provo, Utah: Foundation for Ancient Research and Mormon Studies, 1986), p. 94, note 787. Robert R. Stieglitz, "Long-distance Seafaring in the Ancient Near East," *Biblical Archaeologist* 47 (1984): 138–39, points out the overseas connections of that day.

4. Hugh Nibley, *Lehi in the Desert and The World of the Jaredites* (Salt Lake City: Bookcraft, 1952), p. 72–77. A fuller and more up-to-date picture of "the Arabian nexus" of Lehi's journey is given in Robert F. Smith, "Book of Mormon Event Structure: The Ancient Near East," *Foundation for Ancient Research and Mormon Studies Preliminary Report* SMI-84 (Provo, Utah, 1984, rev. 1986), pp. 23–30.

5. Orson Pratt believed that Ezekiel, in Babylon, knew of Mulek by revelation; I agreed in my "The Twig of the Cedar," *Improvement Era* 60 (May 1957):330 (5); reprinted under the title "Bible Prophecies of the Mulekites," in *A Book of Mormon Treasury* (Salt Lake City: Bookcraft, 1959), pp. 229–37.

6. Smith, "Event Structure," pp. 26–28.

7. Widtsoe, *Discourses*, p. 410.

8. Samuel E. Shepley, "Old World Metal Workers," paper given at Annual Symposium, Society for Early Historic Archaeology, Provo, Utah, 22 Oct. 1983. John A. Tvedtnes, "Was Lehi a Caravaneer?" *Foundation for Ancient Research and Mormon Studies Preliminary Report* TVE-84 (Provo, Utah, 1984).

9. Lynn M. Hilton and Hope Hilton, *In Search of Lehi's Trail* (Salt Lake City: Deseret Book Co., 1976), p. 106.

10. Ibid., p. 113.

11. Jose Maria Martinez-Hidalgo, ed. by Howard I. Chapelle, *Columbus' Ships* (Barre, Mass: Barre Publishers, 1966), p. 93, for that estimate. The data are not firm; Martinez prefers a length ten feet greater—see pp. 93–100.

12. Hilton and Hilton, *In Search*, p. 114.

13. Ibid., p. 141, reprinting Pliny the Elder, Pt. XXXII.

14. Smith, "Event Structure," p. 27.

15. G. R. Tibbetts, *Arab Navigation in the Indian Ocean Before the Coming of the Portuguese*. Royal Asiatic Society of Great Britain and Ireland, Oriental Translation Fund, n.s., vol. 42 (London, 1981), pp. 360–77.

16. Ibid., p. 360ff.

17. *Foundation for Ancient Research and Mormon Studies Update,* April 1986; Ben R. Finney, "Anomalous Westerlies, El Niño and the Colonization of Polynesia," *American Anthropologist* 87 (1985): 9-26.

18. Thor Heyerdahl, "Feasible Ocean Routes to and from the Americas in Pre-Columbian Times," *American Antiquity* 28 (1963): 482–88, and his *Sea Routes to Polynesia* (Chicago: Rand-McNally, 1968), pp. 37–50. Joseph Needham and Lu Gwei-Djen, *Trans-Pacific Echoes and Resonances; Listening Once Again* (Singapore and Philadelphia: World Scientific, 1984), pp. 5–6, agree with Heyerdahl. Compare Needham alone in his magnum opus *Science and Civilisation in China,* vol. 4, part III (Cambridge: Cambridge University Press, 1971), pp., 547–48.

19. Tibbetts, *Arab Navigation,* p. 49.

20. "Wind and Stars Guide Polynesian Voyagers on Year-long Exploration," *Provo (Utah) Daily Herald,* 5 Oct. 1986, p. 42 (Associated Press dispatch).

21. Clinton R. Edwards, "Commentary: Section II," in *Man Across the Sea: Problems of Pre-Columbian Contacts,* ed. Carroll L. Riley et al., p. 302 (Austin and London: University of Texas Press, 1971). Finney, Anomalous Westerlies, 9–26.

22. Ben R. Finney, *Hokule 'a: The Way to Tahiti* (New York: Dodd Mead, c. 1979).

23. John L. Sorenson, *An Ancient American Setting for the Book of Mormon* (Salt Lake City: Deseret Book Co., and Foundation for Ancient Research and Mormon Studies, 1985), p. 138 and Map 5.

24. Ibid., pp. 83–87.

25. Ibid., p. 139.

26. A bibliography of about 5,000 titles on pre-Columbian ships, voyaging and other culture contacts—of what I have called sources of types 2 through 5—will be issued on a computer disk in 1988: John L. Sorenson and Martin H. Raish, *Transoceanic Culture Contacts and Voyaging: A Comprehensive Annotated Bibliography.*

18

THE PROPHECIES OF THE PROPHETS

Robert E. Parsons

Shortly after the Lehi colony arrived in the promised land, the Lord commanded Nephi to make plates of ore and engrave on them the record of his people. Then, in 570 B.C. Nephi received another commandment to make a second set of plates (the small plates of Nephi), to record the ministry of his people. Obedient to this counsel, Nephi recorded on those plates that an angel had told him that Christ would be born six hundred years from the time the Lehi colony left Jerusalem (1 Nephi 19:8). He then proceeded to cite prophets of old who had also prophesied concerning Christ, his ministry, and the Lehi colony. It is in this setting that we find some of the prophecies of Zenos, Zenock, Neum, and Isaiah in the Book of Mormon. And indeed, it is because they testified of Christ that Nephi included them in his record (1 Nephi 19:10). It is my intent here to review their teachings as they appear in the Book of Mormon and to offer some help in understanding Nephi's quotations of Isaiah 48–49 (1 Nephi 20–21).

Robert E. Parsons is Associate Professor of Ancient Scripture at Brigham Young University.

The Testimonies of Zenos, Zenock, and Neum

First Nephi chapters 19 through 22 introduce us to Zenos, Zenock, and Neum and give us our first quotations from Isaiah. Little is known of the prophets Zenos, Zenock, and Neum, although their importance to the Book of Mormon prophets is evident in that Nephi, Jacob, Alma, Amulek, Nephi the son of Helaman, Samuel, and Mormon all quote from them. They are important to the Nephites for at least three reasons:

First, the Nephites appear to be descendants of these prophets and of Joseph who was sold into Egypt (3 Nephi 10:16–17).

Second, these prophets spoke of that which would happen to all the house of Israel as well as to Lehi's seed (1 Nephi 19:16–17; Helaman 15:11).

And third, and probably most important, they testified of Christ, and hundreds of years before his birth prophesied in detail of his atonement and the circumstances surrounding it (1 Nephi 19:10–12; Alma 33:12–17). We also learn that these messianic prophets gave their lives for their testimonies of Christ (Alma 33:17; Helaman 8:19).

Exactly when and where Zenos, Zenock, and Neum lived is not known except we do know that they lived prior to Lehi's departure from Jerusalem, otherwise their writings would not have appeared on the brass plates. It is likely that they lived after the time of Abraham and before the days of Isaiah, and that Zenos preceded Zenock. This assumption is based on the following scripture, and assumes that since Isaiah and Jeremiah are listed in chronological order, the other prophets are also.

> And now I would that ye should know, that even since the days of Abraham there have been many prophets that have testified these things; yea, behold, the prophet Zenos did testify boldly; for the which he was slain.
>
> And behold, also Zenock, and also Ezias, and also Isaiah, and Jeremiah, (Jeremiah being that same prophet who testified of the destruction of Jerusalem) and now we know that Jerusalem was destroyed according to the words of Jeremiah. O then why not the Son of God come, according to his prophecy? (Helaman 8:19–20.)

Since these prophets were descended from Joseph, it is postulated by some that they may have lived in the north of Israel, rather than in Judah and that is the reason their prophecies were not recorded in Jewish scripture. It may also be possible that these plain and precious prophecies were deleted by unrighteous Jews who did not want these statements on the death of Christ in their scriptures (see 1 Nephi 19:13–14). Until the Lord reveals more information, however, we won't know the whole story.

The Teachings of Zenos, Zenock, and Neum

It is of some interest to summarize the teachings of Zenos, Zenock, and Neum as we have them in the Book of Mormon.

ZENOS	ZENOCK	NEUM
1 Nephi 19:10–13	*1 Nephi 19:10*	*1 Nephi 19:10*
Christ to be buried in a a sepulchre	Christ to be "lifted up"	Christ to be crucified
Three days of darkness will be a sign of his death		
Following his death he will visit all house of Israel; righteous will hear his voice and wicked will be visited with fire, smoke, darkness, and earthquakes		
Jews to be scourged because they crucify Christ		
1 Nephi 19:16–17		
Israel to be gathered from the four quarters of the earth		
Every nation to be blessed and see salvation of the Lord		

ZENOS	ZENOCK
Jacob 5	
Allegory of tame and wild olive tree with its teachings on scattering,	

gathering, restoration, and
Millennium

Alma 33:3−11
Pray and worship in all
  places
Judgments are turned away
  because of the Son

Alma 33:15−16
Mercy comes because of
  the Son

Alma 34:7
Redemption comes through
  the Son of God

Alma 34:7
Redemption comes through
  the Son of God

Helaman 15:11
Lamanites to be restored
  to knowledge of the truth

3 Nephi 10:16
Death and destruction to
  come upon wicked at
  crucifixion of Christ

3 Nephi 10:16
Death and destruction to
  come upon wicked at
  crucifixion of Christ

This listing shows the extent to which Zenos is quoted. It also shows that while his teachings center around Jesus Christ they also speak extensively about the house of Israel and its restoration in the latter days. The volume and content of his teachings were probably the basis for the following comment by Elder Bruce R. McConkie.

> I do not think I overstate the matter when I say that next to Isaiah himself—who is the prototype, pattern, and model for all the prophets—there was not a greater prophet in all Israel than Zenos. And our knowledge of his inspired writings is limited to the quotations and paraphrasing summaries found in the Book of Mormon.[1]

Why Does Nephi Quote Isaiah 48 and 49?

Having quoted Zenos', Zenock's, and Neum's very plain teachings that Christ will atone for our sins and that salvation is found only in the Son of God, Nephi says he has written these things to persuade his people to remember that God showed the prophets of old all things concerning the Jews and also that God showed many prophets what would befall Lehi's colony in the promised land (1 Nephi 19:20−21). He then says:

Now it came to pass that I, Nephi, did teach my brethren these things; and it came to pass that I did read many things to them, which were engraven upon the plates of brass, that they might know concerning the doings of the Lord in other lands, among people of old.

And I did read many things unto them which were written in the books of Moses; but that I might more fully persuade them to believe in the Lord their Redeemer I did read unto them that which was written by the prophet Isaiah; for I did liken all scriptures unto us, that it might be for our profit and learning. (1 Nephi 19:22–23.)

The two chapters which follow, Isaiah 48 and 49, contain significant differences from the King James text. The Book of Mormon text contains a more accurate rendition of the original Isaiah text than the King James Version, since the brass plates would have been an older and better record than the later manuscripts used in the King James translation.

These two chapters do testify of Christ, but not as plainly as Zenos, Zenock, and Neum did. Is it possible that when Nephi says, "but that I might more fully persuade them to believe in the Lord their Redeemer I did read unto them that which was written by the prophet Isaiah," he has in mind that a belief in Christ comes not only through what the scriptures say of him per se, but also by understanding the covenants he has made with Israel and how they will be fulfilled? Certainly Isaiah 48 and 49, which Nephi now quotes to help his people believe in Christ, deal mostly with the covenants to Israel and their eventual fulfillment.

Nephi's Explanation of Isaiah 49

While most Book of Mormon readers follow Nephi's teachings in 1 Nephi 22 and recognize he is interpreting Isaiah, they often cannot determine where he finds his source material for the interpretations in his Isaiah quotations.

If we go back and check 1 Nephi 20–21 (Isaiah 48–49) for the basis of Nephi's teachings in chapter 22, we realize that in addition to what Isaiah says, Nephi has added some of his own understanding to make his commentary as plain as it is. We must remember that Nephi had an extensive knowledge of scripture; not only had he read Isaiah but also Zenos, Zenock, and Neum. He had also had his own visions in which he had seen the time of Christ (1 Nephi 11), his own people in the promised land (1 Nephi

12), the restoration of the gospel (1 Nephi 13), the building of Zion (1 Nephi 13), the destructions preceding the Second Coming (1 Nephi 14), and the establishment of the Millennium (1 Nephi 14). Consequently, Nephi could clearly elaborate on and explain much of what he quoted from Isaiah.

Since Nephi concentrated on Isaiah 49, as recorded in 1 Nephi 21, I would like to do the same. Verse one is a long sentence not found in the Old Testament account. This sentence is important because it tells us to whom Isaiah is speaking, namely scattered Israel.

> And again: Hearken, O ye house of Israel, all ye that are broken off and are driven out because of the wickedness of the pastors of my people; yea, all ye that are broken off, that are scattered abroad, who are of my people, O house of Israel (1 Nephi 21:1).

In verses 1–3 we meet the pronoun *me*, identified as the "servant" of God. Scholars generally identify this "servant" as Isaiah or Christ. I believe *servant* has a dual meaning, namely Christ and Israel, with the work of Ephraim, who holds the birthright in Israel, being emphasized. Thus, the meaning of verses 1–3 would be as follows:

> The Lord hath called me [Ephraim] from the womb [and] from the bowels of my mother [Ephraim was called in the pre-existence] and he hath made my mouth [Ephraim's latter-day message of the Restoration] like a sharp sword [the word of God; see D&C 6:2; compare 1 Nephi 16:2];
> [He hath] made me [Ephraim and specifically Joseph Smith who is from Ephraim] a polished shaft.

This is clarified by the Prophet Joseph's teaching.

> I am like a huge, rough stone rolling down from a high mountain; and the only polishing I get is when some corner gets rubbed off by coming in contact with something else, striking with accelerated force against religious bigotry, priestcraft, lawyer-craft, doctor-craft, lying editors, suborned judges and jurors, and the authority of perjured executives, backed by mobs, blasphemers, licentious and corrupt men and women—all hell knocking off a corner here and a corner there. Thus I will become a smooth and polished shaft in the quiver of the Almighty, who will give me dominion over all and every one of them.[2]

Isaiah continues his analogy with "in his quiver hath he hid me" (1 Nephi 21:2). This is also clarified in the Doctrine and Covenants.

> Therefore, thus saith the Lord unto you, with whom the priesthood hath continued through the lineage of your fathers—
> For ye are lawful heirs, according to the flesh, and have been hid from the world with Christ in God. (D&C 86:8–9.)

The work of Ephraim and Christ in the last days is dually outlined in verses 5–9.

1. Both Ephraim and Christ were called in pre-earth life to bring Jacob or Israel to God (verse 5).

2. Ephraim, the servant of the latter days, will raise up the tribes of Jacob—that is, Ephraim will teach and gather the Lamanites, the Jews, and the lost tribes (verse 6).

3. Ephraim will also restore the preserved of Israel—that is, Ephraim will gather those who have the blood of Israel but have been scattered among all the nations of the earth and have lost their identity (verse 6).

4. They, Christ and Ephraim, are to be a light to the Gentiles (verse 6):
   a.　Christ is the light of the world and offers himself and his gospel as that light.
   b.　The restored Church is the custodian of Christ's true teachings and offers the Gentiles the light of salvation which they do not have.

5. The prisoners shall go free—free from the spirit prison when Christ opens the doors there following his crucifixion, and free from the prison of sin and spiritual ignorance when Ephraim preaches the restored gospel to them in the last days (verse 9).

As Ephraim does his latter-day work, Israel will be gathered both spiritually and temporally, and Jerusalem and Zion will be established (verses 10–13).

When Zion, specifically scattered Israel (Jews, Lamanites, ten lost tribes), shall think that God has forsaken and forgotten the covenants he made with them, he will show them that he has not. He will fulfill his covenants to gather and establish scattered Israel in Zion. Although Zion is a term applied to the Americas, the complete fulfillment of restoring scattered Israel to Zion will include the restoration of the Jews and the ten lost tribes to the Holy Land, for they are also part of Zion who hath said, "The Lord has forsaken me, and my Lord hath forgotten me." However, all that God has promised Zion, both in America and in the Holy Land, is constantly before him as if engraved on the very palms of his hands. (Verses 14–16.)

One possible meaning of "engrave thee upon the palms of my hands" is that the marks in his hands which will be shown to the Jews when he appears to them are a token of the covenants he has made with their fathers as well as a sign that their fathers crucified the very Son of God (D&C 45:51 and Zechariah 13:6).

As latter-day Israel is gathered and restored, she will fill up the land and marvel where all gathered Israel has come from, since it seemed she had lost all her children long ago (verses 18–21).

This great restoration will be done through the restored gospel which will come to the Gentiles (most of whom are a combination of Israel and gentile blood descent) through Joseph Smith and through members of the Church. These Gentiles will nurse Israel (Jews, Lamanites, ten lost tribes) (verses 22–23).

Israel (the restored Church) will consist of the Gentiles, who are mainly a mixture of gentile and Israelitish blood descent, and of Jews, Lamanites, and the ten lost tribes who will no longer be trodden down by the world. The house of Israel who have been captives and have been the prey of mighty nations will be saved by the Mighty God of Jacob and will have power over those who once oppressed them (verses 24–26).

If we now go to Nephi's commentary in chapter 22, we can see that he drew at least ten of his thirteen points from Isaiah 49. These thirteen points are listed below, followed with references showing Nephi's source in chapter 21, followed by a slash and his comments in chapter 22.

1. The scattering of Israel (1 Nephi 21:1 / and 1 Nephi 22:4–5).

2. The nursing of Israel by the Gentiles (1 Nephi 21:22–23 / and 1 Nephi 22:6).

3. The raising up of a mighty nation, the United States (1 Nephi 21:22/and 1 Nephi 22:7).

4. The scattering of the Lamanites (1 Nephi 21:14, 17, 19, 25/ and 1 Nephi 22:7−8).

5. The restoring of the gospel (1 Nephi 21:22/and 1 Nephi 22:8).

6. The fulfilling of the covenants made to the house of Israel (1 Nephi 21:14−16, 18−21/and 1 Nephi 22:11).

7. The spiritual and temporal gathering of Israel (1 Nephi 21:12−13/and 1 Nephi 22:12).

8. The destruction of the great and abominable church (no reference in 1 Nephi 21; see 1 Nephi 22:13).

9. The destruction of all who fight against Zion (1 Nephi 21:17, 25−26/and 1 Nephi 22:14).

10. The destruction of the wicked (1 Nephi 21:26/and 1 Nephi 22:15−16).

11. The preservation of the righteous (1 Nephi 21:12−13, 25−26/and 1 Nephi 22:17, 19, 22).

12. The destruction of churches which belong to the kingdom of the devil (no reference in 1 Nephi 21; see 1 Nephi 22:23).

13. The establishment of the Millennium (no reference in 1 Nephi 21; see 1 Nephi 22:24−26).

If we could have Nephi here to give us his personal insights and interpretations of what he quoted from Isaiah and to comment on it all, we could greatly enlarge our understanding. But since he isn't here, at least this can be a starting point for us to enjoy the Book of Mormon and to avoid the condemnation God mentioned for those who neglect this sacred record.

And your minds in times past have been darkened because of unbelief, and because you have treated lightly the things you have received—

Which vanity and unbelief have brought the whole church under condemnation.

And this condemnation resteth upon the children of Zion, even all.

And they shall remain under this condemnation until they repent and remember the new covenant, even the Book of Mormon and the former commandments which I have given them, not only to say, but to do according to that which I have written. (D&C 84:54—57.)

A Brief Explanation of Isaiah 48

Since I have basically omitted 1 Nephi 20 (Isaiah 48) up to this point, I will now give a brief summary of that chapter.

First Nephi chapter 20 (Isaiah 48) teaches that ancient Israel participated in the baptismal covenant (verse 1). The phrase *or out of the waters of baptism* is not found in the Bible and apparently was not on the golden plates. It was added in the 1840 edition of the Book of Mormon to clarify the meaning of "come forth out of the waters of Judah."

The term "or out of the waters of baptism" did not appear in the first edition of the Book of Mormon. It first appeared in the edition of 1840 on page 53, and the sentence in which it appeared was punctuated, as follows: "Hearken and hear this, O house of Jacob, who are called by the name of Israel, and are come forth out of the waters of Judah, (or out of the waters of baptism,) who swear by the name of the Lord," etc. It is not absolutely clear who was responsible for the insertion of this phrase, although the title page of this edition indicates that it was the "Third Edition, Carefully Revised by the Translator" and was published in Nauvoo, Illinois.

In the "Committee Copy" of the Book of Mormon that was used by Elder James E. Talmage and his committee in making the changes for the 1920 edition, the words "or out of the waters of baptism" were not printed in the text although they had been inserted in red ink in parentheses. However, the parentheses were crossed out by red pencil. These words are printed in the current edition of the Book of Mormon without the parentheses.[3]

Israel (Judah) is now in a state of apostasy (verses 1—8). God foretells the future so that his people who are often wicked will not credit God's work to their idols and images (verses 3—6). Israel, because of wickedness, will be refined in the furnace of affliction for the Lord's sake (verse 10). History attests to the literalness of this refinement.

Israel (Ephraim) is called by the Lord to gather Judah again that she might be redeemed (verses 12–17). This work is yet to be completed in this dispensation. If Judah had not sinned she would have received the blessings of Abraham and her righteous seed would be as numberless as the sand (verses 18–19).

Israel (Judah) is called to go forth out of Babylon to be redeemed (verse 20). This redemption will take place in the last days and will be done through Ephraim, whose work has already been discussed in the analysis of 1 Nephi 22.

Conclusion

The Book of Mormon prophets considered Zenos, Zenock, Neum, and Isaiah some of the greatest of the messianic prophets. Nephi's commentary on Isaiah gives us some of our clearest and most detailed understanding of Isaiah's writings. His explanation of Isaiah 49 is particularly enlightening as we watch the work of Ephraim unfold in this dispensation and look forward to the redemption of Zion.

NOTES AND REFERENCES

1. Monte S. Nyman and Robert L. Millet, eds., *The Joseph Smith Translation* (Salt Lake City: Bookcraft, 1985), p. 17.

2. *Teachings of the Prophet Joseph Smith*, comp. Joseph Fielding Smith (Salt Lake City: Deseret Book, 1976), p. 304.

3. Daniel H. Ludlow, *A Companion to Your Study of the Book of Mormon* (Salt Lake City: Deseret Book Co., 1976), p. 120.

19

TEXTUAL EVIDENCES FOR THE BOOK OF MORMON

Paul Y. Hoskisson

In the past forty years Book of Mormon scholars have produced much textual evidence for a vorlage[1] of ancient Near Eastern descent for the received text of the Book of Mormon. Yet most of this material has provided only *necessary* and not *sufficient* evidence for this vorlage. In order for material in the Book of Mormon to be *sufficient* evidence for an ancient Near Eastern vorlage, as I am using *sufficient* here, it must be demonstrated that the textual material is ancient Near Eastern and that it was not available to Joseph Smith.

Likewise, I maintain, if the material were available to the Prophet, if only in theory, and if it were found in the Book of Mormon, then it would become *necessary* evidence. By this definition we must expect to find at least some of this material in the Book of Mormon. Indeed, if some of it were not present we would have to question an ancient Near Eastern vorlage for the received text. That is why this material is *necessary* evidence.

Paul Y. Hoskisson is Assistant Professor of Ancient Scripture at Brigham Young University.

These definitions are not intended to suggest that all sufficient evidence is superior to necessary evidence. Both sufficient and necessary evidences are highly subjective in quantity and quality. In fact, many pieces of necessary evidence are more compelling than material deemed sufficient. For instance, because chiasms abound in the King James Bible, chiasms in the Book of Mormon provide necessary evidence, by the definition used above. Yet, the complicated chiasm of Alma 36 can leave little doubt that a vorlage of ancient Near Eastern descent lies behind the English translation.[2] The first example of sufficient evidence I provide below is far less compelling than this chiasm.

The difference between sufficient and necessary evidence however, should remain in focus. Therefore, we must ask the question, what was available to the Prophet Joseph Smith? Practically no epigraphic or other literary evidence from Egypt was even potentially available. The first great epigraphic discoveries in Mesopotamia began in the latter part of the 1840s and did not reach Europe until more than twenty years after the 1830 publication of the Book of Mormon, though the first primitive attempts at deciphering cuneiform were being made about the time Joseph first saw and then later translated the gold plates.[3] The Levant did not yield its major epigraphic material until this century.[4]

What authentic ancient Near Eastern epigraphic and/or literary material was potentially available to Joseph Smith? With possibly few exceptions, the only authentic ancient Near Eastern epigraphic material in any form potentially available to the Prophet was the King James Bible with its ancient Near Eastern vorlage. Therefore, any ancient Near Eastern material evident in the Bible becomes, by definition, necessary evidence. Material not in the bible, not potentially available otherwise, and not demonstrably part of the cultural milieu of Joseph Smith would be sufficient evidence.

It cannot be overemphasized here that when looking for such sufficient evidence, we must exercise extreme caution and consider all possibilities. It must also be emphasized again that the particulars of sufficient evidence are highly subjective. The following rather involved and lengthy example demonstrates this need for rigor.

Alma 5:9 reads in part, "their souls did expand." The context would call for a meaning such as "they became happy," to parallel the phrase in the same verse, "they did sing redeeming love" to celebrate their freedom from the "bands of death" and the "chains of hell." Nowhere in the King James Bible does *soul* occur in conjunction with the word *expand*; neither does it occur with the verbs *enlarge* and *swell*, each of which accompany *soul* once in the Book of Mormon (Alma 32:28 and 34 respectively).[5] This phrase appears to be unusual. Why should a soul expand? If this phrase is unique in English to the Book of Mormon, could the phrase reflect an ancient Near Eastern vorlage rather than have its origin in English?

The *Oxford English Dictionary* (hereafter *OED*) under *soul* gives no evidence of the phrase "their souls did expand" occurring in English; neither are there usages of *enlarge* and *swell* with soul.[6] This and other evidence appears to indicate that the phrase "expand the soul" does not have its origin in English.[7] If it could be demonstrated that this phrase has an ancient Near Eastern Semitic analog that was not available to Joseph Smith, it might qualify as sufficient evidence of an ancient Near Eastern vorlage for the Book of Mormon.

Ugaritic, a language closely related to Hebrew and spoken down to about six hundred years before Lehi left Jerusalem, bears on the subject.[8] A passage in the Anath epic[9] reads, *tǵdd.kbdh.bṣḥq. ymlu / lbh.bṣmḫt.kbd.ᶜnt / tšyt.* H. Ginsberg translates, "her liver *swells* with laughter, / Her heart fills up with joy, / Anath's liver *exults*."[10] (The italics are Ginsberg's and indicate his uncertainty in translating the Ugaritic words *ǵdd* and *šyt*.) All three syntagms, "liver swells with laughter," "heart fills with joy," and "liver exults" are of the same type as the Book of Mormon phrase "soul expands," and all four phrases denote happiness.[11]

To establish that "soul expands" of the Book of Mormon and "liver swells" of Ugaritic not only connote but also denote the same thing, it remains to be demonstrated that "soul" is a possible translation of "liver."

In Akkadian, an East Semitic language related to Hebrew and Ugaritic, both *libbu* and *kabattu* (the Akkadian cognates for *lb* and *kbd* respectively in the Ugaritic passage quoted above) can be "the seat of feelings, emotions, thought."[12] When *libbu* and *kabattu* are used with the verb *napāšu* ("to enlarge" or "make wide" in the G-stem and "to let breathe again" in the D-stem)[13] they denote secondarily "mind, *soul*, heart"[14] (italics added). Thus here in Akkadian "the soul (that is, liver) expands with feeling" would seem to be at home.

Psalm 16:9 reads, "Therefore my heart is glad, and my glory rejoiceth." The Hebrew text, *lākhen śamaḥ libbī wayyāgel kabōdī*, translates more literally, "therefore my heart is happy and my liver rejoices." Here, just as with their Ugaritic and Akkadian cognates, *leb* and *kabōd* are the seats of rejoicing. But the Hebrew text does not require the English rendering "soul expanding" with joy. It is Genesis 49:6 that forms the link with soul, *biqᵉhālām 'al teḥad kevodī*, "do not unite, my honor, with their assembly." The Hebrew word in this latter passage, translated in the King James Bible as "honor," is none other than *kābōd*, the same word behind the King James Bible *glory* in Psalm 16:9 and the cognate of the Ugaritic and Akkadian words used with the verb "to enlarge" or "to swell." It usually means "weight," "honor," "glory," etc., but can also mean "soul."[15] It is not translated as "soul" in Genesis 49:6, even though the context would seem to require it, because the more common word for "soul" in Hebrew, *nepheś*, is the parallel to *kābōd* in this verse,[16] and good English style militates against repetition of the same word (just as does Hebrew).

In other words, one translation of the Semitic word for "liver," etc., is "soul." And therefore, even though the Hebrew Old Testament does not reflect it, in Semitic languages related to Hebrew (closely, Ugaritic; and more distantly, Akkadian) "the liver expands (with feeling)" can be translated "the soul expands (with feeling)."

In returning to the Book of Mormon, the phrase "their souls did expand" has an ancient Semitic vorlage and does not appear in any readily available English material. Because it would seem the Prophet could not have been familiar with the phrase (and this is partially confirmed by a glance at the 1828 Webster's dictionary where "the heart *expands* with joy" in English, but not the soul[17]), it would be sufficient evidence for an ancient Near Eastern vorlage of the Book of Mormon.

Yet even with this confirmation by a dictionary contemporaneous with the translation of the Book of Mormon, doubt is sown. While the "soul" does not appear to "expand" in English, if the phrase "the heart expands" is an authentic English phrase, it is possible that in some obscure passage, not readily accessible, an English "soul" might also expand. Because English belongs to the Germanic language group and also is strongly influenced by the Romance languages, if either or both of these phrases should appear in one Germanic or Romance language, then we must conclude that potentially it is a pre-1830 English phrase and our data base is insufficient to document its appearance in English. This in turn would force us to admit that "their souls did expand" might not be sufficient evidence of an ancient Near Eastern vorlage.

A search of readily available German phrases revealed that "expand the soul" with joy does occur in German. For example, see Geibel (3, 35) "So schlägst du frech die hoffnung nieder, die kaum die seele mir geschwellt?" and from Hölderlin (1,176), "Bis, erwacht vom ängstigen Traum, die Seele dem Menschen aufgeht, jugendlich froh."[18] Therefore, though the phrase "expand the soul" does not occur in any readily available pre-1830 English text, and though it is an authentic ancient Near Eastern Semitic phrase, because it is attested in German, we must conclude that the phrase "their souls did expand" is at best necessary evidence for an authentic Near Eastern Semitic Book of Mormon vorlage, but *not* sufficient evidence.

This, however, has not been an exercise in futility. It demonstrates the need for caution, rigor, and the test of time. Therefore, allow me to present three examples (given previously in another context)[19] that as far as I am now aware have no analog in English or in any Indo-European language with which I am familiar, and therefore, were not available to the Prophet. I ask for assistance if it is possible to prove otherwise.

I have chosen a variety of examples that illustrate different approaches, (1) from the style, (2) from the onomasticon, and (3) from the context of the Book of Mormon. The examples also represent different levels of persuasion, that is uncompelling, quite convincing, and most interesting.

The first seemingly sufficient piece of evidence concerns style, the use of words and phrases beyond grammatical and logical considerations. First, by way of example, let me explain what is being considered. Those proficient in a language other than their native tongue know that other languages express ideas and concepts differently and that other languages allow constructions that are anathema in their native tongue. For instance, it is not correct to use a double negative in contemporary English. One should not say, at least in formal writing and speech, "I don't know nothing." However, there is no universal absolute prohibiting the use of a double negative. Not only do many languages allow it, but some even encourage it. It is simply a matter of proscription, that is, bad style, that contemporary

English does not allow a double negative. Are there, then, examples in the Book of Mormon of poor English style that could be explained by an ancient Near Eastern vorlage?

For stylistic reasons English syntax frowns on constructions using a cognate accusative, that is, when the predicate is a substantive cognate of the verb. For example, it is not good English to say, "He built a building." Good English style requires rather, "He constructed a building," or, less likely, "He built a construction." We even go to the extreme in English to avoid a cognate accusative. We say, "I present you with this gift," rather than say, "I present you with this present."[20]

Hebrew and other Semitic languages not only allow the use of a cognate accusative but even encourage it. For instance, Numbers 30:2 reads, "If a man vow a vow unto the Lord, or swear an oath [literally, swear a swearing] to bind his soul with a bond. . . ."[21]

There are numerous examples of cognate accusatives in the Book of Mormon.[22] The particular example given here is not found in the King James Bible,[23] though it could easily have been used in ancient Hebrew.[24] In 2 Nephi 5:15 and Mosiah 9:8; 11:13; 23:5, for instance, the phrase "to build buildings" occurs in finite or infinitive phrases. The *OED* does not attest a single instance of *building* used as the direct object of "to build."[25] Therefore, in using the phrase "to build a building," the Book of Mormon adheres to a Hebrew and Semitic practice that is not common in English.

Second, the Book of Mormon onomasticon, that is, a list of proper names, provides another possible instance of sufficient evidence. The name *Alma* has provided much grist for anti–Book of Mormon critics.[26] First of all, unlike many other names in the Book of Mormon, it is attested neither in the Bible nor in any other ancient Near Eastern Semitic source. It could have several Hebrew etymologies, none of which is satisfactory.[27] Is it then possible that the Book of Mormon onomasticon does not reflect an ancient Near Eastern vorlage? Are some of the names in it simply unsophisticated borrowings from Spanish names for girls, as has been claimed?

It was not until 1971, 141 years after the publication of the Book of Mormon, that the name *Alma* turned up in an English translation of documents from Palestine. In that year Yigael Yadin described in the English version of his book *Bar-Kokhba* the discovery, careful excavation, and preliminary evaluation of objects found in caves west of the Dead Sea, particularly in the Nahal Hever area, from the period of the Bar-Kokhba revolt against the Romans about A.D. 130. Among the documents dealing with land transactions at nearby En-gedi the name *Alma* appears, written *aleph, lamed, mem, aleph*.[28] Here, discovered in the Judean desert in 1961, is the confirmation that the Book of Mormon name *Alma*, at which critics of that sacred book have scoffed since its publication in 1830, is an authentic entry in the ancient Near Eastern Hebrew/Aramaic onomasticon.[29]

Finally, in an unusual passage in the Book of Mormon, 1 Nephi 2:9, Lehi noted that the river which he named after his son Laman "emptied into the fountain of the Red Sea." Does a river empty into a fountain? Is it not the other way around? That the passage is problematical is indicated by the attempt to explain *fountain* in a footnote in the 1981 edition of the Book of Mormon. The problem fades, however, when ancient Near Eastern lexical and cosmological considerations are taken into account. In the ancient Near East there were two great bodies of water, the saltwater oceans and the subterranean sweet waters, both of which were thought by the ancients "to be the source of rivers and streams."[30] These "fountains of the great deep" (a phrase used by the translators of the King James Bible in Genesis 7:11), as U. Cassuto explained in commenting on the Hebrew word *thwm*, refer "undoubtedly to the subterranean waters, which are the source of the springs that flow upon the ground."[31] The Hebrews shared this Canaanite concept of the subterranean waters being the source of springs.[32]

These subterranean and oceanic waters then are actually the source of all rivers, streams, and springs. The ancient Semites did not conceive of this, however, as we currently do, namely, through the chain of evaporation, cloud formation, condensation, and precipitation. (No doubt they also had some understanding of this process, but they did not limit their perceptions to this one process.) It was S. N. Kramer who, when first pointing out the remarkable and unusual ancient Near East perception that the source of rivers is the oceanic waters, said:

> The Sumerian "mouth" of the rivers, while it coincides geographically with the actual mouth of the rivers as we understand it today, is nevertheless not to be understood in terms of our modern usage, as the place where the rivers "empty" their waters (*into* the Persian Gulf) but rather as the place where they "drink" the waters (*from* the Persian Gulf). In the light of this conception, the

"mouth" of the Tigris and Euphrates may well be designated as their source, but not the real source, i.e., in the mountains of Armenia, but the source as conceived by the Sumerians.[33]

That is to say, the source of the rivers was the oceanic waters, not in an ultimate sense as we conceive it, but in a more immediate sense, in that the rivers drew directly either from the seas as springs, or from the oceans through their mouths, depending on whether the Canaanite concept or S. N. Kramer's Sumero-Akkadian example applies.

Returning now to 1 Nephi 2:9, it is the statement that the river flows into the fountain that is disturbing. As was just explained, in the ancient Near East the fountain of a river was conceived of as being the oceanic waters, the river actually drawing from the ocean or fountain in a sense that is not clear to our occidental and empirical understanding. Our Book of Mormon is in authentic ancient Near Eastern tradition on this point; and the Prophet Joseph Smith could not have known about it. This then seems to become sufficient evidence.

With these examples of extra-King James Bible and hopefully non-Germanic and non-Romance material in the Book of Mormon, I hope to have illustrated with original remarks what this more focused approach entails. It requires a knowledge of ancient Near Eastern languages and literatures and a thorough grounding in Germanic and Romance languages. I am the first to admit that I am deficient in both these areas and, therefore, appeal for other scholars to become involved. If these three examples can be demonstrated to exist in material potentially available to the Prophet Joseph Smith, I would welcome this information. But as it now stands, I must for the moment classify these examples as sufficient evidence.

The rewards warrant the effort. However, in calling for this more focused approach to Book of Mormon textual evidences, I have already admitted that it is not new. Yet, the idea of consciously pursuing this approach is new and should become more visible and more appealing to Book of Mormon scholars. If this book is an authentic document composed by peoples from the ancient Near East, as I testify that it is, then we must expect many more of these types of extra-King James Bible Semitisms (and Egyptianisms) than the three I have illustrated. Let us make an effort in this direction.

NOTES AND REFERENCES

1. *Vorlage* is a technical term from German that refers to a text before the current one (though not necessarily the original or *Urtext*) from which the present text is descended. In this case, the vorlage of the present Book of Mormon would be the text on the gold plates and/or the texts used to compile the gold plates.

2. John W. Welch first pointed out the existence of chiasms in the Book of Mormon in his master's thesis, "A Study Relating Chiasmus in the *Book of Mormon* to Chiasmus in the *Old Testament*, Ugaritic Epics, Homer, and Selected Greek and Latin Authors," Brigham Young University, 1970, including Alma 36 on pages 128–31. For a complete discussion of chiasmus see John W. Welch, ed., *Chiasmus in Antiquity, Structures, Analyses, Exegesis* (Hildesheim: Gerstenberg, 1981), where John W. Welch's definitive treatment of Book of Mormon chiasms appears on pp. 198–210.

3. In general see C. H. Gordon, *Forgotten Scripts: Their Ongoing Discovery and Decipherment* (New York: Penguin, 1971). For a broader look at ancient writing see I. J. Gelb, *A Study of Writing* (Chicago: University of Chicago Press, 1952), p. 61; and *Writing in Ancient Western Asia* (London: British Museum, n.d.), pp. 14–15, and slides 8 and 9. (This latter work is a pamphlet accompanying a set of forty-two slides.)

4. Next to the Hebrew material from Israelite sources, Ugaritic texts form the largest body of ancient Near Eastern epighraphic material from the Levant. Ugarit was first excavated in 1929, and the announcement of the decipherment of the script followed in 1931. (See Cyrus Gordon, *Ugaritic Textbook*, Analecta Orientalia 38 [Rome: Pontificium Institutum Biblicum, 1965], p. 1; and the preceding footnote.) The category of Levantine epigraphic material also includes, loosely, other Northwest Semitic languages. That this latter material was not available to Joseph Smith in 1828–29 becomes evident with a cursory glance at H. Donner and W. Rollig, *Kanaanäische und aramäische Inschriften*, Band II: Kommentar, 2. durchgesehene und erweiterte Auflage (Wiesbaden: Harrassowitz, 1968), where first publications of nearly all the texts came after 1850. There are of course many Aramaic texts preserved from earlier periods (for example, the post-Babylonian exile) that must be excluded when looking for sufficient evidence, even though these materials were most likely not available to the Prophet in any form.

5. *Enlarge* also occurs with *soul* in the D&C 121:42, but the context does not necessarily call for a meaning of happiness as does Alma 5:9.

6. *The Oxford English Dictionary*, 13 Vols. (Oxford: Oxford University Press, 1961), under the respective words.

7. This does not mean that *enlarge the soul* was not a known English phrase. To prove that it is not would require an exhaustive search of all extant English texts predating 1830. This is of course an impossible task, so we must look for indications that the phrase does not appear in English prior to 1830. The absence of the phrase in the *OED* is good evidence that it is not English, and this is born out by its absence in the concordance to John Milton's poetry and

the concordance to William Shakespeare's dramatic works (respectively, John Bradshaw, *A Concordance to the Poetical Works of John Milton* [Hamden, Connecticut: Archen Books, 1965], p. 331; and John Bartlett, *A Complete Concordance or Verbal Index to Words, Phrases, and Passages in the Dramatic Works of Shakespeare* [London: Macmillan, 1953], pp. 1428–31).

8. As mentioned above, Ugarit was first discovered in 1929 and the first Ugaritic texts were published in the 1930s. Therefore, they would have been of little help to Joseph Smith in writing the Book of Mormon in 1828–1829.

9. *Die keilalphabetischen Texte aus Ugarit*, Teil 1, Hrsg. Manfried Dietrich, O. Loretz, and J. Sanmartin (Neukirchen-Vluyn: Neukirchener Verlag, 1976), 1.3.2.25–27 (also known as *V AB* in some text numbering systems); further references to this work will be by *KTU* plus text number.

10. *Ancient Near Eastern Texts*, ed. J. B. Pritchard, 3rd edition (Princeton: Princeton University Press, 1969), p. 136. See also U. Cassuto, *The Goddess Anath*, trans. I. Abrahams (Jerusalem: Magnes Press, 1971), pp. 119–20. More recent translations add nothing to the discussion here.

11. As C. H. Gordon said, the heart and the liver are the "seat of laughter . . . or weeping." *Ugaritic Textbook*, §19.1348 and 19.1187.) A further passage in the Ugaritic material makes this clear. *KTU* 1.12.1.12–3 *yẓḥq.bm / lb. wygmd̲.bm kbd* "he laughed in the heart and chuckled in the liver." The parallel phrase in Alma 5:9, "they did sing redeeming love," and the context leave no doubt that "their souls did expand" means they were happy.

12. *The Assyrian Dictionary of the Oriental Institute of the University of Chicago* (hereafter *CAD*), eds. I. J. Gelb, B. Landsberger, and A. L. Oppenheim (Chicago and Gluckstadt: Oriental Institute, beginning in 1956), vol. K, p. 13b–14a. The entire quote reads, "Were it not for the late synonym list CT 18 9 K. 4233 + .., there would be no reason to assume that *kabattu* denotes anything else than the inside of a (human) body, and consequently, like its synonym *libbu*, the seat of feelings, emotions, thoughts." See, however, *CAD* L, *libbu* 3, on pp. 169a–172b.

13. For *napāšu* see W. von Sodon, *Akkadisches Handwöterbuch* (hereafter *AHw*) (Wiesbaden: Harrassowitz, 1965–1981), p. 736b. Compare *CAD* N, pp. 289b–90a.

14. For *libbu* and *kabattu* see *AHw* 589a and 416a respectively. The *CAD*, vol. K, and the *AHw* disagree about the primary meaning of *kabattu*. The former makes the point on pp. 13b–14a that it probably does not denote "liver," while the latter renders the main meaning as *"Leber."*

15. See Ludwig Koehler and Walter Baumgartner, *Lexicon in Veteris Testamenti Libros* (Leiden: Brill, 1958), pp. 420–21, especially the note under II *kābed* p. 420a, where *kābed* is suggested for the reading *kābōd*.

16. Indeed, *kābōd* paralleled by *nepheš* proves that *liver* can interchange with *soul* in Hebrew.

17. See *Noah Webster's First Edition of An American Dictionary of the English Language*, facsimile edition (Anaheim, California: Foundation for American Christian Education, 1967), two original volumes in one, "expand, *v.i* . . . 3. To enlarge; as, the heart *expands* with joy." I must thank John Welch of the BYU Law School for pointing this out to me.

18. These two examples are rendered as they appear in Jacob Grimm and Wilhelm Grimm, *Deutsches Wörterbuch*, 9. Band: Schiefeln-Seele (Leipzig: Hirzel, 1899), columns. 2867–68.

19. "The Ancient Near Eastern Background of the Language of the Book of Mormon," in *A Symposium on the Book of Mormon* (Salt Lake City: The Church of Jesus Christ of Latter-day Saints, 1982), pp. 40–42.

20. In some instances we also use cognate accusatives in English, but the instances known to me are limited either to biblical phrases, "I fought a good fight," or to phrases where English cannot avoid it because of the lack of a suitable synonym; for example, "sing a song."

21. Such syntactical constructions in Semitic languages are by the nature of these languages practically impossible to avoid. For instance in Exodus 39:30, the Hebrew was *wyktb . . . mktb* "and wrote . . . a writing" (King James translation). In addition, Hebrew and Ugaritic make extensive use of consonant rhyme, which would naturally tend to frequent usage of cognate accusatives, and not vowel rhyme.

22. As far as I can determine, the first person to point out the presence of cognate accusatives in the Book of Mormon was Thomas W. Brookbank, "Hebrew Idioms and Analogies in the Book of Mormon," *Improvement Era*, 17, 7 (May 1914), pp. 626–27, though he labeled it "Verbs with Cognate Nouns," and did not give the example I use in the following material. E. Craig Bramwell, "Hebrew Idioms in the Small Plates of Nephi," master's thesis, Brigham Young University, 1960, pp. 24–26, does mention the cognate accusative and lists on page 26 the example I use.

23. Several Book of Mormon cognate accusatives are also found in the Bible. For instance, "to dream a dream" is found in a finite phrase in 1 Nephi 3:2 and 8:2 and in Genesis 37:5 and 41:11.

24. The verb I use as an example, *bnh/y*, means in Hebrew to make, build, create. In the sense of make or create it is used in Genesis 2:22. This same verb with the same meaning appears in Ugaritic and is actually used there with a cognate accusative, albeit in the syntactical construction participle plus object, *bny bnwt* "the creator of the creatures," found in KTU 1.4.2.11 and other passages.

25. *OED*, vol. B, p. 291.

26. The following is *not* original with me. I give full and well-earned recognition to Dr. H. Nibley of Brigham Young University, who first pointed out the fact that at last the name Alma has been found in an ancient Near Eastern setting. The following is quoted from his article, "[Review of] Yadin, Zigael (sic), *Bar-Kochba*(sic)," *BYU Studies*, 14 (Autumn, 1973), p. 121: "But strangely enough, the name in the Book of Mormon that has brought the most derision on that book, and caused the greatest embarrassment to the Latter-day Saints, especially among those holders of the priesthood who have borne it among the children of men, is the simple and unpretentious Alma. Roman priests have found in this obviously Latin and obviously feminine name (who does not know that Alma Mater means fostering mother?) gratifying evidence of the ignorance and naivete of the youthful Joseph Smith—how could he have been simple enough to let such a thing get by? At least his more sophisticated followers should have known better! It is therefore gratifying to announce that

at the extreme end of the 'Cave of Letters' on the north side of the Nahal Hever, between three and four o'clock of the afternoon of 15 March 1961, Professor Yadin put his hand into a crevice in the floor of the cave and lifted out a goatskin bag containing a woman's materials for mending her family's clothes on their sad and enforced vacation; and stuffed away under the stuff, at the very bottom of the bag, was a bundle of papyrus rolls wrapped in cloth. These were the Bar-Kochba Letters, and among them was a deed to some land near En-Gedi (the nearest town to the cave) owned by four men, one of whom signed himself, or rather dictated his name since he was illiterate, as 'Alma the son of Judah.' The deed is reproduced in color on p. 177 of the book, and there at the end of the fourth line from the top, as large as life is A-l-m-a ben Yehudah, which Prof. Yadin sensibly renders 'Alma' with no reservations."

27. Proposed etymologies include the stems *ǵlm* "young man, servant"; *ᶜlm* "eternity"; perhaps *'lmn* "widowhood"; and derivations from Latin *alma* from which we get the Spanish feminine first name Alma. Of these possibilities, only the former makes some sense. Given this etymology, Alma would be a hypocoristicon, but the final vowel would remain unexplained, unless it were read as a mater lectionis for a possessive pronoun.

28. The normalization "Alma" of the Hebrew letters is not mine but Yadin's.

29. Since the publication of the Book of Mormon, other West Semitic names ending with aleph have turned up, indicating that the terminal aleph in Alma is not unique to this name. For such names from a language contemporaneous with Lehi's departure from Jerusalem, see K. P. Jackson, "Ammonite Personal Names in the Context of the West Semitic Onomasticon," in *The Word of the Lord Shall Go Forth: Essays in Honor of David Noel Friedman in Celebration of His Sixtieth Birthday* (Winona Lake, Indiana: Eisenbrauns, 1983), pp. 507–21, particularly p. 518 for names ending in aleph.

30. T. H. Gaster, "Ugaritic Mythology," *Journal of Near Eastern Studies* 7 (1948) 185. The close connection between the bodies of water becomes clear from the Ugaritic parallel word pairs *mbk nhrm* "springs of the rivers" and *apq thmtm* "streams of the deep." For the passages see R. Whitaker, *A Concordance of Ugaritic Literature* (Cambridge: Harvard, 1972), pp. 410–11. For this word pair as "a place where the two rivers join the two oceans," see M. Drower, "Canaanite Religion in Literature," in *The Cambridge Ancient History*, vol. 2, part 2: *History of the Middle East and the Aegean Region c. 1380–1000 B.C.,* 3rd ed., eds. I. E. S. Edwards, C. J. Gadd, N. G. L. Hammond, and E. Sollberger (Cambridge: University Press, 1975), p. 154.

31. *Commentary on the Book of Genesis, Vol. II: From Noah to Abraham,* trans. I. Abrahams (Jerusalem: Magnes Press, 1974), p. 84. Note also Psalm 18:16–17; 2 Samuel 22:16–17; Job 6:15; and Proverbs 8:24, 27–28.

32. See the preceding note and also the succinctly discussed and conveniently illustrated article by L. Jacobs, "Jewish Cosmology," in *Ancient Cosmologies*, Carmen Blacker and Michael Loewe, eds. (London: George Allen & Unwin, 1975), pp. 69–70.

33. *Bulletin of the American Schools of Oriental Research 96* (1944) 28, note 41. See his extended remarks beginning on page 27, note 41. For general

comments on *sea*, see also W. G. Lambert, "The Cosmology of Sumer and Babylon," *Ancient Cosmologies*, pp. 55–60.

20

B. H. ROBERTS:
THE BOOK OF MORMON
AND THE ATONEMENT

Truman G. Madsen

Less than a year after B. H. Roberts returned from presiding over the Eastern States Mission, he was asked by an editor of a national magazine, "Why does Mormonism appeal to you?" He sat down and wrote the following nine-point list:

1. Its views of God,
2. Its views of man,
3. Its views of creation and the universe,
4. Its views of the purpose of life,
5. Its views of the atonement of the Christ,
6. Its views of the gospel as a means of man's salvation,
7. The grandeur and consistency of its development as the dispensation of the fulness of times, the completion of the plans of God with reference to the redemption of the earth and the salvation of man, and finally,
8. Its views of the physical resurrection and the
9. future degrees of glory to which man will be assigned as the outcome of his earth life.[1]

Truman G. Madsen occupies the Richard L. Evans Chair of Christian Understanding at Brigham Young University.

Those nine points multiplied by six chapters each, were the structure of a fifty-five-chapter work titled "The Truth, the Way and the Life" (hereafter TWL), on which he was then far along. That volume was the mature summation of his entire life's studies. Its production was arduous. He wrote to a former missionary that he had "poured out a wealth of work" on it—indeed, he expended much of the energy of the last six years of his life on the project. Substantially it was drawn into shape in Brooklyn during a six-month period after his release as mission president. On special leave given him by President Heber J. Grant, he remained in New York, in a little apartment on the Hudson River, and daily dictated elements of this manuscript to his secretary.[2]

The Truth, the Way, the Life

Some time ago, I published a thirty-page account of this volume, its background, its form and features, and the essential themes it treats.[3] More concerned with controversy than clarification, many have read only Roberts's speculative and now obsolete sections on science. Those sections were the main reasons the manuscript remained unpublished. None have written about its pervasive inclusion of the Book of Mormon, both in its historical and doctrinal phases. Here I propose a beginning in that direction.

The Quest for Coherence

Roberts's driving aspiration in TWL is longstanding. In his speaking and writing, Roberts sought to show coherence and system. He frequently lamented that we only understand or teach the Restoration in fragments. Out of all of these fragments, he believed one could, if one had the power and the patience, draw together what he called an "ever mighty system of truth."[4] He did not envision a closed system, for Mormonism is open in nature, open upward to further clarifying and expanding revelation from on high, and open downward to the ever-growing expanse of human experience. Nevertheless, he repeatedly said he would account himself most happy if only he could reduce these truths to some orderly system. His secretary, Elsa Cook, reports that during his labor on this his final work he would often say, "It is wonderful how the gospel hangs together."[5]

As the title of his work manifests, he saw the center of the system as Jesus the Christ: He is the Truth, He is the Way, and He is the Life.[6] And that for Roberts is the permeating message of the Book of Mormon

Roberts's Estimate of TWL

Roberts's own high estimate of his final manuscript is apparent in his correspondence. In 1929 when the manuscript was in most parts complete, he described it as his "latest and greatest work."[7] He later called the summation "the climax" of the "doctrinal department of my work, just as the Comprehensive History made the climax to my historical contributions."[8] His history volumes, 5 of 6, were finished by April of 1930, the Church's centennial. In a commemorative address, he placed the volumes on the Tabernacle pulpit and called them his gospel sermon. In February 1931, he wrote to President Heber J. Grant that in TWL he had crystallized practically all of his thought, research, and studies in the doctrinal line of the Church and that it was "the *most* important work that I have yet contributed to the Church, the six volume *Comprehensive History of the Church* not omitted."[9] In his final month (September 1933) he dictated a note to his secretary in which he said he hoped the ideas in TWL would be embraced by the youth of the Church. He wanted these ideas to reach the youth so they would not only "intellectually assent to [them] as an advanced system of truth, but also become imbued with [their] spirit and feel and enjoy [their] powers."[10] A year before his death, he had written that with his "incurable ailment" (by now the ravages of his diabetes had required a foot amputation), he hoped he would not die before his book could be published. Yet he added, "That work may not likely be printed in my lifetime. . . . I will not change it if it has to sleep."[11]

In accordance with his passion for reconciliation, Roberts writes at the outset of TWL, "let us not have the heart breathing defiance to the intellect." The inscription on the title page says, "Religion to be effective must appeal to the understanding as well as the emotions."[12] He believed TWL had received and would yet receive vindication in human experience, not only in its parts, but as a whole.

Additions and Expositions

Much of what Roberts writes about Christ and the Atonement in TWL was anticipated in his 1908 *Seventy's Yearbook*, an entire year's study course for the Seventy which dealt with the Atonement.[13] Every book of the Book of Mormon (with the exception of Jarom, Enos, and Omni) is utilized in depth in the chapters on the Atonement in TWL. The focus is especially on doctrinal sections and sermons and explications—1 and 2 Nephi, Jacob, Mosiah, Alma, Helaman, 3 and 4 Nephi, Ether, Mormon, and Moroni. In four different chapter introductions, he recommends as background, "Read the Book of Mormon entire." His elaborate scriptural foundation for the Atonement is the heart of hearts of TWL. At the outset of these six chapters on the Atonement, Roberts writes, "I must . . . ask that there be a suspension of judgment on the respective parts of the theme until all shall have been read; as knowledge of the whole, I am sure, will be necessary to complete understanding of the parts" (TWL, 40). Two sections deal with "Book of Mormon Prophecies of the Atonement" (2 Nephi 2:26, 27; Mosiah 3:16–18) and "Book of Mormon Historical Utterances on the Atonement" (3 Nephi 9:15–18, 21; 3 Nephi 11:9–11; Moroni 7:41; Id. See TWL, 40). In his introduction to 3 Nephi he writes, "The most important utterances that can come to man on any subject would be what the Lord Jesus Christ himself would say upon those subjects. For that reason, I am limiting the historical statements of the Book of Mormon on the Atonement to such words as were alleged to have been spoken by the risen Lord Jesus." (TWL, 40.) Then he cites 3 Nephi 9 and later chapters.

Here, arranged in columns, are the major chapters in TWL which are buttressed by the Book of Mormon:

Chapter	Title	Book of Mormon chapter and/or verses
1	Dissertation on Truth	Jacob 4:13
26	Pre-existence of Spirits	Alma 11:38–39
27	Purpose of God in Earth Life of Man	Book of Mormon entire, especially 2 Nephi 2:1–20; 2 Nephi 2:24–25; Ether 3.

32	Life Status of Adam and Eve at Their Advent	Book of Mormon entire, especially Mosiah 16:8, 9, 10, 18; Alma 11, 40
33	The Problem of Evil	2 Nephi 2; Alma 42
34	The Affair in Eden, the Fall of Man	2 Nephi 2; Alma 12:19–25; Alma 42
35	After the Fall, the First Dispensation of the Gospel	2 Nephi 2:14–30; Mosiah 4:4–12; Alma 11:38–46; Alma 42.
39	The Meridian Dispensation	Mosiah 15:4; Alma 11:38, 39; 3 Nephi 11:17; 11:23–26; Moroni chapters 4–5.
40	The Atonement I—The Revealed Fact of the Atonement	Book of Mormon entire, especially 3 Nephi. Also Mosiah 3, 4, 5; Moroni 7:41. Index references on "atonement."
43	The Atonement IV— Could Other Means than the Atonement Have Brought to Pass Man's Salvation?	Book of Mormon entire, especially 1 Nephi 9:7; 2 Nephi 9:21; Alma 13:14, 34:8–14.
44	The Atonement V—The Atonement of Broader Scope Than Making Satisfaction for Adam's Sin	2 Nephi 2, 9, 25; Alma 12, 34, 42; Helaman 14:17–18; Mormon 9; Moroni 8.
49	The Life: Under Commandments of God	Book of Mormon entire.
50	The Life: Sermon on the Mount—I	3 Nephi entire
51	The Life: Sermon on the Mount—II	3 Nephi entire

The Presuppositions of Atonement

We turn now to the weightiest of Roberts's writing, his account of the factors that must be kept in mind to comprehend the Atonement (TWL, 43).

First, a reign of law subsists throughout the universe. Roberts cites Nephi, Alma, and others on law, inexorable law, self-existent law. Law, he insists, prevails in the spiritual as well as in the physical realm. Whether inherent in the nature of things or instituted by divine initiative, all laws have bounds and conditions. This perfect reign of law and the reign of perfect law is in strict harmony with God's attributes, and God's attributes with it.

Second, violations of law, out of ignorance or deliberation, destroy the steady maintenance of the law and involve transgressors in the penalties inseparably connected with law. Without these, law would be of no efficacy at all. Law prescribes the consequences of one's acts. But law is not totally coercive. Certain consequences are inevitable, but our choice of them and our responses to them are not.

Third, two kinds of things exist in the universe. In the language of the Book of Mormon, these are "things to act and things to be acted upon."[14] Men are among the things to act. We are free and, within limits, eternally free. When we obey the laws, certain results follow; whether we ignore or disobey, "Suffering is the consequence or penalty of violating divine, moral law" (TWL, 43).

Fourth, the attributes of God, complete and perfect as they are, exist in harmony with each other, no one supplanting another or intruding upon its domain. Over and over the Book of Mormon says, if so and so, then "God would cease to be God," or again, "God cannot. . . ." He cannot, for example, lie or deny his word, or violate his promises (TWL, 43). The "cannot" does not mean that he lacks the power, for that would mean that God has less power than man. It means that in harmony with the attributes of his nature he *will* not violate law. Ancient debate asks whether God's will is right because he wills it, or whether he wills it because it is right." Roberts opts for the second position and insists that once the "broken harmonies" are overcome, man's will, like God's, will harmonize with eternal law.

Any manifestation of God's initiative in special providence or mercy, even that actuated by Divine love, must not and will not violate this core-conception of the attributes of Deity (TWL, 14).

Fifth, the world cries out for justice and mercy. Roberts had written earlier that nowhere in all sacred literature, not even in the New Testament, is the balance of justice and mercy so clearly taught as in the Book of Mormon. "And now," he writes, "it is justice that cries aloud for their presence in the divine government" (TWL, 43). But is there not a clash between justice and mercy? The Book of Mormon asks, "Do you suppose that mercy can rob justice?" and answers no (Alma 42:25). How, then, are they reconciled? The answer is that those who do not harden their hearts but instead in penitence with a broken heart and a contrite spirit surrender in response to mercy are the only ones unto whom the ends of the law, which are love and mercy, can be answered. To put it differently: When men after transgression, or setback, or willful failure, are contrite, it is *just* that they should receive mercy, which leads to repentance and healing. Otherwise, justice would require that they receive none.[15] To bring love and mercy into the world in harmony with all the attributes of God required the Atonement. Jesus became the voluntary Messiah.

But why shouldn't the Atonement be dispensed with altogether? With Alma, whom he thought "among the greatest of the ancient American prophets," Roberts says it is "expedient," and in brackets he interprets *expedient* to mean necessary. The great and last sacrifice must occur, infinite and eternal, for the highest impact on the family of God (see Alma 34:8–14). "Even God's omnipotence must conform to the attributes of truth and wisdom and justice and mercy. But neither justice nor mercy would require nor permit more suffering on the part of the redeemer than was absolutely necessary." (TWL, 34.) Otherwise, it would be cruelty, pure and simple. The testator's blood is the effectual seal of the testimony of the testator (see 1 Nephi 9:7; Alma 13, 14). Hence came a Lord of life with power of life within himself and power to impart it in a voluntary act.

For Roberts, exalted conceptions arise from all this: greater respect for the moral government of the world, for the majesty and justice of God, for the physical life of the hereafter (resurrection), for the spiritual life, the indissoluble union of man with God, for God's mercy, and over all for the love of God. And why? Because for each of these Christ suffered and died. "Behold, he suffereth . . . the pains of every living creature, both men, women, and children, who belong to the family of Adam" (2 Nephi 9:21).

Implications: Four Kinds of Suffering

Now some personal applications. The Atonement involves suffering. Roberts identifies four modes of suffering. He begins with the premise that mental-spiritual suffering is no less real and no less intense than is physical suffering.

1. We suffer *for* our own sins, in the wake of, because of, and due to them.

2. We suffer *because of* the sins of others; for example, as parents for our children, and as children for our parents.

3. We suffer *with* each other on account of sin "through common human sympathy."

4. We are *willing to suffer for each other* (TWL, 45).

It has been said Christ came into the world not that men might not suffer but that their sufferings might be like his.[16] The more one identifies with Christ, the more one identifies with those who are his and also those who refuse thus far to become his. Hence the soul-cry, "Oh Absalom, my son! Would to God I had died for thee." (2 Samuel 18:33.) So parents cry out for children; so children for parents. In some cases so strangers for strangers (TWL, 45).

Roberts embraced these profoundly intimate verses in the book of Alma on the sufferings of Christ. "He shall go forth," says Alma, looking forward through time as we look backward, "suffering pains and afflictions and temptations of every kind." Alma explains that this was required, but not in the sense that it was fated or inevitable. Rather, it was in order that Christ's bowels (the Hebrew word for the center self) "may be filled with mercy . . . that he may know . . . how to succor his people." It is true that the Spirit "knoweth all things." Yet Alma says, "Nevertheless the Son of God suffereth according to the flesh." (Alma 7:11–13; also 2 Nephi 9:21.)

The clear implication here and elsewhere in the Book of Mormon is that if Christ had not submitted to the pains and afflictions and temptations as a participant and not simply as an ideal spectator, he would have been inacapable of the deepest levels of compassion. Compassion came through his experience,

experience in the flesh. Roberts emphasizes throughout his treatise the primacy, the preciousness, the cruciality of mortal experience as the very meaning of life. It cannot be circumvented. Actually or vicariously we must go through it all. Then will emerge, he says, "New Righteousness" based upon virtue instead of upon innocence; it will be "righteousness founded upon experience, upon tested experimentation and intelligent righteousness" (TWL, 24).

The Law of Opposites

But couldn't God have overcome evil in some other way? Roberts reads the Book of Mormon as a "testimony" to the eternity of opposite existences including evil. He writes, "The sacred writer Lehi . . . boldly carries the necessity of such existences to such an extreme that . . . he makes existence itself, and even the existence of God, to depend upon the fact of things existing in duality" (TWL, 32).

As examples, Roberts cites centripetal and centrifugal forces, action and reaction, composing and decomposing, positive and negative; then light and darkness, movement, and repose, energy and matter, heat and cold, life and death, "the one and the multiple." In the moral order, he names good and evil, joy and sorrow, courage and cowardice, righteousness and wickedness. (TWL, 33.)

Conclusion: "God did not create evil. Neither is he responsible for it." (TWL, 43.)

A dominant philosophical tradition rejects this sequence of explanation and justification. It argues that if there is any self-existent or co-existent reality besides God, it and not God is God. This tradition says, "God only is self-existent and all other reality is utterly contingent upon him."[17] The view is enmeshed with two premises to which the Book of Mormon teaching is a clear alternative: (1) The absolute ex nihilo creation. This means that God by fiat act brought into being everything that is, from nothing. For Roberts, this leads to an intractable problem despite labored special pleading. For it means the very conditions to which the Atonement was in answer were created by God himself. The second is absolute omnipotence and omniscience of God. It follows that with unqualified, absolute pre-vision and pre-power to do otherwise, he tied knots which he then inscrutably untied through his innocent Son. How could a God of love, of limitless power and knowledge, set up such a system? How can we avoid the conclusion that in such a plan he is vindictive, even malicious? (TWL, 33.)

But Roberts is saying in the name of the Book of Mormon that God did not create the dilemma of free selves and inviolate law. God is self-existent but we ourselves are co-existent with him—as spirits, or intelligence. He himself has mastered and fulfilled and become what he is, in harmony with law. He has all the power it is possible to have in this given universe (Roberts would prefer to say pluriverse).[18] In that sense, he is almighty. But he does not have all power. He could not have done it in another way with the same results.[19]

The Resolving of Paradox

Now, let us sketch implications of this eternalism which requires radical reformulation of classical views. Traditional theism absolutely divides the realm beyond, the divine realm, from the physical and the earthly. Usually these are so polarized that not one quality ascribed to the temporal realm can be ascribed to the eternal "timeless" one. When it is affirmed that God, the one necessary being, is immaterial, it is further affirmed that he cannot (the *he* here is itself puzzling for these writers and must be stripped of all physicalistic connotations), except by a "scandal of particularity," involve himself in the materiate, spatial, and temporal realms. Thus arise the "paradoxes of the incarnation" creedalized at the council of Chalcedon, which insists on both the absolute humanity and the absolute divinity of Jesus Christ. Put briefly, they require that the infinite became finite, the immaterial identified itself with matter, the unchanging changed, the nontemporal submitted to time, the nonspatial entered space. When one says, "But those are incompatible," the response is, "Of course; here is the need of faith." Such paradoxes are not taken as flashy ways of saying things, which under analysis become reconcilable. They are instead taken as profound unresolved mysteries in the ultimate character of Being.

Roberts gloried in the recognition that the Book of Mormon doctrine of God, Christ, and the Atonement avoids not just some but all of those paradoxes. A long string of theological pseudo-problems and untenable dualisms is resolved. Among them (on which more cannot be said here):

1. Being vs. Becoming

2. Universal vs. Particular

3. Transcendence vs. Immanence

4. Spirit vs. Body

5. Spiritual vs. Temporal

6. Faith vs. Reason

7. Grace vs. Merit

8. Sacred vs. Secular

9. Other-worldly vs. This Worldly

10. Escape vs. Transformation

11. Symbolic vs. Literal

In a word, Roberts accepted the Book of Mormon doctrine (as later expanded upon by Joseph Smith) that the universe is a collection of particulars which occupy space and time and therefore can interact. It was not God, an immaterial and unconditioned being, who entered a body. It was Jesus, the first spirit Son of God the Father, who came into the world and inherited a physical body and then, moving from grace to grace, became what he became: both our exemplar and our redeemer.[20]

Story, History, and Inseparable Links

Roberts was in many ways the most prolific of Mormon historians of the first century. At the same time, without massive tensions, he was one of its most articulate theologians. It is a left-handed tribute to Roberts that many specialized historians today find his writings too theological or, as they would say, apologetic. On the other hand, many theologians, whether they are dogmatic or speculative or even naturalistic, find his theology too historical.

He observed that in the Book of Mormon there is no yawning chasm between the Jesus of history and the Christ of faith. Well-meaning people are presently at work trying to "save" the book by denying its historical content and context. They say, "Let's treat the Book of Mormon as an allegory; take it as a collection of symbols in quasi-narrative garb. Let's call it nineteenth-century pseudepigrapha. But let's give up the quest for "external evidence."

Of course the book is rich—Roberts says far richer than we yet know—in allegory, typology, symbol, and metaphor. But external as well as internal historicity is the essence of the book. To try to disentangle it from its earthly and sometimes earthy connections, to deny its narratives, its chronology, to isolate its functions from reportage is not to save the book. It is to eviscerate it.

The question was raised by one of Roberts's contemporaries, Kierkegaard.[21] How can one commit his or her own salvation to a mere set of historical or probabilistic judgments? Roberts answers with the Book of Mormon, "The Gospel has a history and 'the life' required in it is based upon the facts of that history" (TWL, 14).

"But," persists the critic, "we cannot recover the precise historical truth about a Moses or a Jesus." The consensus of a century of scholarship, for example in the New Testament, is that either we must be content to see Jesus through the eyes of an already distorting institution called the Christian Church or acknowledge that we cannot see him at all. Roberts answers that the peoples of the Book of Mormon left Jerusalem, not Athens. They left before the rise and canonization of Greek philosophy through Plato and Philo in Christendom and Judaism. They were prompt in recordkeeping. And they were dead and buried before the hellenization of what we call Western culture. "Take off your metaphysical glasses," Roberts pleads, in effect, "and read the Book of Mormon, which is full of plain and precious but also profound things. Cease to impose the Greek assumptions that distort and stifle." (TWL, 20.)

The Book of Mormon in modern translation is only one step removed from the bearers of revelation. These persons are real for Roberts. So are the events. They are accessible. That accessibility does not require one to retreat into mysticism, which strives to retain a claim on the divine by the final disparagement and rejection of perception. Extreme mystics want nothing to do with the senses and if it gets in their way they will have nothing to do with reason. But prophets are not mystics in this extreme sense. Ten prophets in the Book of Mormon, as Roberts's own notebook records, encountered the living God in vision. When they say they saw and heard God, they saw and heard God. The Book of Mormon reinstates all authentic modes of religious awareness. And it does not disparage any.

This same presumption, with the Book of Mormon in the foreground, led Roberts to see to it that the modern Church came to repossess its cradle. "I feel satisfied that we are going to get added inspiration from the fact that we own our birthplace and our cradle."[22] With the approval of the First Presidency (before his release 2 May 1927), he was instrumental in the recovery of the Joseph Smith farm, the Sacred Grove, the Hill Cumorah, the Peter Whitmer home, and the home in Harmony, Pennsylvania, where the Prophet completed the translation of the Book of Mormon.

"I rejoice", says Roberts in a late discourse, "that we have access to these [places]."[23] Why? Here again is the sacramental insight. These origin-events are to our profound religious impulses what the sacrament of the Restoration is to the soul: nurture and nourishment. "As the bugle to the war horse; as the sight of the flag to the patriot, and the drum-beat to the soldier," Roberts taught, a frequent . . . "recurrence to the . . . great events in which our Church had its origin give inspiration and spirit life to us."[24] That history for Roberts includes the story of the Book of Mormon. More than that, it includes the story *in* the Book of Mormon. That story is not a mere story, not contrived fiction. It is history. At the heart of it is Christ's story, the story of him who lived and died and lived again. In anticipation, in enactment, and in retrospect, the Book of Mormon records that monumental series of events.

Other Life Reconciliations

One can see the man Roberts—a man of commingled griefs and joys—behind his final analysis of what he called the "Fifth Gospel," 3 Nephi. A basic tension is reflected in an excerpt he made from Paleys "Two Views" of life and character:

> The one possesses vigor, firmness, resolution; is daring and active, quick in its sensibilities, jealous of its fame, eager in its attachments, inflexible in its purpose, violent in its resentments.

The other is meek, yielding, complying, forgiving, not prompt to act, but willing to suffer; silent and gentle under rudeness and insult, suing for reconciliation when others would demand satisfaction, giving way to the pushes of impudence conceding and indulgent to the prejudices, the wrongheadedness, the intractability, of those with whom it has to deal.[25]

The world venerates the first approach. Roberts pleads "Render unto Caesar what is Caesar's, to God the things that are God's." But does Christ really mean these things about cloaks and miles, and loving and praying for enemies? "Utterly impracticable," Roberts answers for the realist. "It would produce a race of mollycoddles, of non-resisting, unaggressive simpletons." The plea "Take no thought" is "wholly at variance with true economic principles and the stern requirements of common sense." (TWL, 50.)

What Roberts finds in 3 Nephi and the "American Sermon on the Mount" is two realities: On the one hand, Jesus presents to the Nephites an "intensification" of the requirements of "the Life." It is more idealistic, more perfectionistic than the parallel account in Matthew. For example, he admonishes not just against anger, "without cause," but against anger itself, "stopping it at its source." He advocates not just the first and second miles but service "with real intent." And he makes the key words of the several duties of almsgiving, prayer, and fasting "cheerfulness, lightheartedness and joy" not as if they were "burdens hard to bear." (TWL, 50.)

On the other hand, the sermon clarifies with penetrating insight the who, the when, and the what of certain requirements which are falsified when they are absolutized. The counsel "take no thought for the morrow," for example, is not for everyone. It is for the Twelve and dedicated missionaries. So, likewise, in some of its ethical reaches is the command to "turn the other cheek." The counsel on adultery of the heart is coupled with "deny yourself," not as some have supposed with a "fanatical" encouragement of self-mutilation.

More fundamental, all the counsels of the sermon remain unreachable except through a rebirth, a life derived from Christ's life. No fruits are promised without roots. The entire sermon is preceded by the requirement of baptism of fire and the Holy Ghost. Jesus' high ethic presupposes a radically altered personality, one reborn to this new life. For Roberts, the glory of it is in this sentence: "He who delivered it lived it!" (TWL, 51.)

The Sacramental Prayers

That leads to a rediscovery in Roberts's latest thought on the Book of Mormon—the two sacramental prayers. These prayers alone, he had concluded earlier, mark the Book of Mormon as authentic and divinely inspired. "The composition of them in excellence arises far above any performance that Joseph Smith could be considered equal to."[26] Now he insisted they were "the most perfect forms of sacred literature to be found."[27] He had earlier written that to add or subtract a word would mutilate or mar them and diminish their power. Now he described them in a way foreign to Mormon ears. They are like creeds. (TWL, 39.) By this he means that they embody, in masterful, rich, heavily freighted phrases, the whole of the gospel. They encapsulate the whole Book of Mormon. To participate in them is to enter the Holy of Holies of the Atonement. Four pages of TWL add to his earlier exposition of them.

These prayers spiritualize the physical and physicalize the spiritual. They unite the life-sufferings and death of Jesus into our frail flesh. They cry out in prayer and covenant from man's mortal condition to an Eternal Father.[28] They present physical realities—bread and water—to be blessed and sanctified to the soul. *Soul* does not mean, as it does in most traditions, an immaterial entity that is somehow *in* the body, "a ghost in the machine." *Soul* is the revealed name of the spirit and body together, as Roberts says at length in a comparison and contrast account of the Book of Mormon doctrine of joy. These prayers, and the ordinances which they recapitulate, convey more than salvitic grace. They transmit "powers of godliness." We may receive into our souls his spirit. Eventually we may become like him. That is the premise and promise of the prayers—life without which there is no life—life like His.

Roberts, a man who knew how stressed and confused and sinful life can be, emphasized that the key word in the first prayer is *willing*. That is the covenant of the first prayer: Willing to take upon them His name. Willing always to remember him. Willing to keep his commandments. Finally, man may arrive at the point through this "palpable food to the soul" when he loses even the desire for sin. (TWL, 39.) That too, is an intrinsic promise of the prophets of the Book of Mormon.[29]

So impressed was he with this that it became the conclusion of his last address. Only twenty-three days before his death,

Roberts addressed the Chicago Parliament of Religions. His subject was "Economics of the New Age."[30] His presentation ended with the Book of Mormon sacramental prayers. He concluded: "What could be better as the sum of all excellence? And the one thing needful for the solution of all our human woes?" (TWL, 39.)

Summary

The following inclusive paragraph sums up all Roberts had tried to say:

> Spiritual life means relation to and participation in all the higher and better things, the good, the true, the beautiful, the pure, the refined, the noble, the courageous, the unselfish, the merciful, united with truth, justice, knowledge, wisdom, power, intelligence. The heart of all this, the very center and circumference of it and the life of it, is and must be God. And so to deport oneself that he is thrown out of harmony with all this, severed from fellowship with God by separation from him who is the life of all this volume of higher and better things, this body of soul quality, this ocean of righteousness is death, indeed spiritual death. It is death as real as physical death, the separation of spirit and body. (TWL, 38.)

Thus, to B. H. Roberts the Book of Mormon is in the fullest sense a matter of life and death.

NOTES AND REFERENCES

1. Personal Scripture Notebook, B. H. Roberts, Church Archives.

2. Truman G. Madsen, "The Truth, The Way, The Life," chapter 17, *Defender of the Faith* (Salt Lake City: Bookcraft, 1980), pp. 338–45.

3. Madsen, "The Meaning of Christ: The Truth, The Way and The Life: An Analysis of B. H. Roberts's Unpublished Master Work," *BYU Studies*, 15 (Spring 1975), 259–92.

4. See Foreword, *Discourses of B. H. Roberts* (Salt Lake City: Deseret Book, 1948).

5. Letter of Elsa Cook, Roberts's secretary in his last years, to the author 10 February 1970.

6. This title derives from John 14:6. Roberts's notebooks show he was first impressed to use the title when singing the last verse of a classical Mormon hymn, "Prayer Is the Soul's Sincere Desire." "O Thou by Whom We Come to God, the Life, the Truth, the Way!" (No. 145 in 1985 Hymnbook.)

7. From a letter to President Heber J. Grant. See Nels B. Lundwall papers, BYU Special Collections.

8. Ibid.

9. B. H. Roberts to Heber J. Grant, 9 February 1931, Heber J. Grant Collection, Church Historical Department. In a letter to a missionary friend, he wrote on 3 March 1931, "I have been passing through the severest and mental and spiritual strain of my life during the last two months . . . concerning my manuscript, 'The Truth, The Way, and The Life.' . . . Matters, however, have not reached conclusions yet, and I still hope for a favorable decision."

10. From the handwritten title page of the preface to *Discourses of B. H. Roberts*, Elsa Cook's handwriting says, "These were President Roberts's exact words."

11. Roberts to Heber J. Grant, 9 Feb. 1931.

12. Introduction to "The Truth, The Way, The Life." (Hereafter cited in the text as TWL, chapter number.)

13. See *Seventy's Course in Theology*, Fourth Year, The Atonement (Salt Lake City: Deseret News, 1908).

14. TWL, 43. 2 Nephi 2:11–14; 10:23. Roberts quotes Nephi: "The first judgment which came upon man [the judgment of death, spiritual and physical] must needs have remained to an endless duration. And if so, this flesh must have laid down to rot . . . to rise no more." (2 Nephi 9:7). Again, because of the fall of Adam "all mankind were fallen, and they were in the grasp of justice; yea, the justice of law, God, which consigned them forever to be cut off from his presence" (Alma 42:14).

15. Roberts writes, "Not only must there be made satisfaction to eternal justice, but there must be the power of Deity exercised if man is to be saved from death; there must be a power of life so that that which was lost may be restored, both as to the spiritual life of man and the physical life" (TWL, 43).

16. George McDonald in C. S. Lewis, *The Problem of Pain* (New York: Macmillan, 1962), preface.

17. This is a central thesis of the philosophical theology of Augustine, Anselm, and Thomas Aquinas. It remains uncontested in official Catholic, Greek Orthodox, and Protestant thought. Roberts contemplates the cost (TWL, 43).

18. The word *universe* suggests a "block-universe," but Roberts was a particularist. There is no one thing, one plenum. There are many selves, many lives, many goods, many evils (TWL, 9).

19. Roberts's section on "limitations on these powers" is in his Treatment of the "Omnis." God's eternity is without qualification. But God's omnipresence must be qualified—his Spirit permeates space but his personal presence is in some place. His omnipotence must be qualified—he has all the power that it

is possible to have in a universe of laws and free intelligences but he has not the power to create or destroy element. He is also limited and delimited by the exercise of human freedom. God's power does not extend to the creation of freedom. Freedom is an ineluctable fact (TWL, 20 and 42).

20. In chapter 20, "Departure of the Church from the True Doctrine of God," Roberts presents the formuli and creeds, the apostle creed, the patristic view, the doctrine of trinities, the Nicene creed, the Athanasian creed, all of which "stray from the plain anthropomorphism of the New Testament revelation of God through Jesus Christ." This has pagan origin and Roberts cites scholars who acknowledge that the notion that the conception of God is "pure being," "immaterial," "without form" "or parts or passion" has its origin in philosophy, not in Jewish or Christian revelation."

21. S. Kierkegaard in *Concluding Unscientific Postscript*, trans. by David F. Swenson (Princeton: Princeton University Press for American Scandinavian Foundation).

22. *Conference Report,* October 1926, p. 127.

23. Ibid., p. 124.

24. Ibid., pp. 124–25.

25. Roberts's Personal Scripture Notebook, under "Views of Life and Character," Church Archives.

26. See *New Witnesses*, 3:489.

27. See "The sacrament of the Lord's supper" (TWL, 39). "In the Book of Mormon is given a most dramatic and soul-thrilling testimony to the resurrection of the Christ by the appearance of the risen Redeemer to a multitude of people in America, shortly after the resurrection of the Christ; thus to the people of America no less than to the people of the Eastern Hemisphere, did God give assurances through their ancient prophets from time to time of the existence of his gospel and of power unto salvation; and lastly the risen Christ came to them to assure them of the verities of the Plan of Salvation and especially of this feature of it, the Resurrection from the dead, by his own glorious appearance among them, and his quite extended ministry among them. (For all which, see Book of 3 Nephi, the whole book, but especially chapter 11.)" See also his stake conference addresses of January, March, and April 1931 and April and August 1932. In each he occasionally discoursed on these "prayers perfect."

28. TWL, 39. "Eternal Father" for example means to Roberts not first cause as in the classical view, but eternal continuing cause and eternal sustaining power; not the Aristotelian unmoved mover, but the "most moved mover," the most touched, the most impressed, the most compassionate.

29. This means to Roberts that the gospel cannot be reduced to an ethic only. It is a religion of transformation.

30. See his "Economics of the New Age" in *Discourses of B. H. Roberts* (Salt Lake City: Deseret Book Company, 1948), p. 7.

21

CONCLUSION AND CHARGE

Jeffrey R. Holland

May I express my deep personal appreciation for all who have organized, prepared, attended, and participated in this second annual symposium on the Book of Mormon. I am very proud of the Religious Studies Center at Brigham Young University and the Religious Education administrators and faculty who carry the lion's share of the responsibility for pursuing the work of the center. It is one of my highest personal hopes that the Religious Studies Center will be an extremely visible and very influential agency on the Brigham Young University campus, stimulating the strongest and best kind of religious research underscoring and reaffirming the truths of the Restoration.

I am also in hopes that the center and its work will involve not only all of our Religious Education faculty at BYU but also many of our colleagues from the full range of disciplines across the campus, and that we will reach *beyond* the campus to friends, adjunct scholars, and interested participants the Church over. I realize that geography and travel hold some limitations for us,

Jeffrey R. Holland is President of Brigham Young University.

but we hope that just such events as this Book of Mormon symposium will continue to make BYU the center of strong, reliable teaching and research in all of the areas that are of doctrinal importance to the kingdom of God in these last days.

In that spirit I thank all of you for your participation and attendance here these past two days. I only wish I could have been in every session for every hour. I am very proud of your accomplishments and wish to conclude this symposium with a strong expression of encouragement for next year's topic, for the year after that, and so forth. We have an everlastingly rich source of doctrinal ore here to mine, especially in the Book of Mormon, and I encourage all of us to participate in that task. BYU intends to facilitate your work and give expression to it.

May I just add something of my own personal testimony to the theme that has been pursued at the symposium. I commend Dean Robert Matthews, Associate Dean Monte Nyman, and all who have assisted them for their decision to have us focus on a manageable segment of the Book of Mormon and, in effect, work our way through the book over the next several years. That manageable but immensely rich segment for this symposium has been 1 Nephi, "The Doctrinal Foundation."

I don't know just where I was in my teaching career when I began to realize what remarkable pieces of material 1 Nephi specifically and the small plates of Nephi generally really were. I suppose all of us have wondered about the detail and doctrine that were lost with the disappearance of that initial 116 pages of Book of Mormon manuscript. Indeed one of my fantasies since youth has been that I would be the one rummaging around in an old attic or library somewhere and would discover those manuscript pages. I would then triumphantly bear them off as a gift to the President of the Church. I guess that is still kind of a fun fantasy to have, and if any of you have suggestions about old attics in which I should be rummaging I'm open to suggestion.

Nevertheless I have long since come to believe that when the Lord in his omniscient wisdom foresaw the Martin Harris problem and planned for its remedy more than two thousand years in advance of that loss, he knew full well what our needs would be and provided in that replacement matter (that is, the small plates) perhaps an even richer resource for our study and edification than those initial 116 pages of abridged material would have proven to be. I do not want this to sound like heresy, much less even hint that I'm glad the 116 pages were lost, but if such a loss is what it took in order for us to have 1 Nephi and the rest of the small plates given to us, so be it. I confess I cannot imagine what the Book of Mormon would be without those first 145 printed pages you and I now enjoy.

I suppose I am intrigued with this introductory material in part because all of us have to be intrigued—and captivated and led on and inspired—by how a book begins, or else we are likely not to read the rest of the book at all. My life and library contain a lot of books in which I have read the first fifty or seventy-five pages and then have closed the books, never to read there again. Patience is not one of my great virtues, and if a book cannot say something to me forcefully and well somewhere in the course of its first pages, I am not very sanguine that it is going to say much to me thereafter. Perhaps that is an unfair judgment to make, but it is one I do make regularly as a reader, and perhaps you do as well.

For that reason truly great books, and I believe virtually all even reasonably good books, have a strong, compelling beginning. We have been agreeing with Aristotle ever since he said that "a good book must have a calculated structure and development which gives a unified impact from beginning to end."[1] I believe that by Aristotle's standard the Book of Mormon is not only a good book; it is a classic. In spite of the fact that it is written by a series of prophets who had different styles and different experiences, in spite of the fact that it has some unabridged materials mixed with others that have been greatly condensed, in spite of the fact that it has unique and irregular chronological sequences, it is nonetheless a classic book—indeed, Aristotle's kind of book: unified, whole, verses fitting with verses, chapters fitting with chapters, books fitting with books, and always that strong beginning.

Several years ago I was asked to write on this subject for the *Ensign* magazine, and there I tried to suggest, particularly for a younger reading audience, that in the first chapter of 1 Nephi, twenty carefully written and powerfully stage-setting verses, a *great* deal is said about what the rest of the Book of Mormon is going to be. Now, putting aside some other very important items that occur even in such a brief chapter, we note that a rough outline of those first twenty verses indicates that

1. A prophet prays

2. He has a vision

3. In the vision he sees heavenly messengers (including Jesus Christ)

4. In the vision he receives a book filled with remarkable truths and prophecies

5. He is rejected by most of the people

For me it cannot be coincidental that Lehi's experience at the beginning of this book parallels so closely that of Joseph Smith's. For one thing, I believe all prophets have some special experiences in common. One thing we *know* they have in common is receiving revelation from the Lord, revelation that often gets canonized in books of scripture. Furthermore, it seems to me that this parallel experience, sketchy as it is, links an older dispensation of prophets who lived the Book of Mormon experience with a modern-day prophet who would translate and reveal it to the world. That is just one more way in which we realize that if we accept Lehi and the Book of Mormon, we surely have to accept Joseph Smith as a prophet of God: the former cannot be seen as an authentic, ancient prophet without acknowledging the divine work of the latter which revealed such a fact to the world. On the other hand, when we accept Joseph Smith as a prophet we surely must accept and faithfully seek to live by the teachings of Lehi and the others who follow him in this record, because a true prophet will bring forth true teachings.

This first chapter of 1 Nephi is just one of those impressive ways by which revelation leaps the traditional impediments of time and space, giving great unity to the dispensations and to the doctrinal truths of the kingdom which characterize and connect them. In that sense the Book of Mormon is not only the testimony of Nephi and Alma and Mormon and Moroni, but it is also the testimony of Joseph Smith and Brigham Young and Spencer W. Kimball and Ezra Taft Benson. Just as all scripture is, in a sense, one in God's hand, so are all the prophets who provide it.

Above all, what this chapter and the rest of 1 Nephi says to us—and for my purposes here, what the entire Book of Mormon says to us—is that revelation is indeed the great binding mortar of this dispensation and of every dispensation. The Prophet Joseph said that revelation is the rock on which the Church of Jesus Christ will always be built and that there can never be any salvation without it.[2] That is the principle we are forced to deal with in the opening verses of 1 Nephi, and we continue to be inundated with it through all of 1 Nephi. It is clear to us very early that revelation is what the book is about, and if we do not accept that principle rather quickly we are in trouble on the very first page of the book.

I have already noted Lehi's revelatory experience in chapter 1. Notice how chapter 2 begins. "For behold, it came to pass that the Lord spake unto my father, yea, even in a dream, and said unto him. . . ."

Chapter 3: "And it came to pass that I, Nephi, returned from speaking with the Lord. . . . And . . . [my father] spake unto me, saying: Behold I have dreamed a dream, in the which the Lord hath commanded me. . . ." Later in the chapter an angel appears and speaks.

Chapter 4 tells of Nephi being led by the Spirit, not knowing beforehand the things which he should do.

Chapter 5 speaks of the plates of brass (scripture), giving some general outline of their doctrinal, historical, and genealogical contents.

Chapter 6 is an editorial comment about the value of scripture.

Chapter 7 simply continues the theme: "After my father, Lehi, had made an end of prophesying concerning his seed, it came to pass that the Lord spake unto him again. . . ."

Chapter 8, of course, tells of that remarkable first vision of the tree of life. The chapter begins with Lehi's declaration—again—"Behold, I have dreamed a dream; or, in other words . . . seen a vision"; and then the stunning details of that well-known vision unfold.

Chapter 9 is an editorial comment from Nephi about why the small plates had been recorded, and chapter 10 contains the first extensive Book of Mormon commentary on the Savior of the world. Nephi, speaking of his father's sermon, says, "He also spake concerning the prophets, how great a number had testified of these things, concerning this Messiah, of whom he had spoken, or this Redeemer of the world."

Then, of course, in chapter 11 Nephi takes his own rightful place as one of those prophets when he is led by the Spirit to see all that his father had seen and eventually much more, a vision of remarkable content and detail and revelatory impact.

That is enough, sketchy as it is, to suggest the incessant revelatory nature of these opening chapters. Prophets, dreams, angels, visions, scripture, promptings of the Spirit, more prophets, more visions—they come in every chapter, on every page. By the time we get to 1 Nephi 15 or so we have dealt with almost every conceivable form of divine revelation and yet are only thirty pages into the book. Again it strikes me that at this point the intellectually honest reader must make a very fundamental concession: The Book of Mormon presupposes the reality of revelation. Indeed in some ways it is one long revelation about revelation. If that premise is unacceptable to the reader, as it unfortunately is to some, that is why (it seems to me) he or she may as well close the book and conclude the reading, as some unfortunately do.

Consider the role this special book of revelation(s) played in the sequence of the Restoration. With the book finally published in the last days of March 1830, the stage was set for the organization of the church just days later on the sixth of April. The restoration of the gospel of Jesus Christ and its institutional church would have *everything* to do with and everything to say about revelation. Indeed its principal document, the Book of Mormon, was written, watched over, preserved, revealed, translated, published, and carried to the world to declare—again —that revelation had not ceased, that the heavens were again open, that God does speak to men. Nothing else that Samuel Smith and those early missionaries would teach could have much impact if that cardinal, fundamental truth about revelation was not accepted by the people they taught.

And so it still is today. That confrontation with revelation and the reality of God's direction to his prophets is part of the intellectual sequence and spiritual journey into which the reader of the Book of Mormon is immediately forced to step. I believe if we are still reading after the first thirty pages, and reading with intent and honesty and examination, we are ineluctably on our way to accepting not only a millenium of Nephite history but also the boy prophet and the restored Church which published it to the world. All of the revelatory grandeur of the Restoration with all of its glory and abundance lies just beyond 1 Nephi. No wonder the book begins the way it does.

Let me suggest another thing that I believe is happening in 1 Nephi. I mentioned earlier that I believed this was a superbly crafted book, verses fitting with verses and chapters fitting with chapters. Somewhere along the way, as we read 1 Nephi, we realize that these revelatory experiences just alluded to are posing a seemingly endless series of confrontations and choices. Lehi is one kind of local leader, his relative Laban is another; Nephi is one kind of son, Laman is another; and so forth, ad infinitum.

If we read for a while we inevitably begin making something of a mental list showing this significant string of alternatives—all in 1 Nephi: Lehi versus Laban, Nephi and Sam versus Laman and Lemuel, New Jerusalem versus Old Babylon, the tree of life versus the depths of hell, the virgin mother of Christ versus the harlot mother of abominations, the church of the Lamb of God versus the church of the devil, and of course ultimately what we are seeing by the end of 1 Nephi is simply Christ versus Satan.

Along such a path of choices and alternatives we come, with some difficulty, through the wilderness of mortal life, finding virtually no good that seems not to be countered by an opposite evil.

"Opposition in all things." Now, that is a phrase with a familiar ring to it. I suggest it is not accidental that such extensive and skillful preparation is laid in 1 Nephi for the doctrinal exposition we fill find in 2 Nephi. That book, of course, contains one of the greatest scriptural discourses in all the Book of Mormon (and all scripture, I might add) on opposition in all things, dramatized by the issues surrounding the fall of Adam and the atonement of Christ.

I am sure that Lehi could have given a mighty sermon (or, in this case, a patriarchal blessing) on opposition and agency somewhere back in 1 Nephi, but how much more powerful it is for his sons and for us as readers to have lived through fifty pages of such confrontations and alternatives before we hear it verbalized as a doctrinal issue. The faithful few in that little family have had about as much "opposition in all things" as they can stand, but it has taught them something about themselves, about a fallen world, about the plan of God, about the majesty of Christ, and about the eternal exercise of choice.

It would seem, then, that all the hardships of 1 Nephi have had significant purpose in pointing us toward the doctrinal climate of 2 Nephi and the figure of Christ which will entirely dominate that book, including the Isaiah chapters that are included there. I suppose, in a sense, I am being led into next year's symposium sequence. But then that is part of my point. It is very hard—and sometimes even dangerous—to read the Book of Mormon piecemeal. It has been carefully edited and its text highly selected for a particular purpose. I believe those purposes blend together from cover to cover. As a practical matter we have to divide the book up to study it, but it is clear to me that we will read it best and help our students read it best when we keep returning to it in the grand sweep that starts at the first and continues to the last, giving a wholeness and unity to the book, to the dispensations, and to our view of the gospel plan.

With that I close. About a year or eighteen months ago I was struggling with a very real and very difficult problem. It was as difficult as anything I had faced for a long time and it had implications for the university and for me personally. I struggled and hurt and ached and prayed. I wondered whether peace would come and answers would be provided. I think I must have felt at least a little as Lehi felt traveling for the space of many hours in a dark and dreary waste. You have had those struggles, too.

One weekend when I was alone with my own thoughts and praying about this problem, I was prompted to pick up the Book of Mormon and open it at random. I do not intend to make too much out of such an act and I do not suggest that every random opening of the Book of Mormon is heaven directed, but I felt there was a messge for me that day and I would be led to something that was important for me to know.

I got up off my knees and opened the book and these are the words I read directly:

> They said unto me: What meaneth the rod of iron which our father saw, that led to the tree?
>
> And I said unto them that it was the word of God; and whoso would hearken unto the word of God, and would hold fast unto it, they would never perish; neither could the temptations and the fiery darts of the adversary overpower them unto blindness, to lead them away to destruction.
>
> Wherefore, I, Nephi, did exhort them to give heed unto the word of the Lord; yea, I did exhort them with all the energies of my soul, and with all the faculty which I possessed, that they would give heed to the word of God and remember to keep his commandments always in all things." (1 Nephi 15:23–25.)

That is my prayer for all of us as we continue to study the Book of Mormon. To the extent that I have a charge as outlined in the symposium schedule, my charge is to cling to that rod of iron, to cherish the word of God, to study it as the ancient Israelites were commanded to study the law, "both day and night," to have us meet here again one year from now to continue our exchange and study and enlightened discourse on this "most correct of any book on earth" (Book of Mormon Introduction, 1981 edition). I believe that, like these travelers in 1 Nephi, we too will "search them [the scriptures] and [find] that they [are] desirable; yea, even of great worth unto us, insomuch that we could preserve the commandments of the Lord unto our children. Wherefore, it [is] wisdom in the Lord that we should carry them with us, as we [journey] in the wilderness towards the land of promise." (1 Nephi 5:21–22.)

May we so search and journey together, with our grasp firmly on the rod of iron, I pray, in the name of Jesus Christ. Amen.

NOTES AND REFERENCES

1. *The Basic Works of Aristotle*, Richard McKeon, ed. (New York: Random House, 1941).

2. *Teachings of the Prophet Joseph Smith*, comp. Joseph Fielding Smith (Salt Lake City: Deseret Book, 1976), p. 274.

SUBJECT INDEX

SCRIPTURE INDEX

OLD TESTAMENT

NEW TESTAMENT

BOOK OF MORMON

DOCTRINE AND COVENANTS

PEARL OF GREAT PRICE